ARCHITECTURAL
IRONWORK

Dona Z. Meilach

Consultant, Stephen Bondi

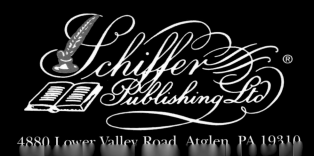

Schiffer Publishing Ltd

4880 Lower Valley Road, Atglen, PA 19310

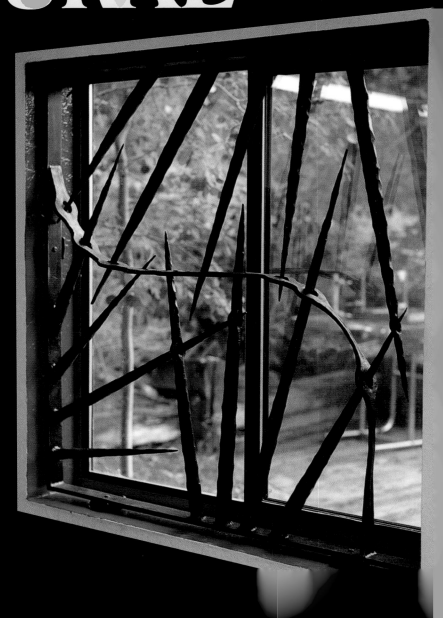

Front Cover - French style staircase, Jean-Pierre Masbanji
Frontispiece - Security Grille, Helmut Hillenkamp
Dedication Page - Drawing, Thomas Wilson
Back Cover - Escallier stairs in the Hotel de Ville, Nancy, France, Jean Lamour. Zilker Botanical Gardens gate, Lars Stanley. Oriental Theme gate, Michael Bondi. Entry gates, Jean-Pierre Masbanji. Rainforest gates, Jean Whitesavage and Nick Lyle. Circle Railing, Kirsten Reese. Fireman gate, Lars Stanley.

Library of Congress Cataloging-in-Publication Data

Meilach, Dona Z.
    Architectural ironwork/Dona Z. Meilach.
    p. cm.
    ISBN 0-7643-1324-X
    1. Ironwork--History.   2. Decoration and ornament, Architectural--History.   I. Title.
    NK8206 .M45 2001
    739.4--dc21
                              2001000406
Copyright © 2001 by Dona Z. Meilach

Designed by "Sue"
Type set in Americana XBd BT/Zapf Humanist 601 BT

ISBN: 0-7643-1324-X
Printed in China

Schiffer Books are available at special discounts for bulk purchases for sales promotions or premiums. Special editions, including personalized covers, corporate imprints, and excerpts can be created in large quantities for special needs. For more information contact the publisher:

Published by Schiffer Publishing Ltd.
4880 Lower Valley Road
Atglen, PA 19310
Phone: (610) 593-1777; Fax: (610) 593-2002
E-mail: Info@schifferbooks.com
Please visit our web site catalog at www.schifferbooks.com
We are always looking for people to write books on new and related subjects.
If you have an idea for a book, please contact us at the above address.

This book may be purchased from the publisher.
Include $5.00 for shipping.
Please try your bookstore first.
You may write for a free catalog.

In Europe, Schiffer books are distributed by:
Bushwood Books
6 Marksbury Ave.
Kew Gardens
Surrey TW9 4JF
England
Phone: 44 (0)208 392-8585
Fax: 44 (0)208 392-9876
E-mail: Info@bushwoodbooks.co.uk
Website: www.bushwoodbooks.co.uk
Free postage in the UK. Europe: air mail at cost.

Dedicated to
Christopher T. Ray, whose philosophy, wisdom, and creativity I shall sorely miss.

◆

"Fine art is that in which the hand, the head, and the heart go together." - John Ruskin

◆

Every effort has been made to trace the artists and owners of any works that are not credited.
The author apologizes for any unintentional omissions and would be pleased, in such cases,
to place an acknowledgment in future editions of this book.

◆

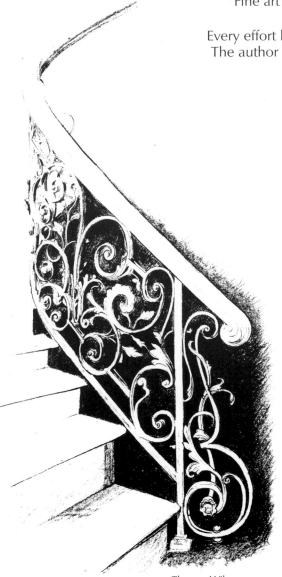

OTHER ART-CRAFT BOOKS by DONA Z. MEILACH
Blacksmithing:
The Contemporary Blacksmith
Decorative & Sculptural Ironwork
Direct Metal Sculpture
Also
Contemporary Stone Sculpture
Sculpture Casting *with* Dennis Kowal
Creating Small Wood Objects as Functional Sculpture
How to Create Your own Designs *with* Jay & Bill Hinz
Collage and Assemblage *with* Elvie TenHoor
Macramé-Creative Design in Knotting
Woodworking: The New Wave
Contemporary Art with Wood
Creating Modern Furniture
Batik and Tie Die
Ethnic Jewelry
Printmaking
Box Art
And others

Thomas Wilson

Acknowledgments

Each person who submitted photos for this book has contributed to its success. Without their gracious and willing sharing, there would be no book. I am grateful to all the photographers whose art is equally as important as that of the artists whose work they have photographed. To the artist blacksmiths who have learned to use a camera as well as a forge, I am doubly grateful. The photo quality can determine whether or not a piece is selected for an art book.

My sincere thanks to my consultant, Stephen Bondi, who had ready answers to my questions or knew where to find them. Sculptor Ken Capps' experience and opinions were invaluable for a first selection from the approximately 1500 photos piled on my ping-pong table. Sue Kaye also helped select photos and blue pencil the manuscript. I treasure her extensive art background and wholehearted willingness to participate. Willene and Russell Jaqua's expertise played an important role and I'm forever grateful for their technical information and editing suggestions.

Special thanks to John Medwedeff and Thomas Wilson for enthusiastically volunteering to create the drawings I needed. Thanks, too, to Werner F. Bocqué for the many photos he took of Art Nouveau examples in Brussels, Belgium; to my brother and nephew, Seymour Zweigoron and Doug Zweigoron, for their special photo efforts in the Dallas, Texas, area. The serendipitous meeting with blacksmith Jean-Pierre Masbanji of Santa Barbara, California, at a lunch table during the ABANA 2000 conference, resulted in the examples of his extraordinary work plus the acanthus leaf photo that graces the top of each chapter.

Jock Dempsey, Webmaster of www.anvilfire.com, was kind enough to announce that I was launching into this book so that many smiths contacted me whom I might not have found otherwise. Announcements in The Anvil's Ring (ABANA Publication), and in the BABA (British Artist Blacksmith Association) Website and newsletter also brought the project to the attention of European smiths. Combined with the artists whose work I already knew, I corresponded by phone, fax, mail, and email with over 150 artists and associations from several countries. Add to that my photos of ironwork from various travels and it tallies up to over 375 illustrations from eighteen countries: Belgium, Canada, Czech Republic, England, France, Hungary, Italy, Japan, Mexico, Monaco, Morocco, New Zealand, Russia, Scotland, Spain, Switzerland, Turkey, and the United States.

When I requested a survey-type feedback, many blacksmiths quickly responded. I especially appreciate the answers, short and long and always helpful, from Michael Bendele, E.A. Chase, Bill Fiorini, Kirsten Skiles, Jim Gallucci, Keith Johnson, Robert S. Jordan, Craig Kaviar, Scott Lankton, Jefferson and Mary Jo Mack, Dan Nauman, David Ponsler, and Christopher Thomson.

My deep appreciation to the staff at Schiffer Publishing, Ltd., for their ability to take a finished manuscript and magically transform it into a beautiful book.

There are no words to adequately express my appreciation to my husband, Dr. Melvin Meilach. He willingly, uncomplainingly, and patiently, drags around the world with me. He carries and watches equipment and smiles with amusement at people who wonder what catches my eye when I point my camera at some indefinable ironwork object.

Preface

This introduction to ironwork as it applies to architectural embellishment provides an overview of how the styles evolved. It also provides the tools one needs to understand how the artist blacksmith designs and creates his art. With this knowledge, you will inevitably focus on what you see and appreciate what you may have missed before you were aware of iron as an art form. Beyond that, you also will have insight into the motifs used and how they are assembled into a whole. Hopefully, you will never again climb a staircase or open a gate without noticing its construction and details.

Should you collect, design, or buy ironwork, whether it's a staircase for a home, a wind vane atop the roof, or a gate into a garden, you'll gain a new appreciation for the work of the artist blacksmith.

Our cityscapes are open-air museums of the blacksmith's art. Yet even people who are well informed about art may overlook the artistic ironwork all around them. Most people see ironwork fences, gates, door handles, window grilles, staircase and balcony railings, but give them little thought, though they use and touch them daily. This book will offer an insight into ironwork, who does it, and what is involved.

The objects shown are all the work of the metalworker-blacksmith. If your image of a blacksmith is the village smithy who fixes farm equipment, and the farrier who shoes horses, you're in for a pleasant awakening.

The book is organized with an historical overview, then a short discussion of the artist blacksmith's background, his studio, and his tools. Following that, I have covered the blacksmith's "alphabet" or elements of design. These should help the viewer understand what to look at and look for when encountering artistic ironwork. I have also included close-up photos of several projects to illustrate the detailing and texturing that is inherent in hand forged work. A few process shots show how a project progresses from inception of idea to finished work. Ironwork, from a small project to a large one, takes planning, design knowledge, heating, bending, welding, fabricating, and installing procedures. The men and women who create architectural ironwork toil long and hard. . . and it's always a labor of love.

The chapters are organized as one might encounter architectural ironwork. One enters a building under a canopy or an archway, then through doors. On the way inside, or once within a building, one would probably find staircases. Window grilles, railings, balconies would be inside or outside a building, and finally, there are gates and fences.

Within each chapter the examples are organized on their design principles rather than function. After a short historical perspective, stairways, for example, are presented by their distinctive elements. These include styles such as Gothic, Romantic, Neo-Baroque, Art Nouveau, and 20th century renaissance since about 1975. Some examples have been completed just in time to be photographed for this book.

There are detail photos that show how the metals are joined. A successful piece, visually and structurally, requires beautiful and often innovative joinery. The quality of the joinery, whether by welding or mechanical methods such as riveting, and passing one element through another, is a clue to the quality of a work. Focusing on joinery, textures, finishes, and details, along with the design, will foster a greater understanding of this pervasive art form that enriches our environment.

With this, my fourth book covering work of the artist blacksmith, I'm often asked, "How did you begin writing about blacksmithing?" In the 1970s I was involved in writing about many craft forms. At that time, blacksmithing was emerging from the farmer and farrier shops into the art world. That brought about the seminal book, *Decorative & Sculpture Ironwork*, in 1977 that became a catalyst for what has now been recognized as a renaissance in decorative ironwork. I watched interest in ironwork grow among makers, consumers, and industry. About twelve years later, Crown Publishers let that book go out of print but people constantly requested that I re-issue it.

In 1999, I proposed the idea of a revised edition to a receptive editor from Schiffer Publishing. For the revision, I received an outpouring of photos along with pleas that I write another book. The result was *The Contemporary Blacksmith* (2000). I had bitten off more than I had planned. From the 3000 photos submitted, 550 were used in *The Contemporary Blacksmith*. How could I showcase the wonderful unpublished examples for the world to see?

Schiffer agreed to publish a revised edition of *Direct Metal Sculpture* (2000), originally written with sculptor Don Seiden in 1966, to tap into the incredible activity of sculpture made with forging methods. Still more photos were needed and, in time, I updated that book in a revised edition that includes new contemporary sculpture and a chapter on public art.

I had still more photos in other categories, especially staircases, gates, and fences. Here is the result of that horn of plenty combined with many more examples gathered over the following year. As an art historian, I felt it was important to supplement the modern examples with the heritage and the inspiration for architectural ironwork. Fortunately, I had many photos in my archives from my travels. A trip to Prague and Budapest richly supplemented those with examples not seen in other books.

I already hear rumblings of, "Why don't you do a book just on such-and-such an aspect of ironwork? No one else is doing so much to bring the art form out of the country shop and into the art mainstream."

I am grateful for the continuing interest, encouragement, and appreciation. Stay tuned.

Dona Z. Meilach
Carlsbad, California
June 2001

Contents

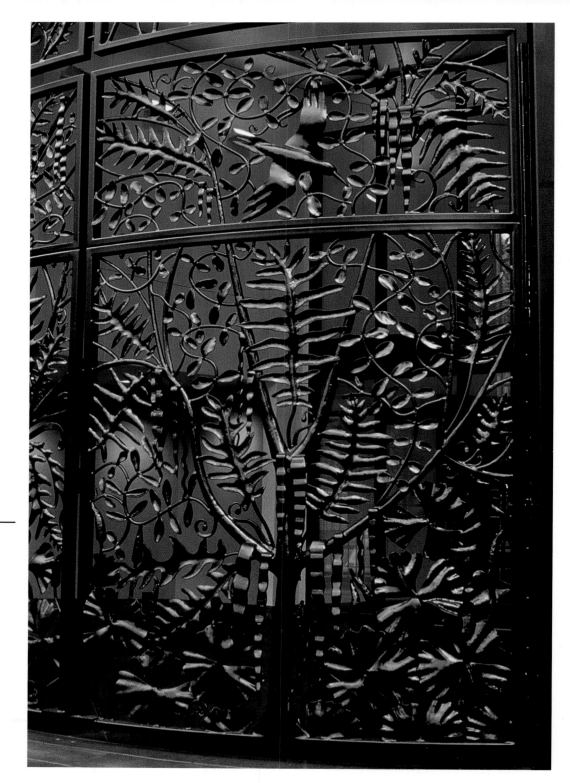

Jean Whitesavage and Nick Lyle. Rainforest Gates, detail. An architectural enhancement for the King Street Center, Seattle, Washington. The project consists of main entry gates, two sets of bi-fold gates, two large building brackets, a decorative sculpture band, and an eyebrow. Shown is a detail from the right side of the main gate. Gate opening is 22' high, 22' wide. *Commissioned by Wright, Runstad & Company, The National Development Council, and the King County Public Art Program. Photo, artists*

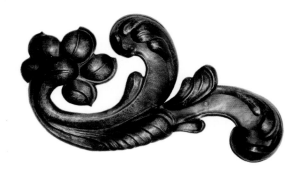

Chapter 1
The Magic of Metal

There's magic about metal that mesmerizes those who work with and appreciate it. The ability to take a stack of hard rods and bars, heat them, and reshape them into beautiful useful objects is a constant source of awe, wonder, and pride.

Every object you see in this book started out as hard, cold, milled metal. Then, through someone's imagination and labor, it became a utilitarian and decorative object. Whether it's the upright for a fence, a staircase baluster, a building support, or a door handle, it went through a similar metamorphosis.

The focus of this book is on the decorative and functional results of working metals as opposed to structural applications. Think of these as fences, gates, doors, screens, and staircase railings, within or outside a building. Think of structural work as metal used in iron bridges, the Eiffel Tower, the Pompidou Center, or the multitude of modern buildings throughout the world today that use iron as its framework and support.

Why and when is ironwork used for decoration as opposed to other materials such as stone, wood, or tile? Iron is often a choice rather than a necessity. When someone selects metal over wood, plaster, adobe, or another building material, it is because of its longevity, low maintenance, design potential, and appearance for the particular environment.

Metal is often preferred for grillwork because it is considered a more secure medium than wood and may last longer in a particular site. Metal is a strong material that can be designed to let in light while providing decoration for a structure. It will last a long time with minimum maintenance. Rust and weathering attack metal in time but many examples from antiquity have been rescued, restored, or preserved, and can be seen at museums around the world.

The history of decorative ironwork is long, involved, vague, and varies by country. There are overviews of ironwork in many books but compiling a world history of ironwork would be a daunting task that might require several volumes. There is an infinite variety of objects. Styles vary by country and with the times. Hand wrought pieces and cast iron would have to be included as their threads are braided throughout their histories.

Many outstanding early ironwork gates, fences, chandeliers, fireplace equipment, hardware, and jewelry, have been traced. Most likely the blacksmiths remained anonymous and the designer, architect, or patron was credited with the work. When artists are known, they are named but despite their anonymity their work speaks volumes. It offers insight into their times and the influences they have exerted on subsequent artist blacksmiths. The modern smith, however, has progressed with the times. Since the Industrial Revolution in the late 1700s, machines have improved the blacksmith's lot immeasurably. Today, power hammers, extruding devices, welding equipment, mechanized cutting systems, and more efficient tools are readily available and in use in most blacksmith shops. But hand forging is still the norm for much of the work.

The Information Revolution and computers have also changed the way blacksmiths work. Computer Aided Design (CAD) can be used for accurately and quickly committing a design to paper. It can help visualize a project in its ultimate environment, view it from different positions under various lighting, with different finishes, and accurately determine the amount of materials required. It may estimate the number of hours needed to complete the job. All this before a bar of iron is ever ordered, cut, hammered, or welded.

In the following pages, several examples from the past are shown that have, and still are, inspiring the modern smith. They offer designers, clients, and smiths, ideas for developing architectural ornamental ironwork that will reflect today's best ideas and become the historical basis for the burgeoning ironwork activity of the 21st Century.

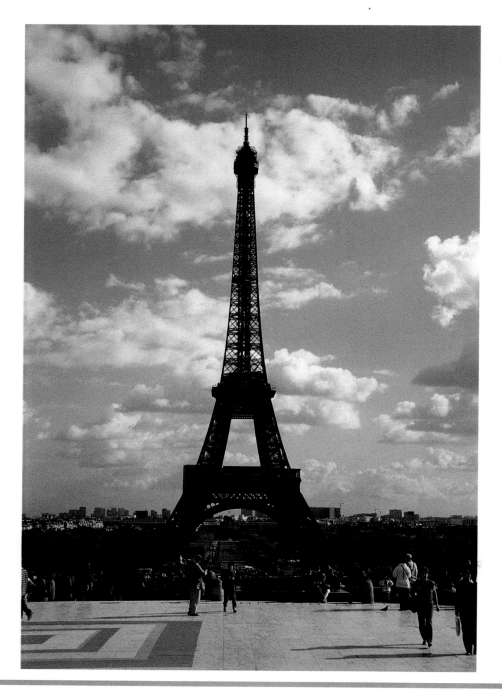

Yes, today's artist blacksmiths are forging a new chapter in iron-work history. They are signing their work with registered touchmarks so that they will be recognized as artists whose contributions to the culture of our society are as important as those created by their peers working in other media. Ultimately, more people see ironwork on a daily basis than they do paintings and sculptures. Ironwork is all around us while other media most often is in museums and galleries where people must walk through doors to view the work... doors that could have been made by an artistic metalworker.

Gustave Eiffel. Eiffel Tower, Paris, France. 1889. Eiffel chose pig iron girders using a complex pattern that would stabilize the tower in strong winds. The design quickly won admirers for its pleasing symmetry. The building begins with a dense use of iron at the bottom, then becomes lighter and lacier as it rises. *Photo, author*

Understanding the Material

All ironwork is not iron. Wrought iron is an iron with no carbon in it and it is no longer available in large enough quantities for big projects. Today mild steel is used but it is commonly called wrought iron.

Mild steel is iron with a small amount of carbon added for extra strength. Any ironwork project may combine steel with other materials such as copper, brass, bronze, or aluminum, for color and detailing. Steel can also be colored. Sometimes, an entire project may be made of aluminum or another metal still using the blacksmith's artistry and methods. Following are frequently asked questions and answers.

Differences Between Wrought Iron and Cast Iron

Wrought iron refers to "mild" iron or steel that is low in carbon content, and has been heated up to 2000 to 2500 degrees Fahrenheit. It can be worked with a hammer or bent while hot.

Cast iron is iron that has been melted at 2800 degrees or hotter and then poured into a mold and allowed to cool and harden. Much of the ironwork in New Orleans is cast iron. It was made from melted scrap iron brought from Europe as ballast in empty ships that were coming to the colonies to pick up goods.

Will Iron Rust and Deteriorate?

Iron, (mild steel), is commonly coated with a linseed oil finish but can still rust if left outdoors. However it will not rust if kept indoors. Should signs of rusting appear, boiled linseed oil or beeswax might be applied frequently to prevent further rusting. When metal will be used outdoors, there are processes that retard, or prevent, rusting such as hot dip galvanizing, electroplating, and powder coating. There are companies that specialize in such processing, they may be found in a telephone book under galvanizing or metal finishing. Many smiths include the weatherproofing processes in their quotation. Well maintained metal will last indefinitely.

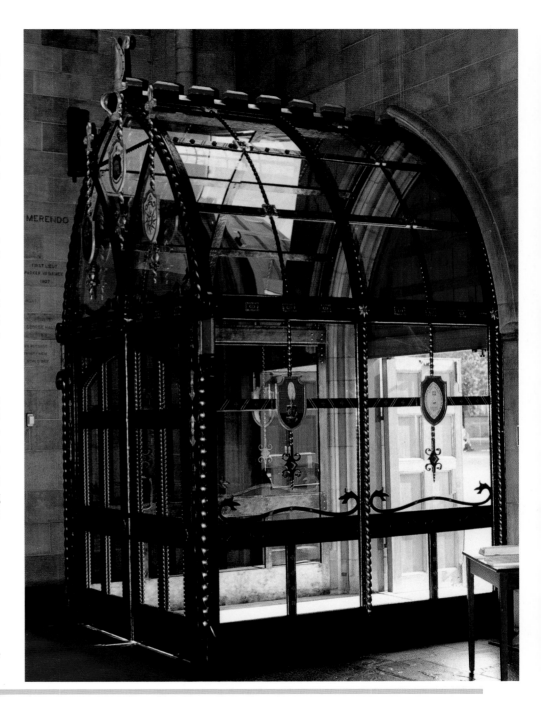

Peter Happny. Gothic vestibule for the Trinity College, Hartford, Connecticut. Forged steel with bright finish. The pointed arch is characteristic of Gothic architecture. Glass is sandwiched between the structure and the decorative pieces. It took Happny 1-1/2 years to create this work, and 7 days to install it. Happny, like many of today's artist blacksmiths, can work in many styles either as new work or as restorations. 16' high, 8' long, 8' wide. *Courtesy, artist*

How and Where did it Begin?

Whoever first used the phrase, "There's nothing new under the sun" didn't study the history of iron and blacksmithing. The Iron Age is, of course, ancient history. Iron is one of the oldest materials known to man. The blacksmith has been working it into myriad items for centuries.

Ancient Times

The legend of Hephaestus, the artistic smith of the Gods, dates back to Greek mythology. Legends say he was able to tame fire to his will and turn ores of the earth to make invincible weapons and simple tools. He allegedly forged thunderbolts of metal that he hurled in rage from Olympus to tame and rule a world occupied by rebellious people. In Roman mythology, Vulcan made a net of iron in which he trapped Venus and her lover, Ares, the God of War. Each of the Gods is reputed to have used the same basic tools that the human blacksmiths of the day used: the heat of the forge, the anvil, hammer, and tongs. Amazingly, these are still the essential tools in today's ironwork shop.

Medieval and Middle Ages

In medieval times, and until the late Middle Ages, the blacksmith was able to make iron objects only by heating the iron in a forge and shaping it with a hammer, hence the term wrought (worked) iron. By the late 1400s technological advances enabled iron to be melted and poured into forms, thus initiating the use of cast iron that could produce identical shapes and objects.

The blacksmith made mostly knives, weapons, farm equipment, some household items, and equipment for horses and riders such as stirrups, bridles, swords, guns, and armor. Several historical references are made to the blacksmiths who traveled with European armies where they were needed to repair equestrian equipment.

Certainly smiths in medieval times and the Middle Ages made a variety of functional objects with overtly decorative elements. Examples of door hinges, firedogs, jewelry, religious items, locks and keys, can be found in museums of the world. Probably the most extensive collection of European ironwork is in the Victoria and Albert Museum in London, England. Museums in Spain, Germany, Portugal, Vienna, and Hungary all have extensive examples, also. In America, though its history is not so old, museums on the East coast especially, have collections of ironwork from the early settlers. There are ironwork items from the boats that brought the settlers here, and many utensils that they used daily in the home, on the farm, and in the church.

The heritage, and precursors, of today's architectural ironwork are the examples from Spain, France, Italy, and Flanders in the 15th Century. There are examples of church and cathedral rajas (screens), gates, and fences for royal buildings and large estates, window and door grilles, and balconies.

The 17th Century

Despite the anonymity of most blacksmith work of the past, some names have been chronicled. Jean Lamour (1698-1771) has left a legacy that can be seen in the masterfully crafted Rococo gates in the Place Stansilas, the main square in Nancy, France. He is also known for a lacy iron banister and fifty-six railings of the city's Hotel de Ville de Nancy (see Chapter 3). Lamour used design details that remain popular today including heraldic emblems, gilded acanthus leaves, medallions, intricate scrollwork, and carved figures.

Lamour's patron was King Stanislas of Poland who had the Square Stanislas developed in honor of his son-in-law who had married his daughter, Marie-Antoinette. The gates can be viewed at Internet sites on Nancy, France or in situ if one travels to that city.

Jean Tijou, a French designer, is known for the ironwork he did after he arrived in England in 1689 and until 1711. William and Mary had just begun their reign that encouraged architecture. Tijou introduced a purely French Renaissance design that influenced English ironwork. His "New Book of Drawings" (1693), and his many apprentices furthered his influence. Tijou's gates and railings on the grounds of Hampton Court Palace, made between 1689-1700, are probably most well known. He also fashioned several screens and grilles for Christopher Wren's St. Paul's Cathedral. Tijou's ironwork screens and grilles included the lavish use of rosettes, flowers, embossed leaves, and gold leaf. They marked the high point of French and English wrought ironwork.

In England, staircases created in the Neo-classical style were created in the workshop of William Palmer for the architect William Chambers. They incorporated leaves, anthemia (honeysuckle), scrolls, and elements still popular in today's staircases.

Similar designs with variations followed in staircases in Germany and Italy, often with the addition of acanthus leaves and gilded elements.

Before the 17th Century, ironwork patterns were essentially symmetrical and linear with a formal repetition of elements. They had their basis in the designs of illuminated manuscript borders. The main differences were regional, according to Otto Höver's "Style in Decorative Wrought-Iron Work" in *The Encyclopedia of Ironwork*. He notes that three main forms of the bar dictated inherent style characteristics: flat, round, and square. During the beginning and middle of the Gothic period the flat wrought iron bar, in parts narrow and in parts wide, was favored. The round bar dominated in the late Gothic period and, in northern Europe, continued into the Renaissance. In Italy and the south, during the Renaissance, the use of square bars dominated.

During the 17th and 18th centuries, in France, the smith's designs were often taken from engravings that were ornamental and linear with ribbon like swells and curves. Many of the linear elements were held together with intricately engraved bands, or collars, and straps.

The 18th Century

As the Industrial Revolution spurred manufacturing procedures, cast iron became increasingly popular. It was used extensively for everything from bridges to stair balustrades to household objects including furniture, lamps, railings, fireplace screens, trivets, irons, pots and pans, and an endless number of tools and parts for machinery.

After industrialization brought down the cost of producing cast iron, and pieces could be mass produced easily and quickly, hand wrought, decorative architectural enhancements fell from fashion. With cast iron, entire sections of sculptural forms could be made and used for intricately designed balustrades, grilles, stair risers, and balconies. Early American blacksmiths concentrated on making objects for survival and work, rather than embellishment. They were used extensively along America's Eastern seaboard, in Charleston, and in New Orleans. These were most often cast iron replicated styles that were popular in France and England.

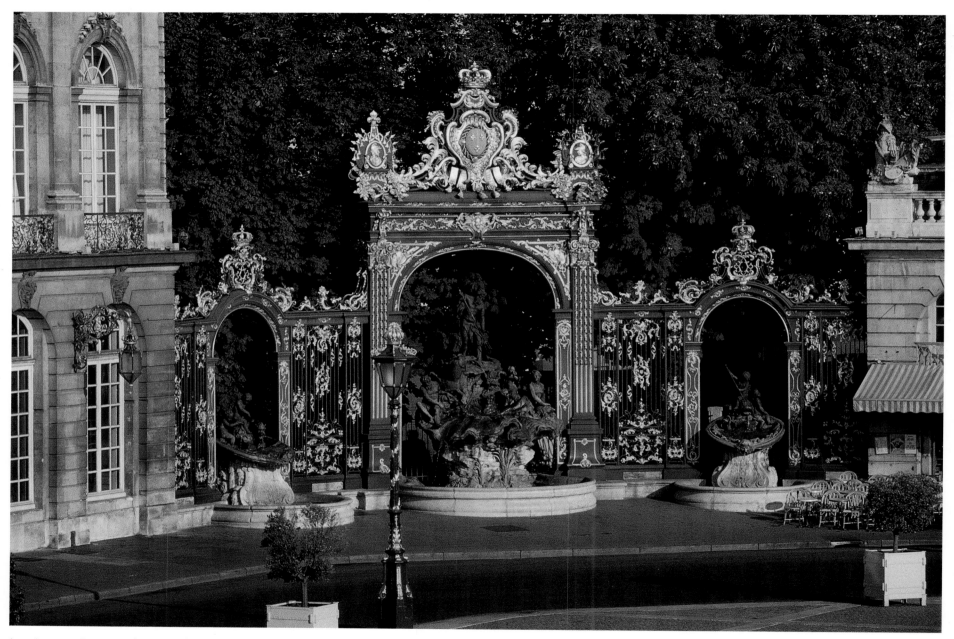

Jean Lamour. Rococo style ironwork in the Place Hamilton, of the Hotel Ville de Nancy, Nancy, France, created between 1751-1759. Lamour's rich gold motifs with floral themes, crowns, heraldic symbols, and portraits set into medallions, helped set the style for French Rococo ironwork in the 18th Century. *Courtesy, Office de Tourisme de Nancy, France*

14

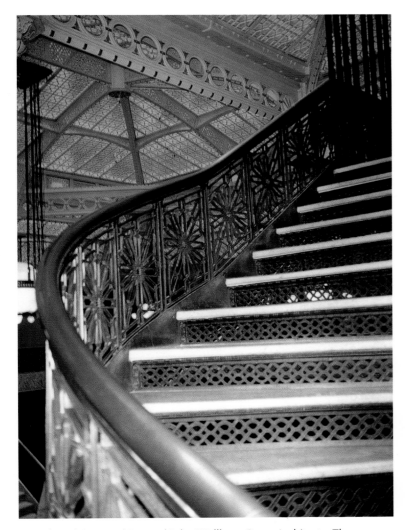

The 19th Century

In Chicago, Illinois, architect Louis Sullivan designed a new style of cast iron. He used it in several buildings that were replacing much of the city's downtown business area that had been destroyed by the 1871 Chicago fire. Rebuilding as economically as possible was essential. The cast iron entry enclosing the vestibule of Carson Pirie Scott & Company, (1899-1906) is still as elegant as it was when it first was built. Cast iron ornamentation on the Madison Street first floor exterior is incredibly intricate.

Architects Richard Burnham and John Welborn Root had already built The Rookery in Chicago, completed in 1886. Construction involved cast iron columns joined by wrought iron spandrel beams. The skeleton construction bearing the weight of walls gave rise to the so-called ribbon windows, which have since become a standard feature of commercial and sometimes domestic buildings.

An open interior court, elegantly designed with gold and ivory by Flank Lloyd Wright and executed in 1905, was later painted over. The combination of Root's delicate ironwork and Wright's decoration "suggested a nineteenth-century counterpart to the profusion, magnificence, and delicacy of Baroque architecture," wrote Carl W. Condit in his book, *The Chicago School of Architecture*.

Daniel Hudson Burnham and John Wellborn Root. Architects. The Rookery (1885-87) building in Chicago, Illinois, takes its odd name from a temporary city hall at this location that was the favorite gathering place of pigeons. One of the oldest precursors of modern skyscrapers, this eleven-story iron framed structure was designed as an office building. The exterior walls are load-bearing masonry. The staircase risers and decorations are cast iron. *Photo, author*

Right: A decorative panel beneath the staircase in the Rookery illustrates the characteristics of cast iron. It emulates forged iron scrollwork but the design is not as open; there is no joinery or banding, and the surfaces may appear concave. *Photo, author*

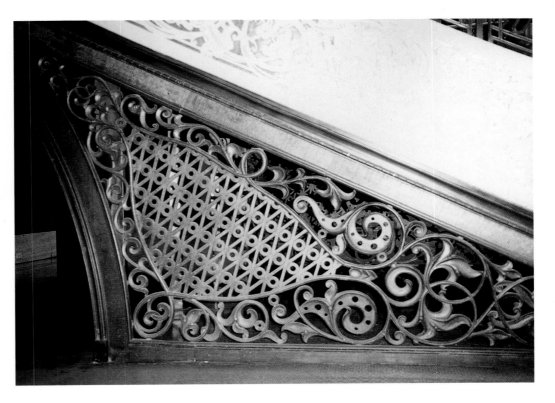

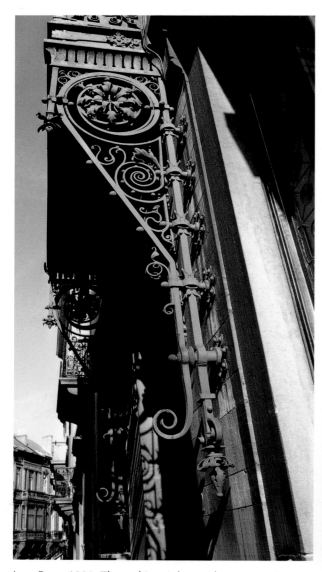

Art Nouveau

About 1850, English architects who were restoring medieval churches and cathedrals had to renew or replace wrought iron screens that had been removed earlier. Inspired by this use of wrought iron of the Middle Ages, they reacted against the increasing use of cast iron. In turn that led to the Arts and Crafts Movement of the late 1800s. But the most dramatic change occurred from about 1890 to the beginning of the First World War in 1914.

A momentous shift in attitude about the use of architectural ironwork occurred first in Brussels, Belgium, in the late 1800's with the work of Architect Victor Horta (1861-1947). It quickly spread to France, Italy, Spain, Germany, Vienna, then throughout the continent and the world. Much has been written about the sinuous asymmetrical forms that were a powerful departure from previous two-dimensional linear symmetrical designs. Thus was born the Art Nouveau period.

Horta's digression began during a trip to Paris. He was deeply moved and influenced by Alexander Gustave Eiffel's Tower, completed in 1889. Horta returned to Belgium with a new vision for ironwork that was like a "shot heard around the world." Horta's early houses are slender iron constructions with an unprecedented use of glass and linear ornamentation. His models for the linear elements were the stalks and stems of plants. Later, other Art Nouveau artists used the blooms and the leaves as well. Horta's own house still stands in Brussels, and has become a museum of the artist's work.

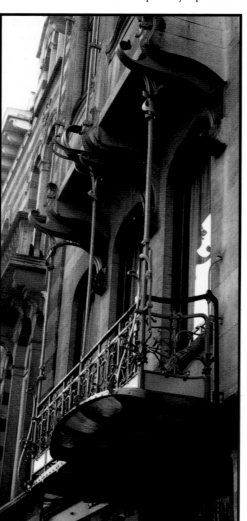

Jean Baes. 1889. The architect's home shows a transition from the romantic Baroque and Rococo styles to less ornate motifs that heralded the Art Nouveau and modern movements. The balconies and supports combined cast and forged ironwork. *Photo, Werner F. Bocqué*

Victor Horta. Art Nouveau canopy, railings, uprights, and brackets for Victor Horta's House, that is now the Horta Museum. 1898 to 1901. Brussels, Belgium. *Photo, Werner F. Bocqué*

As other architects picked up on Horta's lead, Belgium became the hub of Art Nouveau. Gustave Strauven began by working with Horta and later he opened his own practice. His "House of St. Cyr" is a veritable dictionary of Art Nouveau shapes and philosophy. Gaspard Devalck's ironwork details on a door are coordinated with the glass and woodwork. Art Nouveau architects routinely designed everything in a building, including furniture and fixtures, to avoid using traditional period furniture that would destroy the look for which they were striving.

Hector Guimard (1867-1942) furthered Art Nouveau in Paris about the same time. His most notable works are the cast iron railings and lamps for several of the Paris Metro stations (1899-1904). Despite the status of the railings in the history of ironwork, today they are smeared with graffiti and pasted over with posters, and advertisements.

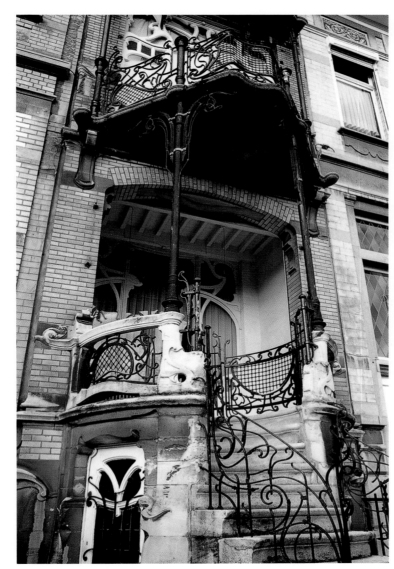

Gustave Strauven. 1903. House of the painter St. Cyr illustrates the architect's enthusiasm for using ironwork in the Art Nouveau manner. Strauven, an architect and an inventor, had worked under Victor Horta until he opened his own offices in Brussels, Belgium. *Photo, Werner F. Bocqué*

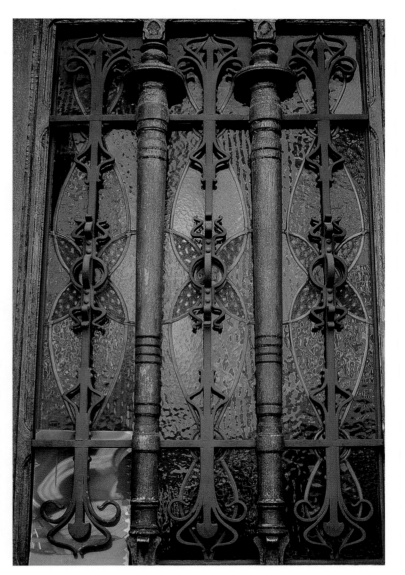

Gaspard Devalck. Door hardware for a house that still stands in Brussels, Belgium. The architect integrated several materials into a structure to create a coordinated entity. Wood, iron, glass, and interior furnishings, are all Art Nouveau *Photo, Werner F. Bocqué*

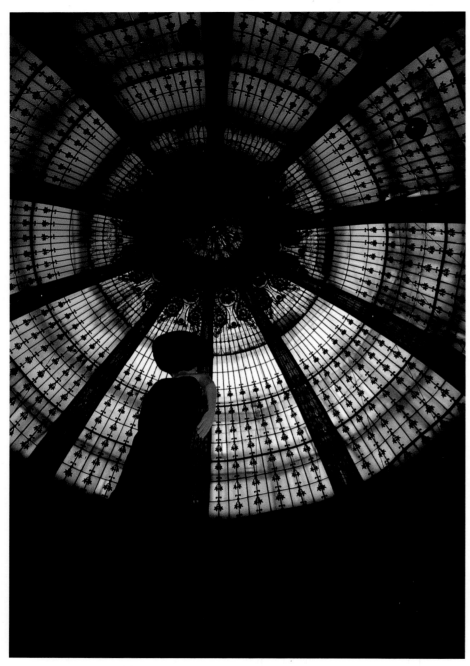

Paris, France. Dome of the Galleria La Fayette Department Store, Paris, France. 1912. Lacy ironwork over glass culminates at the top in a more dense design. The dome ceiling is painted. *Photo, author*

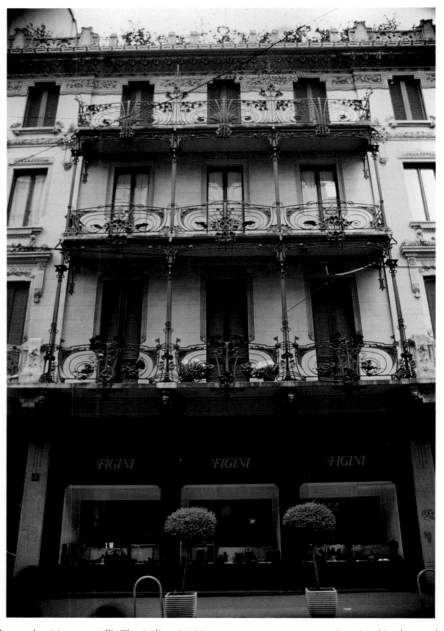

Alessandro Mazzucotelli. The Italian Art Nouveau movement was epitomized in the work of Mazzucotelli in his building, the Casa Ferrario, built in Milan about 1900. As Eiffel did with his tower, Mazzucotelli's composition becomes less dense, with ever decreasing detail as it ascends. Despite the rigidity of the composition, the artist's rendering of floral, insect, and real and fantasy animal forms, shows his mastery for the plastic, and spontaneous, qualities of iron. *Photo, Stephen Bondi*

Paris architects were using ironwork for a variety of commercial buildings. The original department store, La Galeries Lafayette, on Boulevard Haussmann, was built in 1895 and the glass dome with ironwork by Ferdinand Chanut was added in 1910 to 1912. Architect Franz Jourdain built the department store, La Samaritaine overlooking the Seine in 1905 in the Art Nouveau manner. In 1926, Henri Savage built an extension in the Art Deco style that became popular in the late 1920s.

The 20th Century

Edgar Brandt was well known in Paris in the 1920s. He is credited with embellishing the City of Lights with his great works of iron including Paul Poiret's house of couture, the Au Bon Marche department store, and the Louvre.

According to Brandt's biographer, Joan Kahr, Brandt (1880-1960) created "an entirely new aesthetic for the medium of wrought iron that epitomizes the Art Deco style." The author stresses that Brandt was a virtuoso at using several materials, often combining wrought iron with bronze or steel and patinating it with gold and silver. During his day, the craftsman operated a large showroom in Paris, offering everything from grilles and fire screens to lamps, doors, and tables.

The Italian designer and blacksmith, Allesandro Mazzucotelli's (1865-1938) influence on architectural ironwork has been understated to American audiences until recently when blacksmith and iron art historian Stephen Bondi published monographs about Mazzucotelli's work. Horta and Guimard were designer/ architects and the ironwork for their structures were fashioned in workshops by anonymous blacksmiths. Mazzucotelli was first a designer who had a unique feel for handling the metal.

Bondi cites the Casa Ferrario in Milan, Italy, as one of Mazzucotelli's most significant works. Mazzucotelli worked directly with the architect and applied his design concepts to visible structural members of the building. In most works, the architectural structure supports and displays the decorative ironwork. With Casa Ferrario there is a symbiotic relationship in which the ironwork and the architecture support one another.

Antoni Gaudí, (1852-1926) in Barcelona, Spain, furthered Art Nouveau with a unique approach that is still being explored, emulated, and built upon. Ironwork on the balconies of his Casa Milá are like free form ribbons of steel on an undulating façade. Each of the balcony railings is different and none are symmetrical. Gaudí avoided flat surfaces, straight lines, and any kind of symmetry. His buildings, though made of stone, appear to have been modeled with a malleable material. Ironwork on balconies, gates, windows, and staircases are a dramatic departure from the stiff, symmetrical ironwork of styles before 1900.

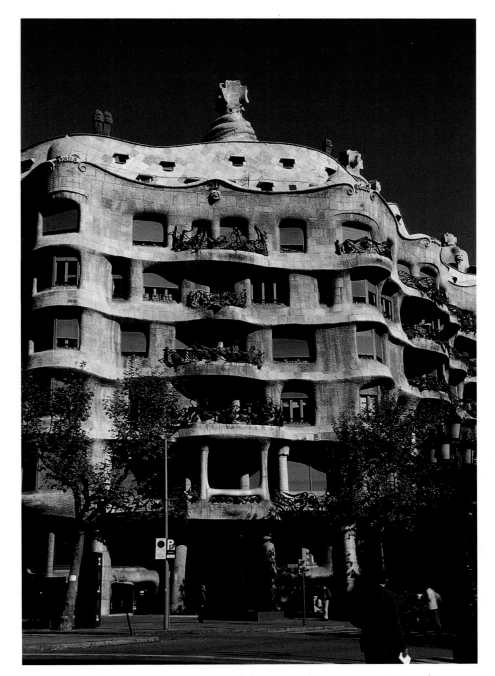

Antoni Gaudí. Spanish architect, Antoni Gaudí's Casa Mila (1906-1910) in Barcelona, Spain, is often referred to as the greatest abstract sculpture ever built. The undulating facade, free form balcony railings, and twisted chimneys were a dramatic departure from the work of his contemporaries. *Photo, author*

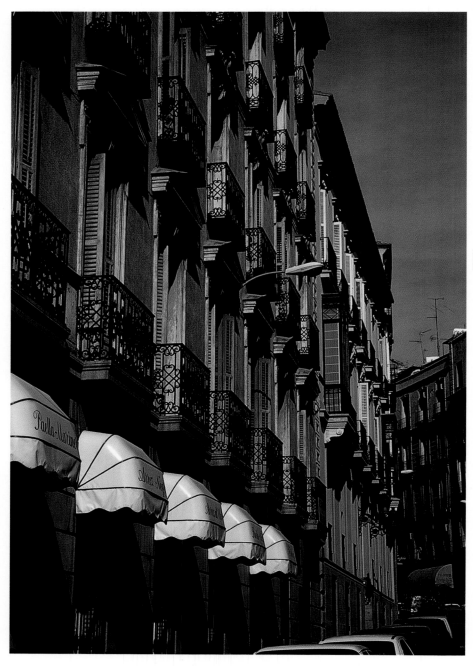

The Scottish architect, Charles Rennie Macintosh (1869- 1945), was a designer, graphic artist, and painter, and later he studied architecture. He won his first architectural commission for the Glasgow School of Art. His simplified, reserved style used in the building's fences and other ironwork was basically Art Nouveau with linear elements taken from Symbolism and Japanese Art rather than the plant forms his contemporaries were using. European artists largely ignored Macintosh's style until much later, but it inspired Louis Sullivan's designs in Chicago, Illinois, at the time.

The painter Alfons Maria Mucha's (1860-1939) work, along with other activity in Central Europe, profoundly influenced the Art Nouveau architecture in Prague, Czech Republic, and Budapest, Hungary, in the early 1900s. Not much of the architecture from these countries has been shown in English art history books. But a recent trip to those cities revealed examples that are significantly different from those in other countries. Many are illustrated throughout this book. Time and language constraints made it impossible to discover the architects and blacksmiths involved. Additionally, because of wars and the age of some buildings, different artists have restored much of the ironwork at different times. But the styles remain. Budapest has made every effort to replicate structures that fell prey to World War II bombings, including the iron Freedom Bridge that was first built in 1896-99. Prague has refurbished much the city that had deteriorated under Communist domination.

Most Spanish ironwork continued to follow traditional forms. The ironwork balconies on a building of a shopping street in Madrid, Spain, are typical. *Photo, author*

Opposite page: Renzo Piano and Richard Rogers, Architects. The Pompidou Center in Paris, France, (1977) was dubbed an "oil refinery" when it was built but it quickly won the accolades of tourists and Parisians. The metal framework and elements are exposed and brightly painted. This building, that houses a library and museum of modern art, is an uncovered framework much like the Eiffel Tower. Remodeling in 1999-2000, was a much less difficult and costly job than if the structure were enclosed. *Photo, author*

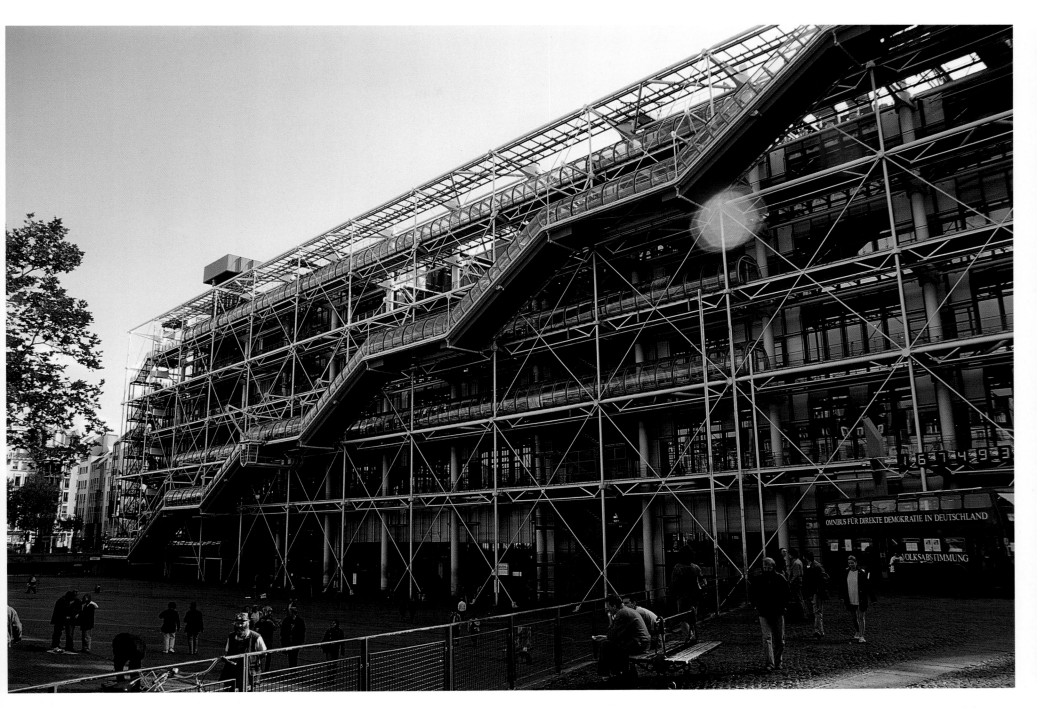

World War I quelled the burgeoning artistic activity in ironwork in Europe with only a few workshops riding out the bad times. Mazzucotelli continued working into the 1930s.

In post World War I America, Samuel Yellin's name stands out in the history of American ironwork. Yellin had emigrated from Europe and set up a shop in Philadelphia. His work began to appear up and down the east coast. Eventually, his shop employed 300 men who had been working blacksmiths in Europe. Today, his granddaughter, Clare Yellin, runs the shop but on a smaller scale.

In the Midwest, Cyril Colnik, who had also emigrated from Europe, showed his work at the 1893 Chicago World Columbian Exposition. Soon after, he settled in Milwaukee, Wisconsin, where he provided a potpourri of imaginative ironwork for several homes in and around the area. These included grilles, fences, escutcheons, locks, rosettes, sconces, floral motifs and his "Masterpiece" grille. No one is sure how this grille was used, but it illustrates his virtuosity with metal.

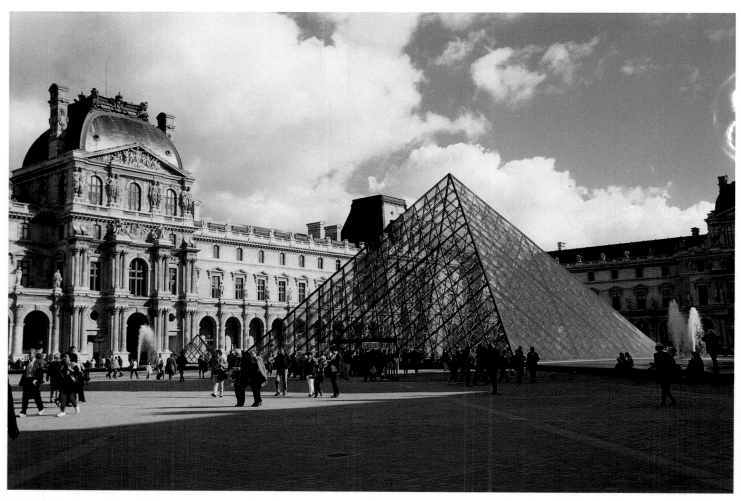

I.M. Pei. The Louvre Pyramid (1989) is an example of an ironwork frame structure covered by glass. The ironwork is the structure and its rhythm of crossed bars forms geometric shapes that provide the decoration. *Photo, author*

Edwin Trinkkeller, (1872-1942), had immigrated to the United States from Germany in 1890, at the age of 18. In 1896 he opened a shop in Los Angeles, California, and much of his work is still standing. Beginning in about 1915 Trinkkeller created architectural ironwork for William Randolph Hearst's San Simeon Castle in California, and for buildings in the Los Angeles area.

After 1925, Art Deco appeared. More stone and brickwork came into vogue and ironwork was an adjunct rather than the prevalent decoration. In a short time, the swinging pendulum brushed away the need for decorative ironwork completely. Germany's Bauhaus School of Architecture gave birth to the modern high rise building. It espoused straight lines, minimal decoration, and an emphasis on pure functionalism. Large windows were meant to make the outdoors the decoration. This was the new architectural style of Walter Gropius and Mies Van der Rohe. Added to that were the International Style of the Swiss born architect, Le Corbusier, and the Prairie style of America's Frank Lloyd Wright. All were shunning decorative elaborate exterior detailing in favor of simple iron framework, unadorned stone, and glass and brick buildings.

John Deere Exhibition Pavilion & John Deere Store. A modern iron framed building (1997) in Moline, Illinois. Architect, HOK, St. Louis, Missouri. *Courtesy, John Deere & Co.*

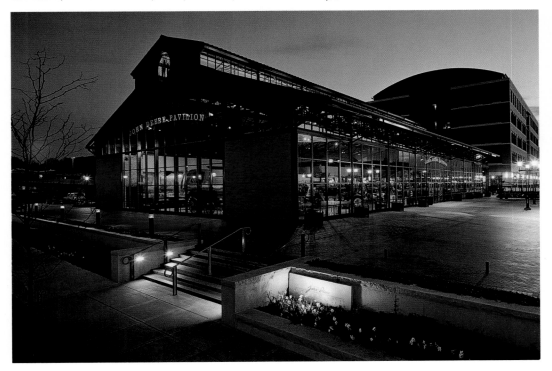

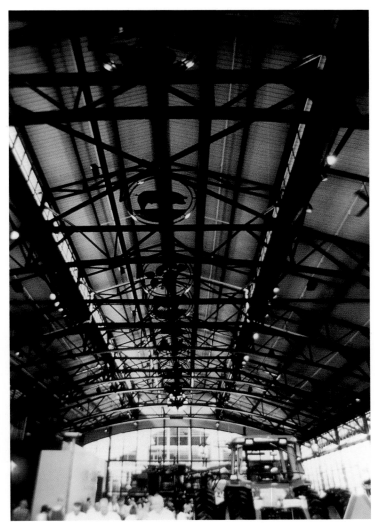

John Medwedeff. Ten hand forged medallions titled, "Agriculture Realized" are installed along the top trusses of the Deere Pavilion. Each 8' diameter medallion has a symbolic image such as corn, wheat, and other plant forms. The total project required 4-1/2 months to complete. *Photo, John Medwedeff*

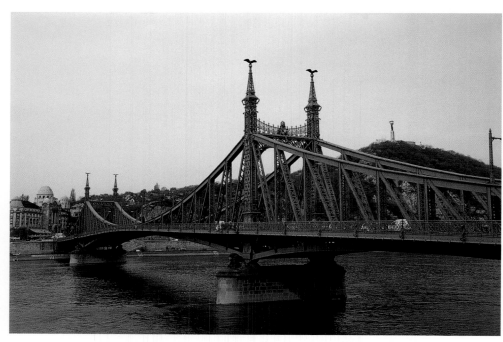

Liberty or Freedom Bridge. Budapest, Hungary. Iron bridges throughout the world often combine cast and forged iron for structure and ornamentation. The architecture and patterns created by the iron girders provide the design. Additional ornamentation can be fabricated. *Photo, author*

Right: Liberty or Freedom Bridge. Budapest, Hungary. Detail of top portion has an enameled royal crest in the center and the legendry Hungarian Turul bird perched on each of the top posts. The bridge was first built in 1894-99, destroyed in 1945, and rebuilt in 1946. *Photo, author*

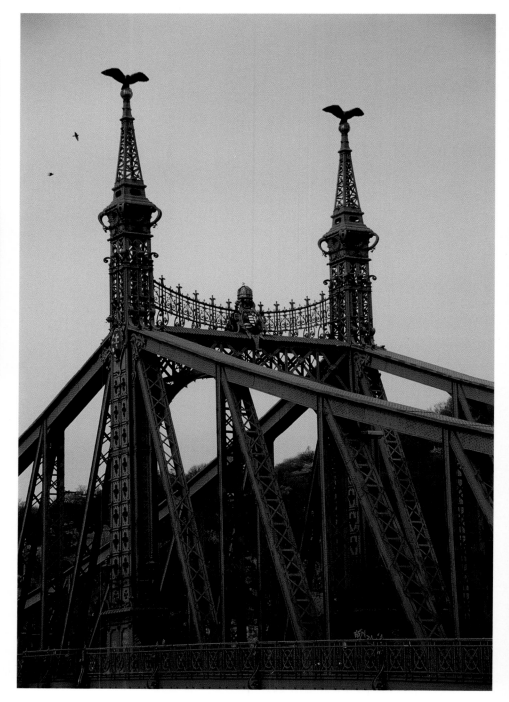

Bridge Construction

Another aspect of iron used as architecture throughout the world, is the iron bridge. Most bridges use cast iron girders but some forged work is also applied. One example is the elegant Freedom Bridge (also called the Liberty Bridge) that spans the Danube River in Budapest, Hungary. The original bridge, built by engineer János Feketehazy between 1894-99, that connected the towns of Buda and Pest, was known as the Franz Joseph Bridge for 50 years. In 1945 during World War II, the bridge was destroyed. It was rebuilt in 1946 by architect Aurél Czekelius retaining all the original features plus new decorations, and renamed the Freedom, or Liberty Bridge. The enameled blazon surmounted at the top center with the Hungarian crown, is by artist Virgil Nágy, and symbolizes the Coat of Arms and various territories. The legendary Hungarian Turul birds are perched atop each post.

Sydney, Australia's Harbour Bridge is probably as well known and often photographed as the Sydney Opera House that it overlooks. The massive steel arch of the Harbour Bridge, begun in 1923 and opened in 1932, is a feat of modern engineering. Other iron bridges with their own beauty and decoration can be found in San Francisco, New York, and in many places where man has found a need to cross water more easily than by wading, by horseback, or boat.

Upsurge

Following World War II, after 1945, when the building trades picked up, no one trend dominated, but more iron was being used for large structures. In Europe, almost all metal had been recycled into munitions during the war and buildings had been destroyed. Rebuilding generated a renewed interest in ironwork for modern buildings in a modern idiom. Fritz Kühn (1910-1967) of Germany led this revival with gates that were more free form and restrained than traditional French and English style gates. Kühn, along with the Italian artist, Antonio Benetton, pioneered new ideas for forged ironwork, even using it for public sculptures for which cast bronze or stone had dominated.

In America a new arts and crafts movement was emerging as people enthusiastically embraced the do-it-yourself concept. Art schools were teaching jewelry courses in which students were exploring the uses of metals for a variety of expressive applications. Albert Paley, originally a jewelry designer, began working with iron and a forge and developed gates that caught the attention and imagination of the art community in the early to mid 1970s.

People were enrolling in art classes and experimenting with new techniques. In that environment, and by demand, ironwork equipment was introduced into workshops and art schools in America and Great Britain. Books appeared and classes in blacksmithing were offered. For the next 25-30 years part time and full time blacksmiths created thousands of items in scores of categories. By the end of the century, the United States was experiencing a booming economy and people wanted hand forged staircases, fences, gates, doors, and door hardware in addition to furniture and interior objects. A growing number of blacksmiths was able and eager to supply them.

By the mid 1990s clients, designers, and architects who understood the value of ironwork, were seeking artist blacksmiths. The country was riding a new wave of prosperity. The design and furniture industry had discovered ironwork. Handcrafted furniture and accessories were added to complement the architectural detailing throughout a building. Ironwork was back in vogue! By the year 2000 the demand for the artist blacksmith's work was higher than ever. The Artist Blacksmith Association of North America Convention (ABANA 2000), attracted over one thousand smiths who attended workshops and lectures, and displayed their works.

2000: The New Golden Age of Artist Blacksmithing

The 21st Century already is being declared the new Golden Age of Ironwork, just as the 18th Century in Europe was dubbed its first golden age. In her book, *Decorative Ironwork*, Marion Campbell writes; "All over Europe, the eighteenth century was a golden age for blacksmiths whose skills created the screens and gates for parks, grand staircases and balconies, for the increasing number of houses of the newly prosperous. Much of their work is still in place in England, particularly in Oxford and Cambridge."

In America two factors are contributing to this growing use and appreciation of ironwork. First, a generation of artist blacksmiths has been honing its skills and artistic vision during the craft's renaissance over the past quarter century. Second, the country is prospering. People are building bigger, more expensive homes. Industry is creating more impressive structures and public art is enhancing our cities. Entertainment, resort, and hotel facilities are using more lavish ironwork for their interiors and exteriors. Designers and architects are bringing the artist blacksmith into the design team at a project's initiation.

With these developments, it is important, and in their best interests, that people understand what's involved when they decide that ironwork is the best material for enhancing a particular project.

About Custom Ironwork

The person who wants custom made ironwork for an architectural application may work directly with an artist blacksmith, through a designer, or through a builder or architect. It will depend on the job and the arrangements. Large projects for buildings are generally architect or builder initiated. These professionals usually know ironworkers who can produce the type of work needed and have the experience of working with them. Smaller projects may be developed between the client and the smith.

In all cases, the most essential beginning involves dialogue and an understanding of what the client wants and expects. All the smiths interviewed emphasized the importance of communicating ideas clearly between designer and client.

What Will It Cost?

Good forged ironwork is labor intensive. It requires safe handling of very hot (2000 degrees or hotter) steel, and manipulating it into various shapes by hammering. Surfaces may be textured. Welding, grinding, smoothing, and finishing are required. Installation adds to the cost. Maintaining a professional metal smith's shop requires gas or coal forges, steel forming equipment such as cutters, rollers, benders, punches and grinders, as well as safety equipment. One acanthus leaf detail, for example, may take 1 to 2 days to create. A large stair railing may use as many as 50 to 75 such details and that's only a minor aspect of the job.

Compare the equipment, the need for additional workers, and installation requirements, for an ironwork project to the time and materials needed for an artist to paint a canvas. This is a good basis for evaluating the reason that ironwork projects can be costly.

Assembly Line vs. Hand Forged Ironwork?

When considering ironwork, it's important to see and understand what you are buying. Once understood, it's easy to differentiate hand-forged work from assembly line projects. Ordinary fences or gates with uprights welded to horizontals, and a few scrollwork elements added, would be examples of assembled projects. They're referred to in the industry as "cut and paste" and may be compared to using clip art in a computer program.

In assembly line production, bars and scrolls are pre-cut to size and assembled by welding. The scroll ends, usually made by cold forming and bending on a jig, are flat, straight, and blunt. There is no texturing from the hammer or other tools. The parts that are joined, the uprights and horizontals on a fence, for example, are welded much as one would glue two sticks together. Often the welded joints are not ground down to a smooth joint and can have bumps, protrusions, and beads. These processes may be fine for many applications. They are meant to be and are purely functional.

Sometimes, builders will feature custom ironwork in tract homes that may have several similar floor plans. When iron staircases or gates are featured, usually they would be composed of uprights and simple scrolls. A builder might justify these as "custom" but they are, in reality, assembled to fit a plan and all are the same. They probably do not show any of the hand made features, such as texturing and slight differences in the same elements.

Wisconsin blacksmith Dan Nauman offers this explanation: "Hand forged work generally has more design appeal to the trained eye. There is some wonderful fabricated work out there, but this work is not 'from the hand'. It is this element that separates truly fine hand forged work from fabricated work. A machine is incapable of reproducing the human touch. The spontaneity of the hammer's blows, each one a bit different produces similar but different elements, even if they are designed to be identical. It is this irregularity that gives the work its character. Often, the piece is a portrait of the makers character and unique imagination."

Michael Bendele says that cold bending is not necessarily a sign of non-custom work. "Depending on the nature of the curve it may be best bent cold. I often do long subtle curves cold. Very long bends with large diameter steel is awkward to get in and out of a forge. Usually I will bend the center part of a long element cold using mechanical advantages. Then I will finish the ends, which may have tighter curves, with a torch and bending tongs. A torch does not replace a forge; it does allow the fire to come to the piece rather than the piece having to go into the fire."

A custom-made piece can be identified by its one-of-a-kind design and attention to the various characteristics of the ironwork and its construction. A hand forged piece will have no identical elements. Even similar elements will have slight variations. The work may have a more spontaneous look to it. Here are features to look for:

DESIGN: The design would be unique and individualized for the location.

TEXTURE: The iron pieces would exhibit texturing from hand hammering that enhances the metal rods or surfaces.

WELDING: Joined areas should be gracefully accomplished. Many types of joinery may be used that can add to the design. Joints should be accomplished with well-formed rivets, or collars, or other good clean logical connections. When mechanical welding (arc, MIG and TIG) is used, the welds should be counter sunk, ground clean and perhaps hidden under a wrap. Corners should be smooth.

ENDINGS: Hand forged scroll ends will be hammered out into different shapes (see drawings) and each one might have slight variations. Fabricated scroll ends often have a straight spot at the interior of the scroll where the machine grabbed the bar to produce the scroll. These machined scrolls often do not have finished ends such as tapers, snubs, splits, and other flourishes that come from the smith's hammer.

SHAPING: Hand forged bars often change shape from the parent bar, and may show absolutely no evidence of the original stock size. Dimensions may vary in each piece of iron from thick to thin. One piece may graduate from 1" square at one end, to 1/2" x 2" in the middle, to 1/8" x 1/8" at the other end. Only heating and hammering the piece at high temperatures can achieve this detailing. Heavier elements, 3/4" and heavier, have more labor involved than 1/4" dimension work which sometimes does not even involve heating the metal.

JOINERY: Combining elements will be accomplished by banding or collaring, (a piece of iron wrapped around one or more bars), rivets, forge welds (often referred to as fire welds, that are performed without electricity), or wrapping the bars around themselves.

ROD CHARACTERISTICS: Are rods tube-steel or solid? Tube steel is much thinner metal and will start to rust from the inside out even if painted regularly. It is much lighter and will have a different character than solid metal.

The best way to learn is to ASK if you think the vendor really knows. Is this handmade? One-of-a kind custom designed? Are the parts manufactured or hand made? Manufactured parts can make ironwork more affordable, but usually some quality, character, and originality are sacrificed.

The Commission-Working Together

The first procedure is finding a blacksmith who designs work in the style the client likes. People may see work installed in a home or building, then track down the people responsible. Blacksmiths are listed in phone books under blacksmiths, ironwork, or ornamental metal work. Blacksmiths whose ironwork appears in this book, and others, may be contacted by writing to the publisher who will forward the request to the author. Authors often have Websites and can be contacted by E-mail. Many artist blacksmiths maintain Websites with examples of their work and contact information. People can also contact ABANA, The Artist Blacksmith Association of North America, (see resources) for references to local chapters and smiths.

The Internet has made it possible to work with artists in different areas and monitor a project's progress. The computer savvy artist blacksmith can easily photograph the project as it develops and upload it onto the Internet so the client can see it evolve. This is valuable for the architect, too. Should construction vagaries occur, necessary changes could be determined and made quickly. The blacksmith need not be on site for installation; local workers should be able to install any project anywhere. Entire staircases can be fashioned in California or New Zealand, and shipped to an Arab republic for installation in a palace.

Most smiths get their work by recommendations rather than from someone walking into their shop off the street. One smith works directly with a client, another works with architects who act as an agent for the client, another has interior designers who bring him all the work he can handle. Many get their commissions from corporations and public art agencies.

What questions should a potential client ask of a smith? Always ask to see a great quantity of high quality photos of the smith's work, or see other completed work on site if it's accessible. Request and check references.

The client should have an idea of what they want: style, period, material (iron, stainless steel, copper, brass, etc.), size, delivery schedule, and budget. Can the smith faithfully address all criterions? Is the smith willing to give references? Once terms are agreed upon, a formal bid is made and, when acceptable to all parties, a contract is signed with dates of completion and all pertinent information agreed upon clearly stated.

Enrique Vega says: "I have found that giving the client exceptional drawings that detail my approach to producing custom ironwork for their unique environments before they make the final decision on the commission is good business for all parties and it prevents misunderstandings, or future delays. Almost all commissions on which I work require some sort of drawing associated with the project. To cover some costs associated with the design time, a 5-10% non-refundable design fee is included in the total budget for the project and is required prior to starting the design drawings."

Tools and Techniques

Most blacksmithing involves heating the iron in a forge and working the iron when it is in a malleable state using an anvil, hammers, tongs, and other tools. The smith who works on large architectural projects needs a large working area, power hammers, and, often, a crew of helpers. Industrial lifting equipment and heavy truck transport may be needed to get a project to a site and to install it. There is so much more to a finished work than meets the eye once it is installed. It's not unusual for a project to take several months to be completed.

Heating, bending, twisting, and shaping into linear designs is the basis of ironwork, but many embellishments can be created. Iron can be manipulated in an almost clay-like fashion. When it is hot and malleable it can be shaped and carved using chisels and other tools. A single rod can be heated, hammered, the end shaped, then features carved for a dragon face, for example. The top can then be reheated and the bar separated to make ears. A nose, and other features, can be modeled, as the iron is workable.

A single bar can be split into branches and from each branch floral shapes can be hammered. It is also possible to make flowers by shaping the petals, layering them, then welding or riveting them together to fashion the flower. Several examples are shown.

Repoussé is another technique used to shape objects from thin metal sheet such as iron, copper, brass, silver, or other metals. This involves hammering the shape into the form using a block or mold for stretching, indenting, and shaping the metal. Essentially, this is the procedure used to make leaves and flower petals.

Often cast pieces will be combined with the forged pieces and these may be of any kind of material including bronze, brass, iron, aluminum, or silver.

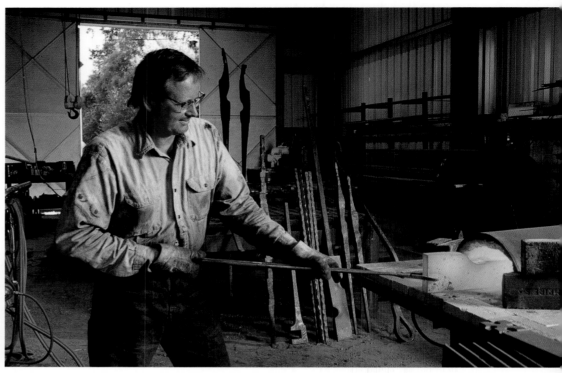

Russell Jaqua removes a red hot bar from a forge…

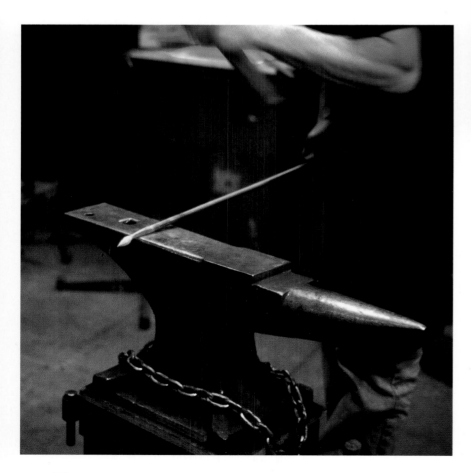

Hand forging is accomplished by heating a piece of iron in a forge until it is malleable, then pounding it on an anvil with any of a variety of hammers to shape it. *Photo, courtesy John Rais*

. . .and shapes it with a power hammer while it is in its red-hot malleable stage. A power hammer is a mainstay of most modern blacksmith shops. But shaping with hand held hammers may still be necessary for details. *Photos, Frank Ross*

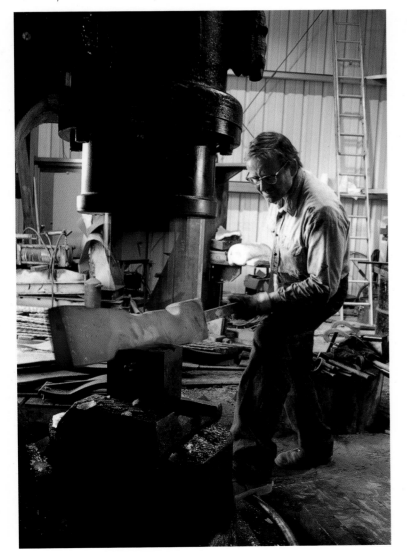

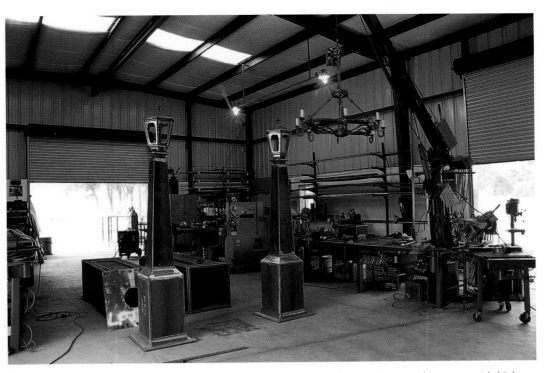

The shop that fashions large architectural decorative projects needs a spacious working area with high ceilings, such as Robert C. Bentley's shop in Paso Robles, California. *Photo, Bruce Woodworth*

Finishes and Maintenance

Metal finishes can vary considerably depending on whether the finished piece will be used indoors or outdoors. A finish may consist of paint (if color is desired), a clear coating, an acid finish, a patina, galvanizing, and/or waxing.

For interior pieces, many smiths prefer a clear finish such as several coats of acrylics that may be applied by brushing, dipping or spraying. Excess and drips are blown off with air. The finish dries in about 30 minutes. Wax may be used on bronze and sheet metal. Clear finishes bring out the beautiful subtle nuances and highlights inherent in hand forged metalwork.

Exterior work may be sandblasted, then hot dip galvanized , electro plated, powder coated, or primed with a cold galvanizing compound. Then it can be top coated with high quality acrylic or epoxy paint.

Surfaces may have to be re-waxed or refinished in time, depending upon the location of the piece. Anything exposed to weathering requires periodic maintenance. Maintenance instructions should be included with a work. Pieces installed as public art may have a maintenance clause built into the contract.

Ironwork Elements

Decorative ironwork is generally composed of rods, bars, and flat plate worked into shapes. Bars are round, flat, and square in different widths. Almost all decorative details are made from these whether they are scrolls, the pineapple for a newel post, a leaf, a fish, a cupid, a basket, a cluster of grapes, a flower, a medallion or any of a variety of spears. They are the basic design elements that may be mixed or matched in infinite variety. These are the blacksmith's alphabet and he uses them to form his unique vocabulary to create essays in iron.

As you study the iron pieces throughout the book, focusing on individual details will be an education. Here are details to observe:

The Twisted Bar

For generations the decorative ironworker has used the simple process of twisting an iron bar in one or two directions. The texture and visual effect depends on the amount of twisting, tightness of the twist, number of rotations, space in which the twist is concentrated, different spacing between twist sections, length of the twist, thickness of the bar, the heat under which the iron was twisted, and even who is twisting.

Twists may be created exactly the same under controlled factory production conditions, but the custom made piece of iron may have minor variations, or even exaggerated and purposeful variations for surface interest. Enrique Vega refers to twisting bars in two directions as the "yin and yang" in metal, or the results of using opposite forces. It is very evident in the twisted bars shown that they can become a "visual landscape of texture."

Vega uses a home built twisting machine and either heats the rod in the forge or with an oxyacetylene torch to control twisting. The key to twisting, especially on large 2" diameter solid steel, is to get the area really hot before starting the twist. Once the material passes the initial twist action the tightness of the twist is controlled by allowing more rotations and/or by the length of time the heat is on the iron. The iron should be at an orange heat throughout the material before starting the twist.

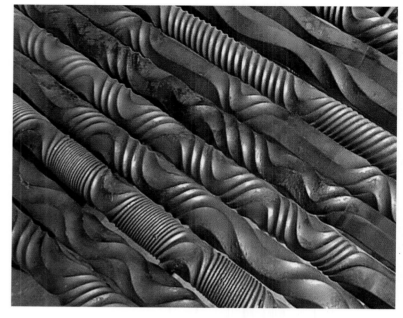

Enrique Vega. The twisted bar is a standard decorative element in forged ironwork. The twist patterns can differ tremendously as illustrated in these 5/8-inch hex bars by Enrique Vega. Vega refers to the alternate twisting as a yin and yang effect. *Photo, Enrique Vega*

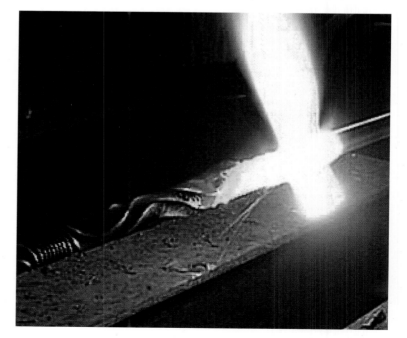

Enrique Vega. One end of the iron rod is in the twisting machine and the other end is in a hand held tool. The area being heated by the oxyacetylene torch can then be twisted to create the desired tightness and twist direction. *Photo, Enrique Vega*

Scrolls and Curves

S- and C-scrolls are the most common scroll shapes. These may be used alone, combined in multiples, or used with other shapes. They may be reversed and made into trefoils and quatrefoils. The ends may be shaped differently to add interest and dimension to a project. The type of end may vary on a project for additional variety.

These elements are like the blacksmith's alphabet, the chef's pantry of staples, and the embroiderer's stitches. The basics are infinitely combined to create the whole. After you learn what they are, and can identify them, being able to analyze a project makes it easier to understand and appreciate it. Try to find the elements in the examples shown here, and throughout the book, before you read the captions. Soon, you will have discovered that observation and knowledge are powerful tools for helping you appreciate and understand what's involved in ornamental ironwork.

Here are the elements, the motifs, the alphabet of ironwork shapes that black-smiths arrange in infinite combinations.

Scrolls and Scroll Endings

1. C Scroll: shaped like the letter C with a curved element at each end. Next to the straight bar the C scroll is probably the basic unit of any decorative iron railing.

There are many ways to finish the curved end of a scroll but most smiths use any or all of the followingt:

2. Ribbon end
3. Half penny snub-end
4. Barrel end
5. Bolt end
6. Fish tail end
7. Snub-end

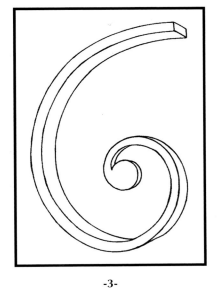

-3-

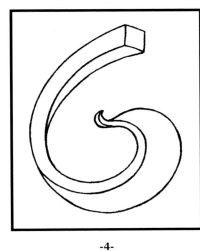

-4-

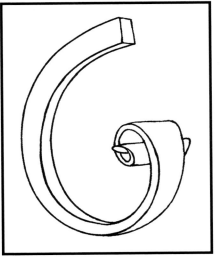

-6-

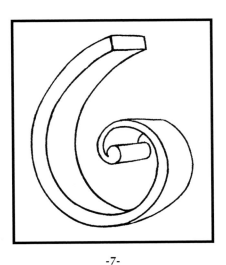

-7-

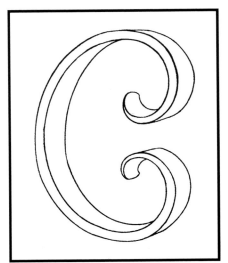

-1-

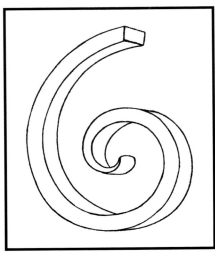

-2-

31

Linear and Geometric Elements

Straight lines
Waves
Greek key

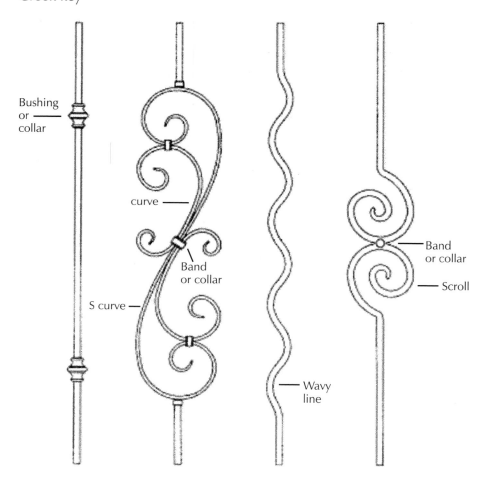

Bushing
or
collar

curve

S curve

Band
or collar

Band
or collar

Scroll

Wavy
line

Other elements frequently used and repeated in different configurations are:
Bushing or collar: holds two bars together, conceals a joint, and is decorative
C curve: The shape of the letter C with ends scrolled. The shape may be used elongated with one end longer than another, in combination with other forms and in infinite other ways.
S curve: The letter S also used in myriad ways.
Wavy line: used by itself, in combination with other bars, and twists.
Band or collar: Holds bars and curved elements together.
Scroll: a curved shape with a decorative curved ending
Drawings, John Medwedeff

Nature's shapes

Acanthus
Animal heads
Anthemion
Branches
Buds
Camellias
Corn
Fleur-de-lis
Grapes
Human faces
Imaginary heads such as dragons
Iris
Leaves
Oak leaves and acorns
Pineapple
Rose
Seashells

Objects

Basket
Cornucopia
Garland
Spears, arrows, spikes, tridents
Coronet
Heraldry shapes
Medallions

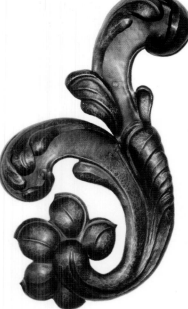

Jean-Pierre Masbanji. Most decorative pieces are hand raised using repoussé techniques. The anthemion (or honeysuckle) leaf is used in many sizes and shapes, and with a variety of metals and finishes. Shown is one with a the *vert-de-gris* finish, but they may be finished with gold or silver leaf, bronzed, and painted. The acanthus leaf, oak leaf, fleur-de-lis, and sea shell are also popular, and can be identified in work throughout the book. It's not unusual for a project to require 50 to 100 or more such items and each one may take several hours to create. *Photo, artist*

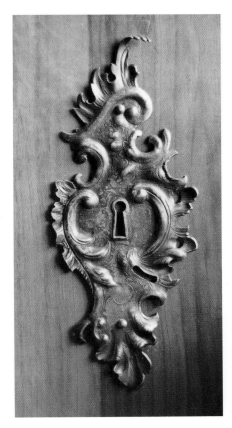

Thomas Wilson. Variation on an acanthus leaf is used for this escutcheon in an antique finish French style. *Photo, Grant Marino*

Jean Lamour. Detail of the gate in Place Stanislas, Nancy, France, illustrates the use of the acanthus leaf in many forms. There is a sea shell near the top. On top, there is a flower-filled loving cup with handles covered with anthemia. Most of the sroll work is covered with anthemia and other leaves. Note the gold balls between the scrolls; those are joinery units. *Courtesy, Office de Tourisme de Nancy, France*

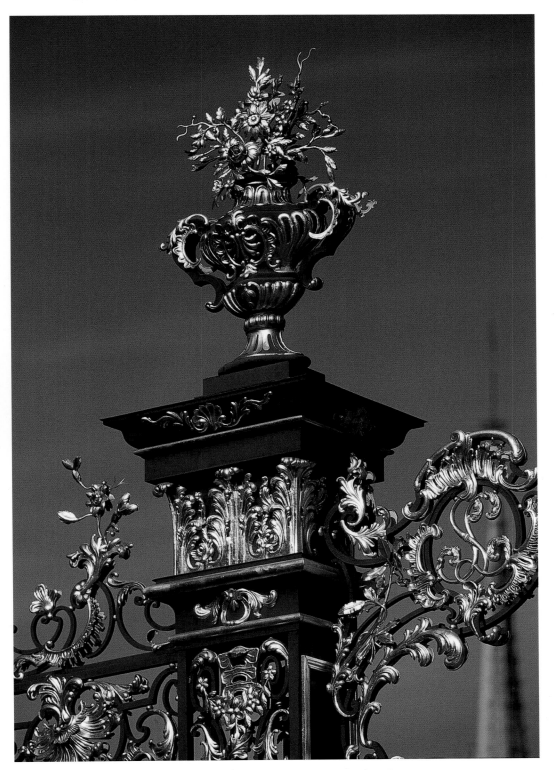

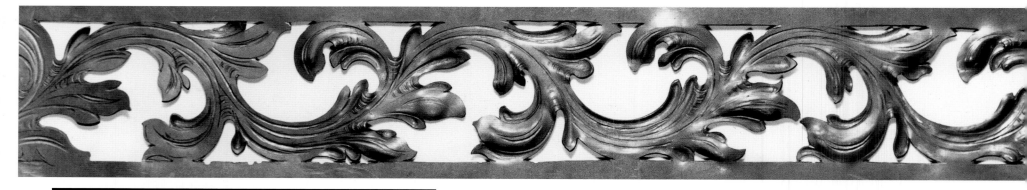

Thomas Wilson. A frieze composed of connected anthemion leaves. Often a leaf is curved and used on the rod elements of a staircase or railing. *Photo, Grant Marino*

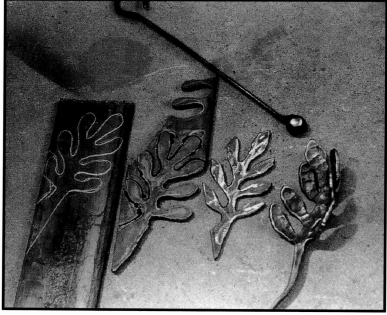

Lars Stanley shows how an oak leaf for his Zilker Gates (see Chapter 5) is developed. First the leaf is drawn on the metal. Next it is roughly cut out with an oxy-acetylene torch. The leaf is heated to a malleable state and the ball end of the rod shown, called a "ball fuller," is hammered repeatedly into the leaf causing the indents and also curving the leaf as the metal is deformed and expanded. The process is fast and many leaves can be forged in a short amount of time. *Photo, artist*

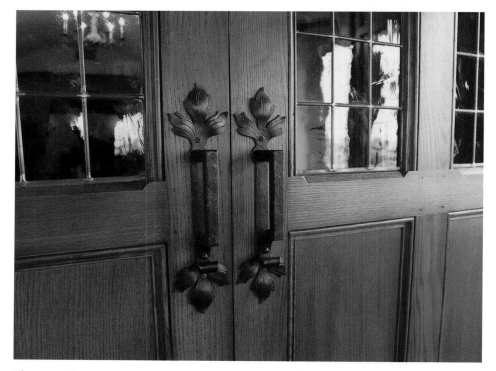

Thomas Wilson. A variation on an oak leaf for a pair of door handles. *Photo, Grant Marino*

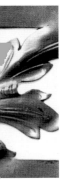

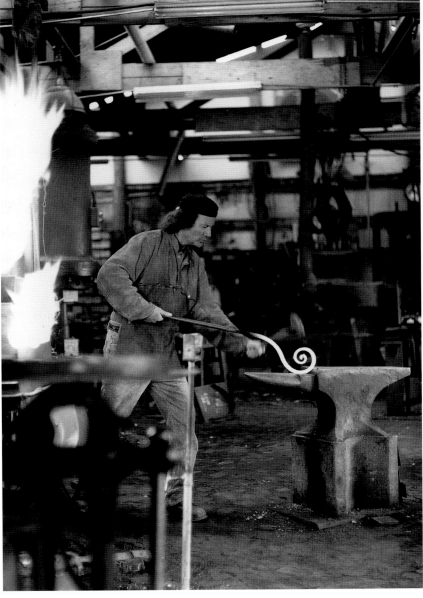

Christopher Thomson. Each scroll is hand forged by placing the heated end of the iron rod on the anvil and, with a hammer, shaping the end, and then carefully rounding and shaping the rod. *Photo, Lizzy Kate Gray*

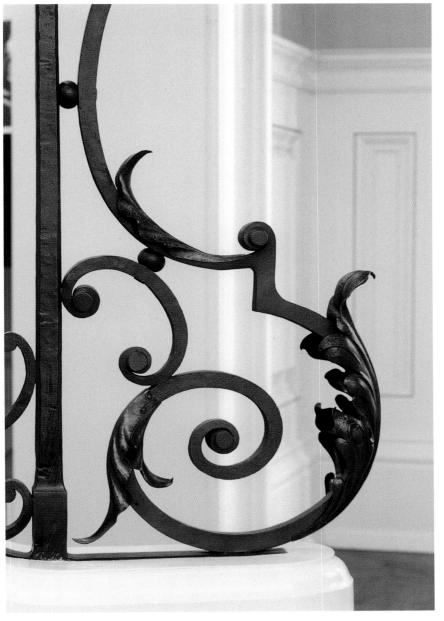

Jean-Pierre Masbanji. Several hand forged elements can be identified in this one section of a staircase:
C Scroll.
Half C scroll at one end; the other angled and joined to another curved shape.
A full acanthus leaf and other portions of leaves.
Balls joining the parts with rivets to the upright.
Photo, James Chen

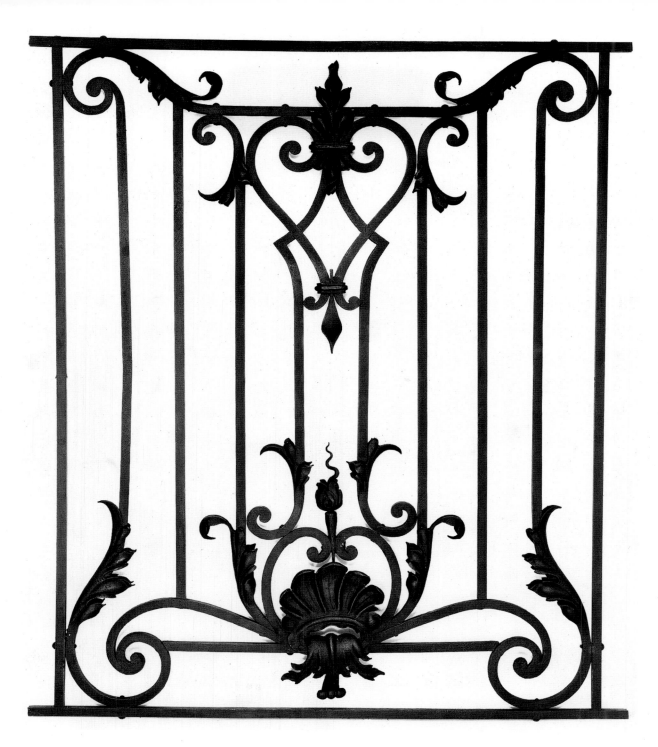

Thomas Wilson. Several traditional ironwork elements can be identified in this grille.
The straight bar
- C scroll with snub ending on the scroll. Acanthus leaves used as a transition from the curved to the straight bars.
- A seashell form at the bottom.
- An anthemion at the top.
- In the center a band joins two ends of the S scroll and a spear shape is between them.
- Below, a tapered, drawn-out corkscrew end "grows" from the flower.
- The curved corners are mounted to the frame with rivets.

Photo, Grant Merino

Enrique Vega. Details from a gate. Twist, leaf end and pointed end scrolls, leaves, bands, circles, and curved members, are part of a larger composition. Observe how the bars with the twists are split to become the leaf end scrolls banded to the circular center. *Photo, artist*

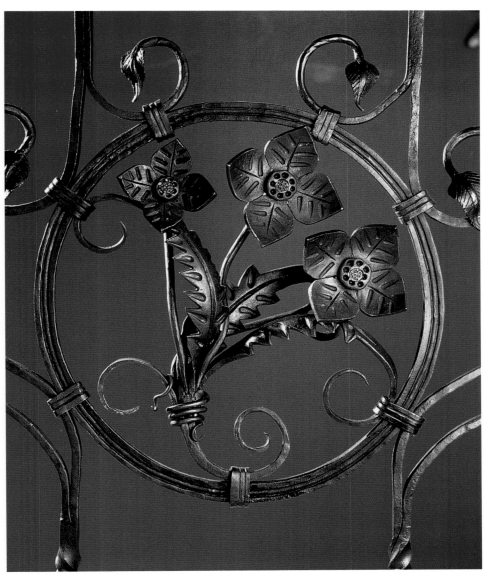

Enrique Vega. Details from a gate. A similar theme as in Vega's bird example, but in this central detail the flowers have punched centers. *Photo, artist*

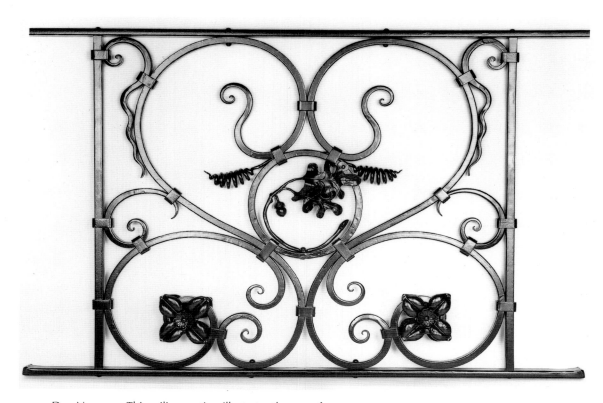

Dan Nauman. This railing section illustrates the use of
- C curves.
- Exaggerated S curves.
- Scroll ends drawn out to graceful points.
- Corkscrew shapes suggest plant forms.
- Four petal medallions.
Courtesy, artist

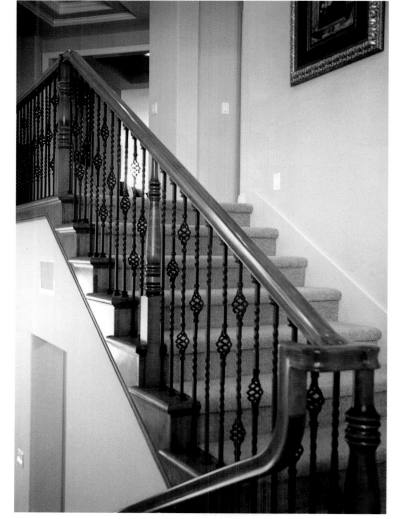

Another often used ornamental motif is called the "basket" or the "bird cage". In this staircase one and two baskets are used on alternate balusters. Using two to four rods welded together on opposite sides of the basket area, then heating the rods where the basket is to appear, makes these motifs. One side is secured in a vise, the other end is twisted with another tool and the rods open up to form the basket. This work must be done quickly. *Photo, author*

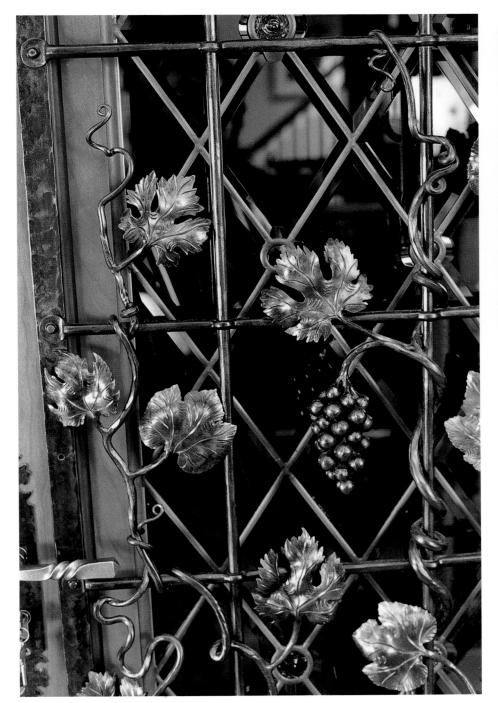

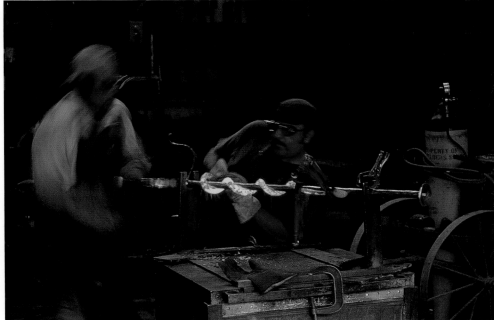

Christopher Thomson. Lest you think that winding iron around iron is an easy task, Thomson and a helper illustrate how it's done. The straight bar is clamped into a vise on each end. The iron is then heated to a malleable state, wound around the straight bar, then further shaped and textured. Several heats may be required to finish any one length of a wrap. *Photo, William Fuller*

Scott Lankton. Grille for a wine cellar door, detail. Grapes, vines, and leaf motifs are frequently used in ironwork. Each leaf is different, the vines wind around the horizontal and vertical bars, and tendrils wind around the vines. Leaves are shaped using the repoussé technique. Grapes are made by raising, or shaping, two half balls, welding them together to make one grape, then combining them into the grape cluster. *Photo, artist*

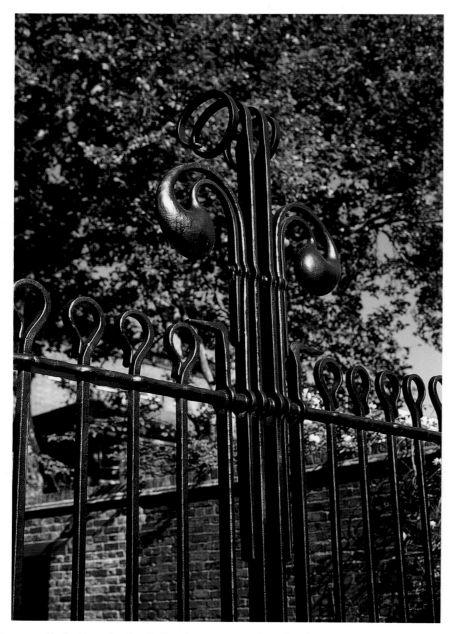

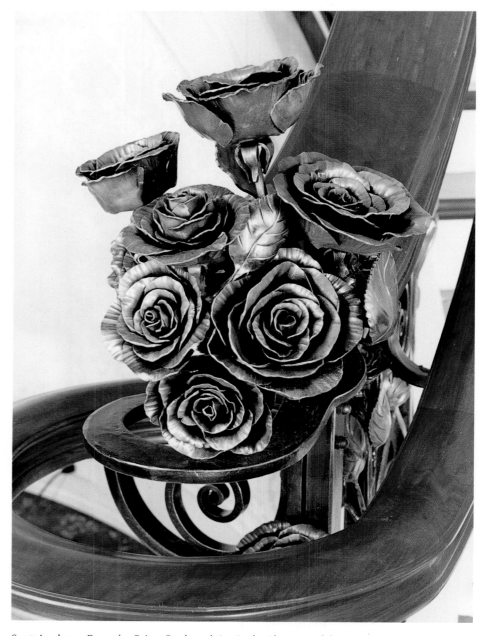

Terrence Clark. Gates for the Geffrye Museum, London (detail). Large-scale projects must have sturdy, decorative methods for joining the horizontal and vertical elements. Punching, which is essentially making a hole in a bar for another bar to pass through is a stronger joint than just welding two pieces of iron together. When a punch is made, the iron is not actually removed; rather it is spread to allow the intersecting bar to pass through. The sides expand, yielding a design variation. Clark also uses rivets for joining the uprights, again by using a punched area for the rivet to pass through. *Photo, artist*

Scott Lankton. Roses by Brian Cook and Jim Roth. Close up of the roses and leaves from the Rose Staircase. Each petal is raised by hand and textured, then combined to form the flower. The roses, leaves, and stems are bronze brushed while hot, using mechanical or abrasion plating, and then finished with clear acrylic. The old world look bronze color is subtler than gold leaf. *Photo, Scott Lankton*

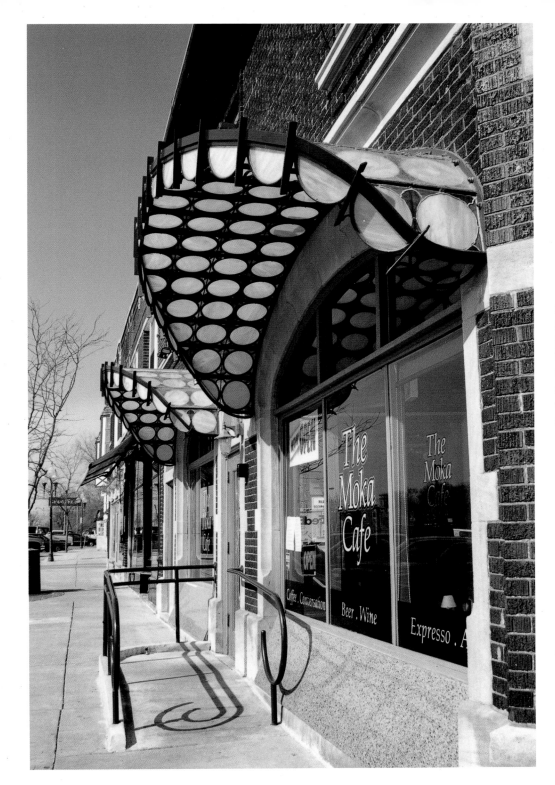

Chapter 2
Entries and Door Hardware

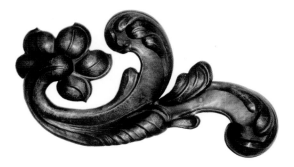

Entryways and doors are taken for granted when one approaches and enters a building or a room. Yet the architect, builder, and designer give much thought and attention to them. An entryway protected by a canopy or awning gives a building a class, a caché that makes it extraordinary. Certainly, one can buy any number of mass produced doors but making them unique requires custom designing and hardware. A plain door can be embellished creatively with a variety of overlay solutions. Among them are grilles, custom designed hinges, hasps, latches, and knockers.

Mark J. Hubrich. Two of three canopies and an entry railing for The Moka Café, Illinois. The ornamental iron-work with glass insets involved an inordinate amount of innovative engineering to achieve the curvature required. *Photo, Victoria Doolittle*

Canopies and Awnings

The ultimate embellishment for an entryway might be a canopy or awning-like structure that can serve many purposes. It is decorative, of course, but it can also shade the area. It delineates the entry in a commercial building, identifies the building, and may carry signage such as the name or address of the establishment. Sometimes, a decorative canopy is so unique, it is an identifiable image used as a logo.

Mark Hubrich's three canopies for the windows of the Moka Café in Illinois are composed of ironwork with glass insets. Engineering the framework was a nightmarish endeavor because of the many curves involved and the intractability of glass. It's one thing for a designer to visualize and draw such a canopy in a rendering. It's another to accomplish the feat. Mark also created railings for the entry.

Says Hubrich; "This was my favorite and most challenging fabrication. It had over ten different radii. Each piece had to be custom cut to fit. The most challenging process of fabrication was forming the return of the fascia to the wall at either end. Each panel was measured and made to fit while keeping the design uniform and also removable to aid in cleaning. I made the job a lot easier by ordering 90% of this project as various diameters of pipe cut into rings 1/2-inch wide. There were many home-made jigs used in this job."

The large canopy over the entry to the Place du Casino in Monte Carlo, Monaco, is iron and glass, but the canopy is a flat plane; only the front framing is curved. This 19th Century building is in the Napoleon III style. Charles Garnier, who also designed the Paris Opera House, designed the interior theatre and much of the exterior decoration of this building.

The Casino at Monte Carlo, Monaco. Iron and glass canopy with iron hanging light fixtures. *Photo, author*

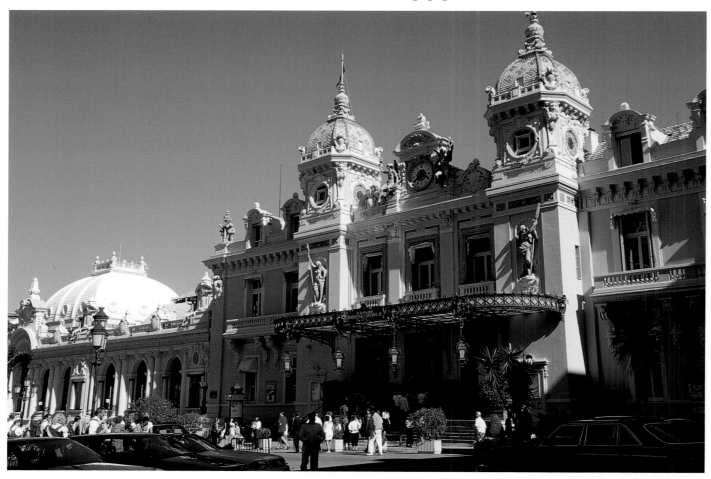

Paul Saintenoy's (1862-1952), early Art Nouveau canopy and ironwork tracery on the windows and bays of the Old England Department Store building in Brussels, Belgium, have been emulated in other cities. First built in 1889, it was remodeled in 1998, and in 2000 it became the home of the Museum of Musical Instruments. I saw a replica of this façade in a small city in North Carolina.

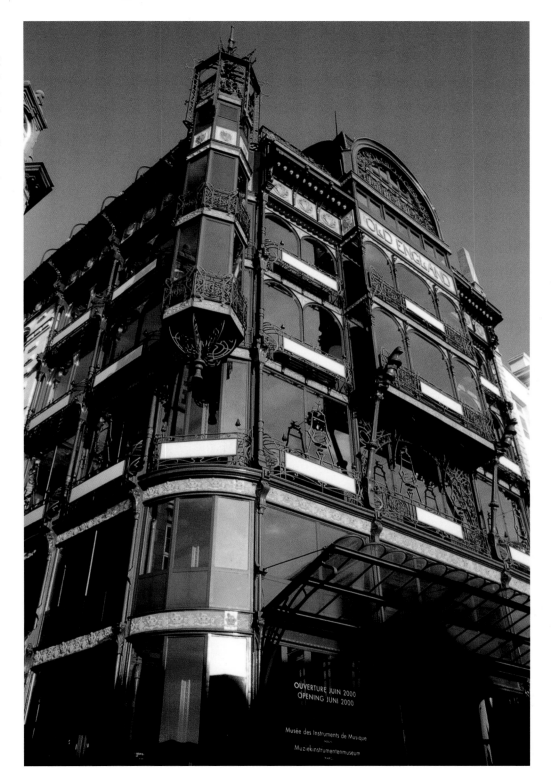

Paul Saintenoy. 1862-1952. The Old England Department Store, 1899, Brussels, Belgium. This totally metal framed and ornamented building was restored in 1998. It opened as the Museum of Musical Instruments in 2000. Canopy, side tower, railings, two-story bow window, façade, tympanum, and other ironwork ornamentation. *Photo, Werner F. Bocqué*

Simon Benetton's canopy for a restaurant in Italy is open at the top and provides a containment area for the outdoor dining tables in a strictly modern style. It is supported by posts and shaped brackets. Benetton also uses a series of curved shapes in the overhang, side supports, and the balustrade for the staircase at the Instituto Suore Canoissiane in Treviso, Italy.

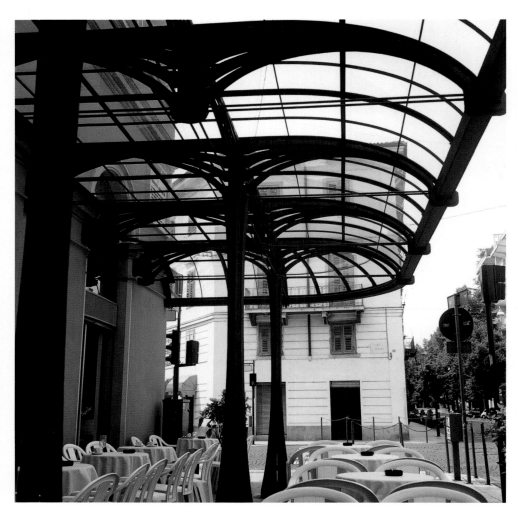

Simon Benetton. Canopy for the Complesso Cafe Theater Verdi di Gorizia. *Courtesy, artist*

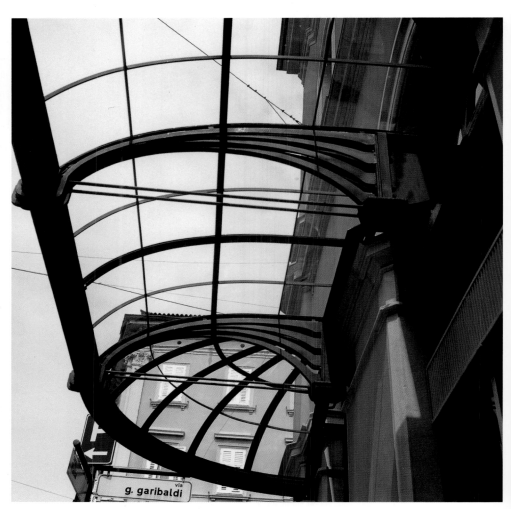

Simon Benetton. Detail illustrating the structural components of the canopy for the Complesso Cafe Theater Verdi di Gorizia. *Courtesy, artist*

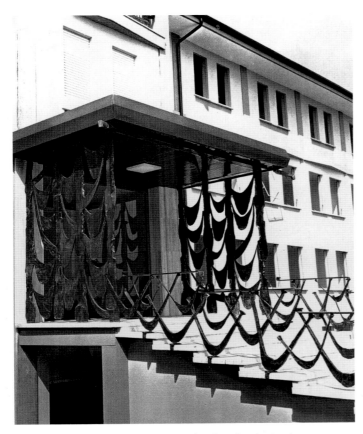

Simon Benetton. Entry structure and railing for the Instituto Surore Canossiane di Treviso, Treviso, Italy. *Courtesy, artist*

A 19th century Baroque canopy marks the entry to a small hotel off a main square in Budapest, Hungary. It also has glass on the top surface integrated with the ironwork. There are iron scrollwork, medallions, and anthemion leaf forms along the top.

Budapest, Hungary. Glass topped hotel canopy off the Central Square has medallions, scrolls, and stylized flowers. *Photo, author*

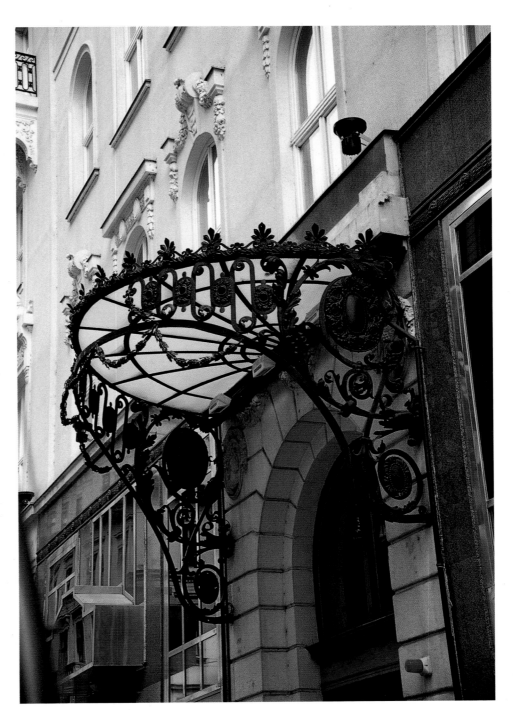

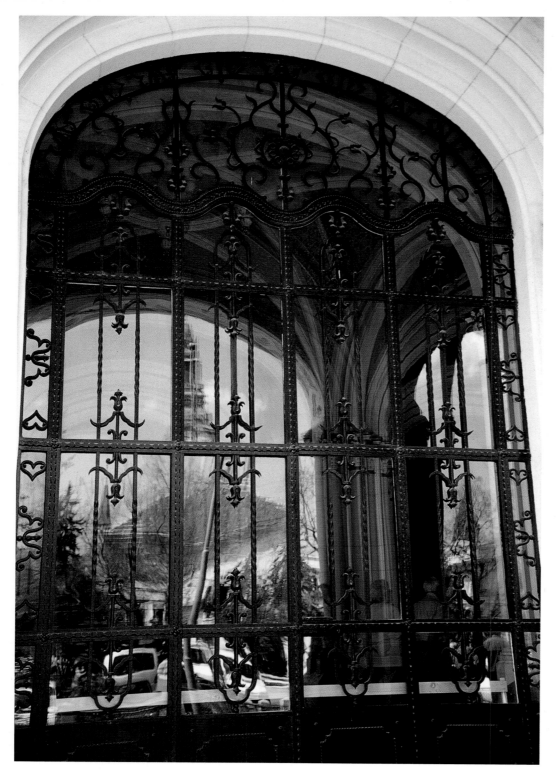

Ödön Lechner's ironwork over the two story glass windows of the Town Hall in Kesckemet, Hungary, represents his masterful Art Nouveau designs. Other buildings he designed are the Central Market, and the Museum of Applied and Decorative Arts in Budapest. All have the patterned tile work roof in a French style.

Ödön Lechner. Iron window tracery. Town Hall, Kecskemét, Hungary. *Photo, author*

A dramatic entry becomes the façade for the King Street Center in Seattle, Washington, by Jean Whitesavage and Nick Lyle. This was a public art project commissioned by Wright, Runstad & Company, The National Development Council, and the King County Public Art Program.

A gazebo structure, also by Whitesavage and Lyle, with symbols of fruit made in iron becomes the entry to the Farmers Market in Seattle, Washington.

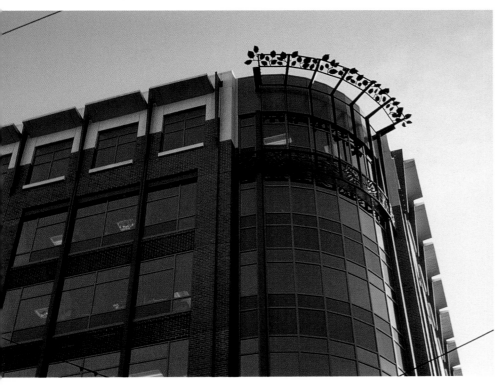

Jean Whitesavage and Nick Lyle. Rainforest project of forged steel has elements around and within the building. The project includes main entry gates, two sets of bi-fold gates, two large building brackets, a decorative sculpture band, and an eyebrow. The Rainforest canopy of alder leaves is at the top. A sculptural band below has alder leaves and deer fern.18' high, 22' wide, 12' deep. King Street Center, Seattle, Washington. *Commissioned by Wright, Runstad & Company, The National Development Council, and the King County Public Art Program. Photo, artists*

Right: Jean Whitesavage and Nick Lyle. Rainforest Project. Gates and frieze. King Street Center, Seattle, Washington. *Commissioned by Wright, Runstad & Company, The National Development Council, and the King County Public Art Program. Photo, artists*

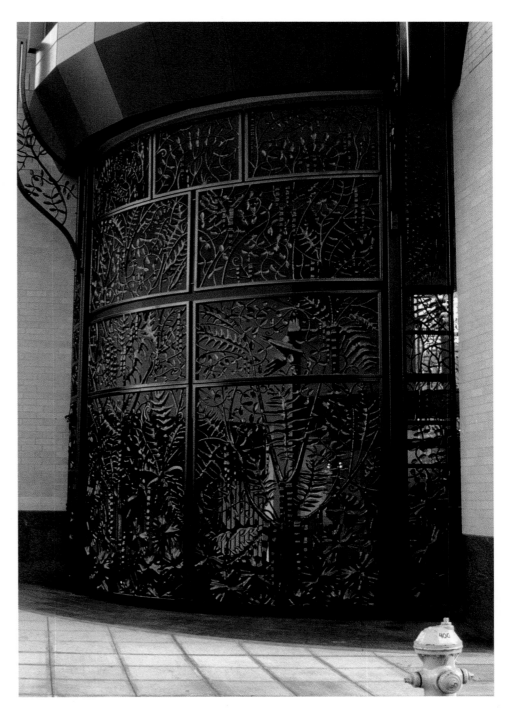

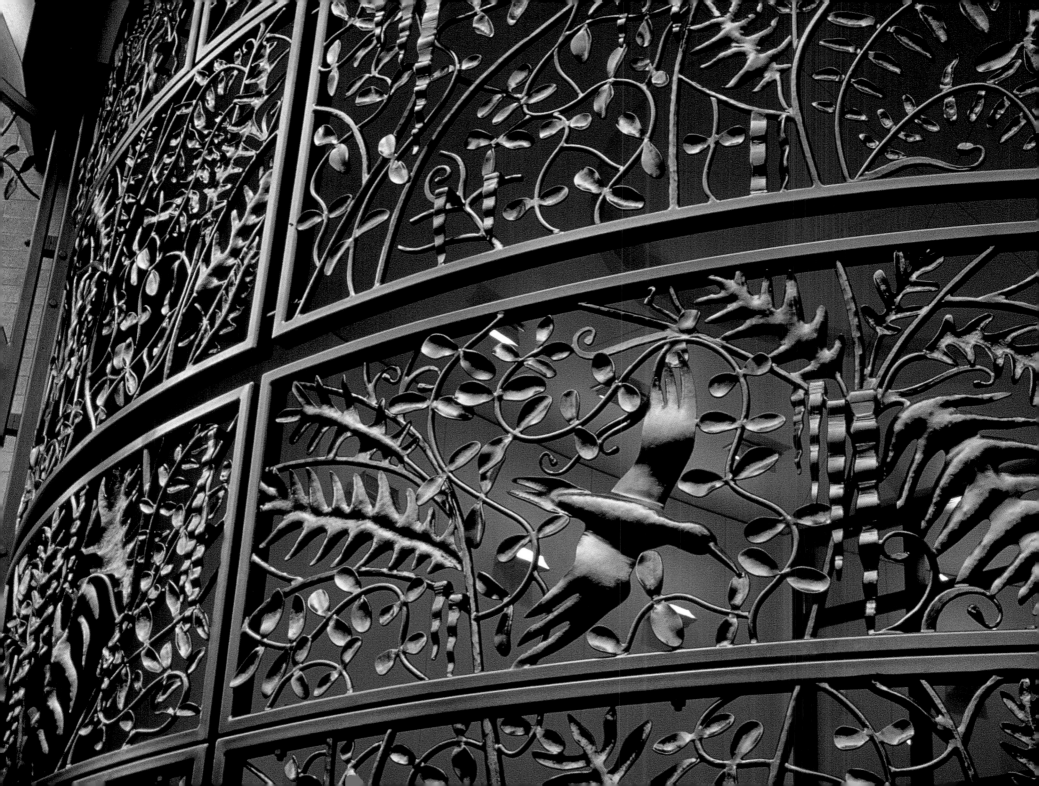

Opposite page: Jean Whitesavage and Nick Lyle. Rainforest Project, (above). Detail of the frieze with the Northern Flicker bird and surrounding foliage. The architectural bracket is at the left. *Photo, artists*

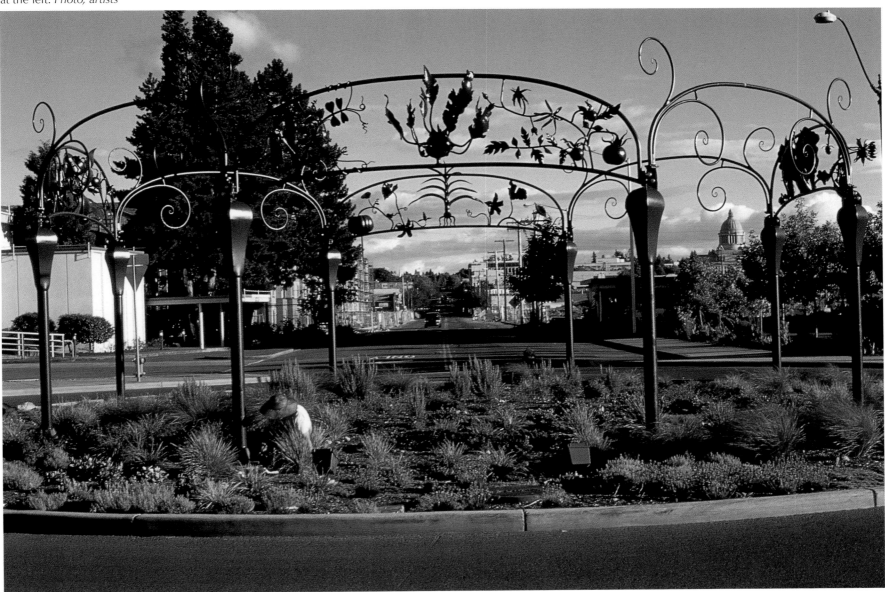

Jean Whitesavage and Nick Lyle. Triumph of the Vegetables. Forged steel and landscaping for the entry to The Olympia Farmer's Market. Each of the four panels displays different food plants. *Project administered by the City of Olympia Arts Commission, Olympia, Washington. Photo, artists*

The single sign for a walkway at Carroll College, Waukesha, Wisconsin, is an arch, integrated with the stone pillars by Dan Nauman. The assignment was to make the arch appear like it was made in the 1800s and to incorporate motifs from the college's history. Nauman's research led him to incorporate items from the college's past.

Joseph Bonifas's surrounds, and entry and exit areas, for the Knight Library, at the University of Oregon, are contemporary, and in keeping with the library's architecture. The elements also have symbolic meanings that relate to the effects of education. The artist writes, "The idea was based on a stone hitting a still body of water and the effects it causes. As the stone contacts the water it creates a transverse wave; the distance the wave travels is in direct correlation to the initial impact. I feel that learning is much like that stone. Although the initial impact of learning may be subtle, the oscillatory effect of that information on an individual can be influential for a lifetime. The gentle curves at the top are symbolic of the waves, and the twisted steel and splashing curves cascading down are representational of water and education that may be forgotten or lost in time."

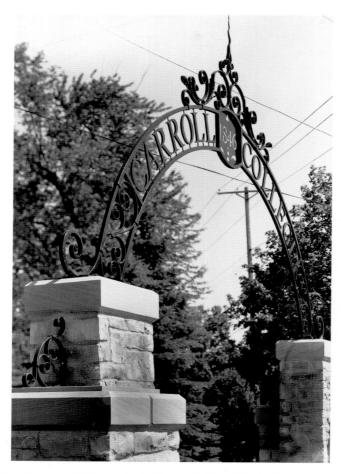

Dan Nauman. Walkway Arch. Carroll College, Waukesha, Wisconsin. Mild steel. The commission required that the arch look like it was made in the mid-nineteenth century, and it had to make a statement about the college. 8' high, 15.5' wide. *Photo, George Lottermoser*

Joseph A. Bonifas. "Transverse Wave Portal," Knight Library, University of Oregon, Eugene, Oregon. One of two entryways. The concept was developed as a metaphor for the learning process. *Photo, Jack Liu*

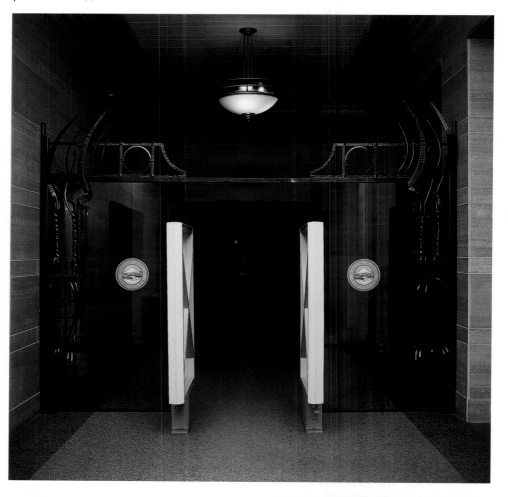

Doors - Inside and Out

The usual perception of iron doors is for security. That's a valid perception and the reason that bank and vault doors are always made of iron. When such doors are also designed as a decorative part of the architecture, the ambiance of the environment takes on a different aura. Think of jail doors with their austere, foreboding, unadorned linear construction and then look at the examples that follow and you'll have a new appreciation for iron as it is used in doors.

In medieval and Renaissance times, iron was used for church architecture as doors, decoration, as hardware for sturdy wooden doors, for dividers within the church, light fixtures, candleholders, and myriad other functional items. Today, iron is still used for churches, cathedrals, synagogues, banks, and anyplace a combination of security and beauty are desired. Perfect examples are the doors throughout the National Cathedral, Washington, DC. Most have been created, and signed, by well-known current and past blacksmiths such as Samuel Yellin, Tom Bredlow, and Theodore Voss. To ironworkers, these names are as well known as many master painters are to the art world.

Many of today's ironworkers specialize in restoring iron objects from various historical periods. Such designs have been well chronicled in myriad other books. The objective here is to hammer out new territory by showing derivations for today's ideas and to illustrate possible idea sources for new work.

It's not surprising that the sinuous, creative forms of the Art Nouveau period still exert a great influence on today's designers and ironworkers. The embellishments and integration of iron and wood in the doors from the Belgian architects Prosper Schryvers, Victor Horta, Jean Teughels, and Franz Hemelsoft can still be seen in Brussels. Generally, the architects have been credited with the designs, and there is little historical reference about the people who did the actual blacksmithing. Nevertheless, these anonymous workers left their stamp upon art history with an indelible and incredible body of work. Whether they were interpreting the architect's sketches, or innovating and improving as they created, is not known.

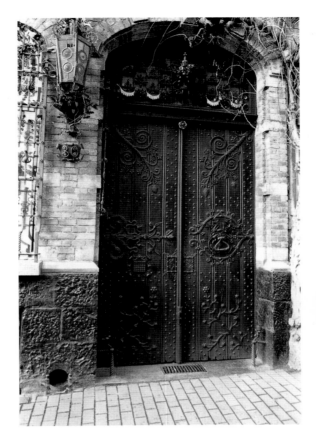

Prosper Schryvers. House of Prosper Schryvers entry door. Schryvers was among the few well known blacksmiths at the end of the 1900s. Rich details and a doorknocker are incorporated into the design. Brussels, Belgium. *Photo, Werner F. Bocqué*

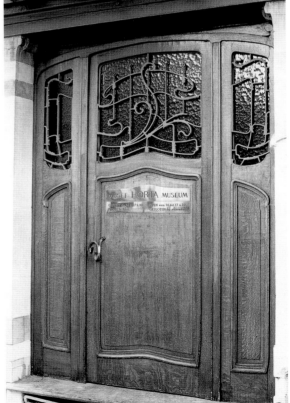

Victor Horta. 1861-1947. Doors to Horta's House are now the entry to the Horta Museum. The ironwork and the wood show the curving elements that characterized Art Nouveau in Brussels, Belgium, in the early 1900s. *Photo, Werner F. Bocqué*

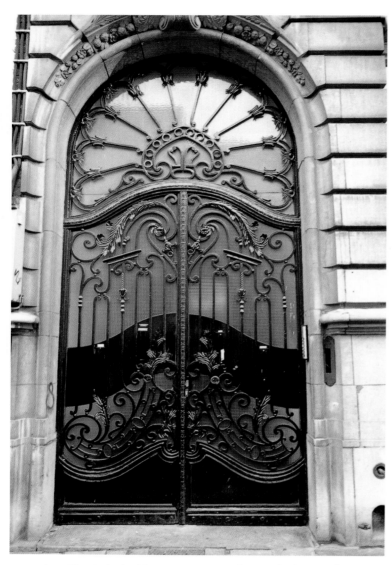

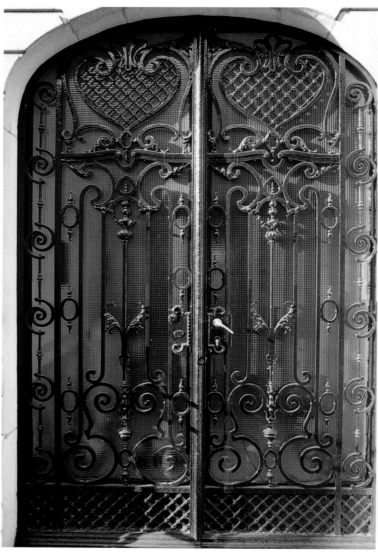

The symmetry in the cast iron doors from Budapest, Hungary, are Art Nouveau, though in a more restrained style than the Brussels, Belgium, examples. The abstract flowers, geometric shapes, and lack of twists, swirls, and scrolls indicate that they were probably made at a later date than 1900-1910.

Jean Teughels. Art Nouveau entrance door to the house of Jean Teughels. Turn of the 20th Century. Brussels, Belgium. *Photo, Werner F. Bocqué*

Franz Hemelsoft. Any portion of a detail from these Art Nouveau doors could be inspiration for a contemporary door design. Brussels, Belgium. *Photo, Werner F. Bocqué*

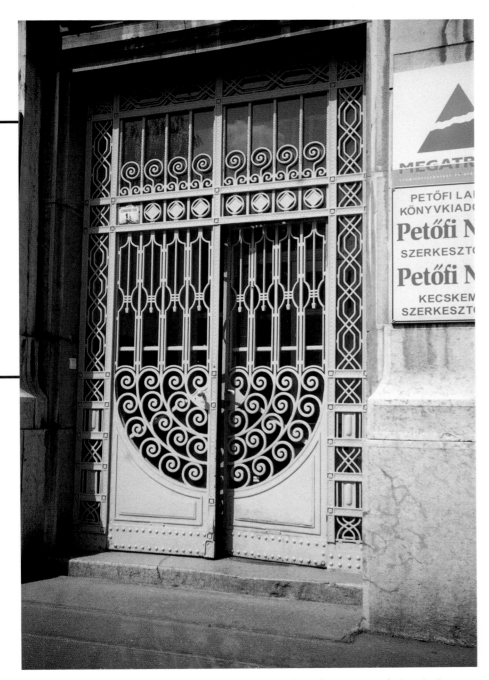

Cast iron door represents the Art Nouveau departure from the Baroque designs in Budapest, Hungary. These doors have stood the test of time in both design and sturdiness. *Photo, author*

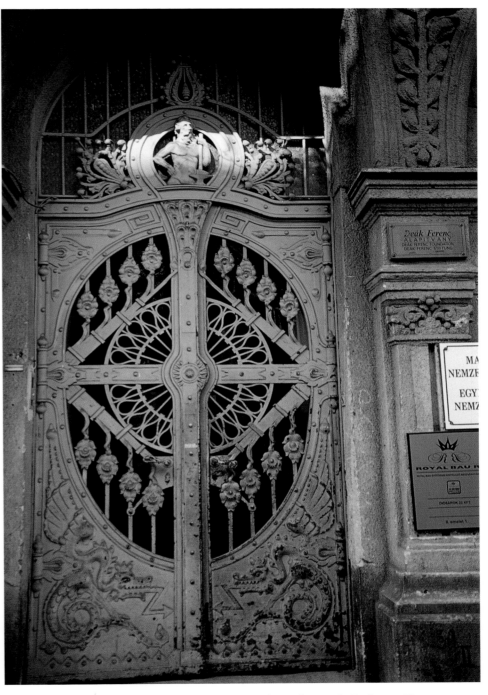

Another cast iron door, Szentendre, Hungary, is similar to the one in Budapest. The same architects often worked in both cities that are only about 75 miles apart. *Photo, author*

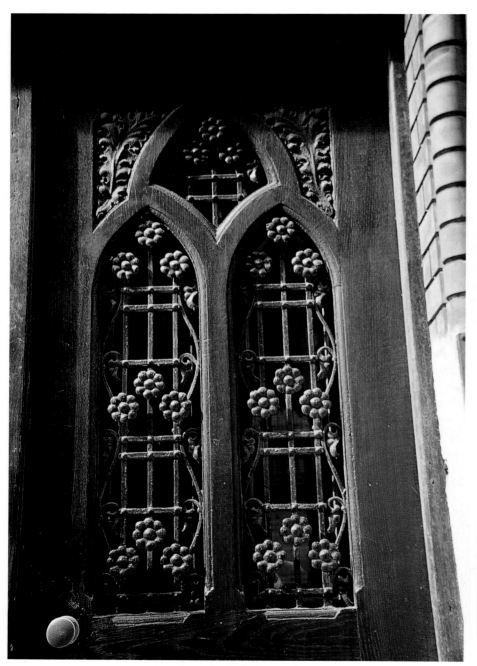

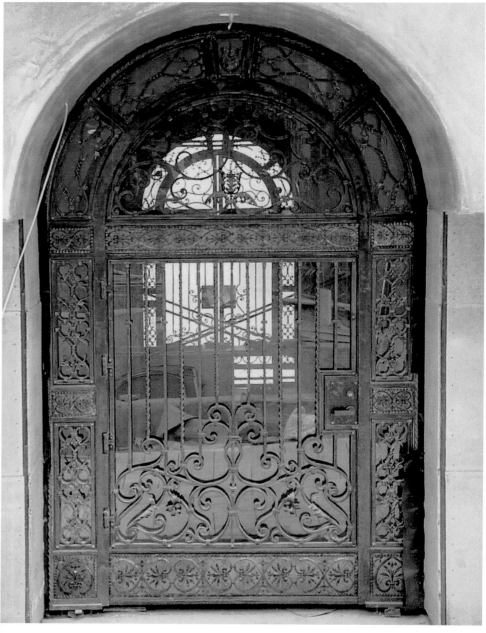

The pointed arch, perfect symmetry, and rosettes are throwbacks to Gothic but the curving lines indicate an Art Nouveau heritage. Budapest, Hungary. *Photo, author*

Alan Drew and Dorothy Stiegler. Drew and Stiegler Metal Designs. A pair of hammer textured, silicon bronze doors designed by Alan Drew. They are sited so that the ocean is in view when you look through them. Richly detailed side panels have floral elements, twists, and other motifs. Repoussé panels are along the top and bottom. *Photo, Michael Murphy*

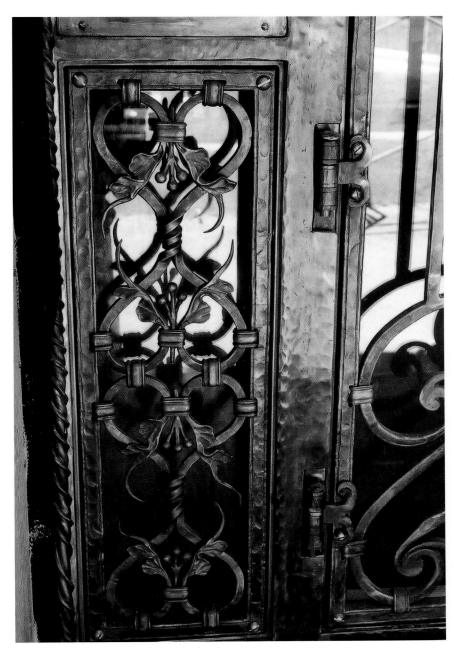

Alan Drew and Dorothy Stiegler. Bronze door detailing shows the texturing, twists, banding, leaves, and buds. *Photo, Dorothy Stiegler*

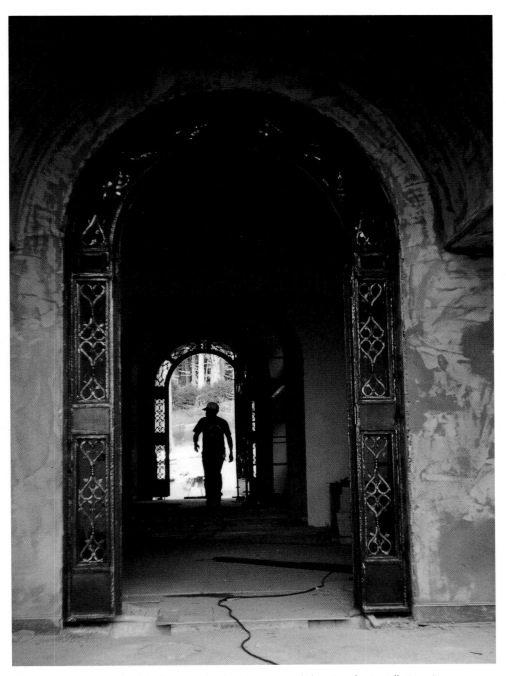

Alan Drew and Dorothy Stiegler. Doorjambs in place, and showing the installation site. Without the glass, each doorjamb weighs about 2300 pounds and the door itself weighs another 1600 pounds. Heavy lifting equipment was required in the shop and on site to handle the doors. *Photo, Dorothy Stiegler*

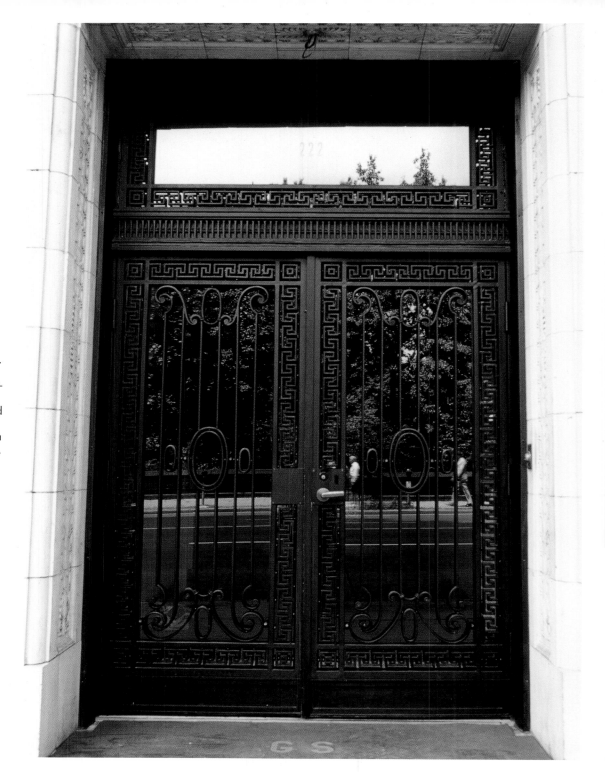

Joel A. Schwartz. Gainsborough Studio entry doors. Vertical bars with ovals end in scrolls. A Greek key design is used for a border on the doors and the transom. James Rhoades, architect. *Courtesy, artist*

Japan's Kotaro Kurata and Goro Hatanaka create many doors for apartment building entries that combine security, strength, and ornamentation. They lament the fact that many of their clients request more western looks to their properties rather than building on traditional Japanese design. They try to combine both by emphasizing the simplicity of their cultural heritage using design repetitions, gracefulness, and restraint.

Transfer Co., Kotaro Kurata and Goro Hatanaka. Entry to an apartment complex. Repeats of circles collared together with a three-sided frame on each door. The top row has broken circles with slight scroll endings. Three-dimensional square shapes with protrusions provide support and additional design touches. *Photo, Shinichi Sato*

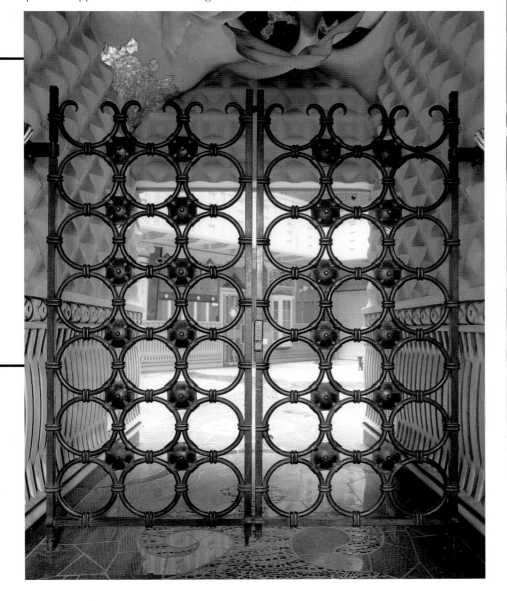

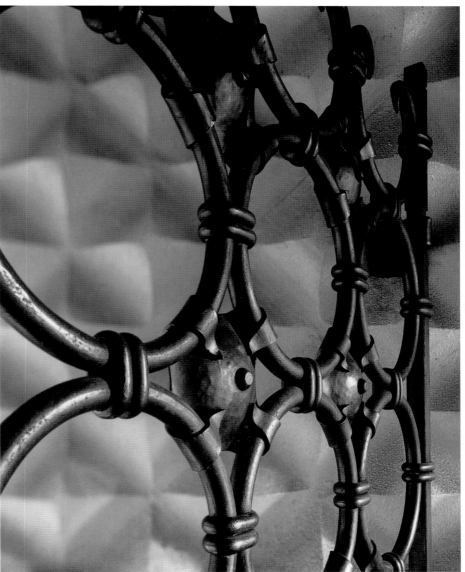

Transfer Co., Kotaro Kurata and Goro Hatanaka. Detail of collaring and square structures. *Photo, Shinichi Sato*

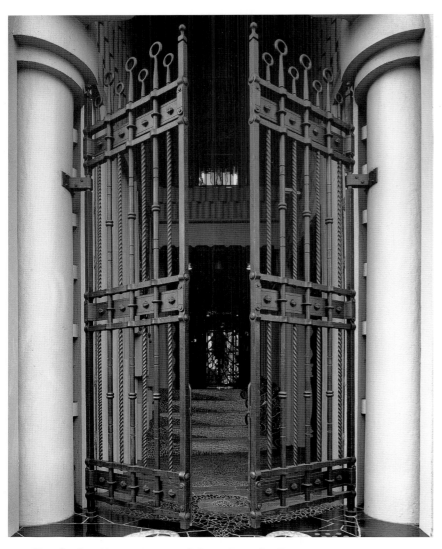

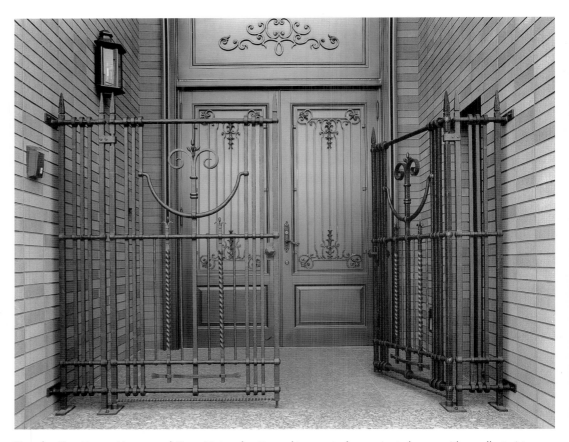

Transfer Co., Kotaro Kurata and Goro Hatanaka. Forged iron gate for a private home with scrolls, twist uprights, and spear endings at top. 6.8' high, 7.5' wide. *Photo, Shinichi Sato*

Transfer Co., Kotaro Kurata and Goro Hatanaka. Entrance gate to an apartment complex. Forged iron. Twisted and plain bars with collars are set into horizontal bars. Wider horizontal plates behind the uprights create another dimension. Alternating long and short circular shapes at the top are a nice touch rather than a solid horizontal frame. *Photo, Shinichi Sato*

California artist blacksmith, Michael Bondi produces an infinite variety of elegant architectural items as shown by the three doors illustrated. One is combined with chip glue glass in a modern interpretation of the examples from Hungary with iron over glass. The door detail and texture of the steel show his exquisite craftsmanship.

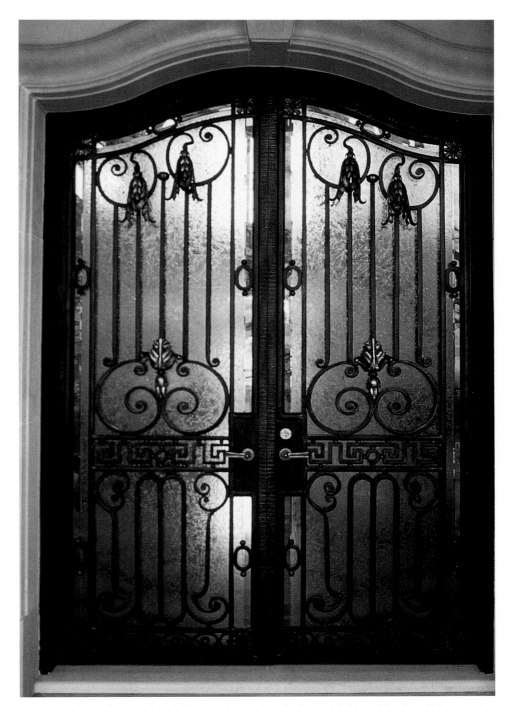

Michael Bondi. Forged and fabricated French style door with blue chip glass. Private residence. *Photo, artist*

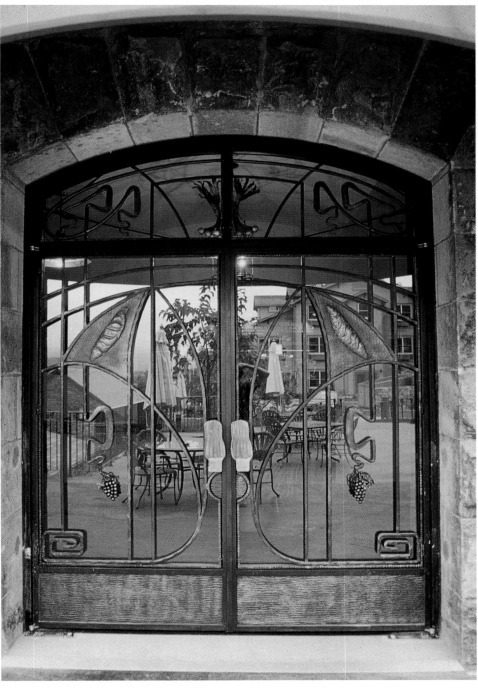

Michael Bondi. Forged and fabricated door with pictographic details and bronze pulls. Culinary Institute of America. *Photo, artist*

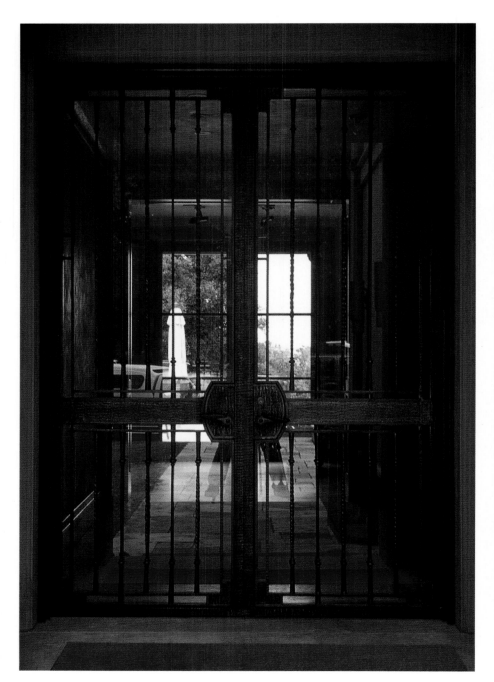

Michael Bondi. Forged and fabricated steel door. Private residence. *Photo, artist*

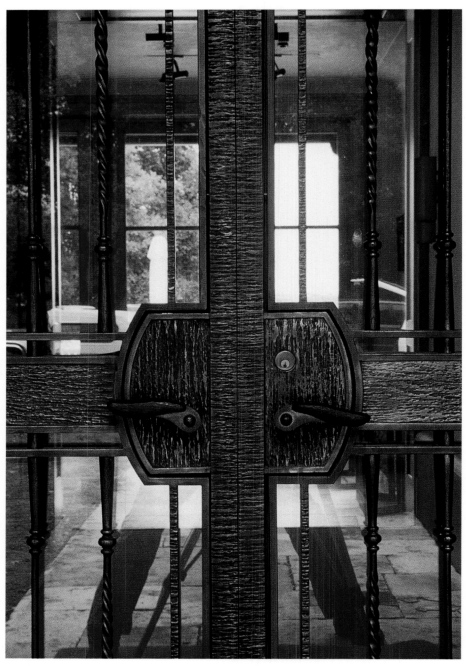

Michael Bondi. Detail of the door handle, doorjamb, and some of the uprights with the carefully worked texture. *Photo, artist*

ArtsWork Unlimited of Miami, Florida, designs outrageously different doors that may have their foot in the Art Nouveau heritage, but are uniquely individual. In the aluminum abstract door a variety of materials and construction techniques were used. The design was drawn on CAD, and then water jet cut from 1/2" thick plate. A frame was routed to accept the plate and the plate was attached with over 200 stainless steel countersunk screws. All the three-dimensional leaves were formed from 1/8" aluminum sheet using custom dies on a Pullmax sheet metal tool and conventional repoussé tools. The metal was repeatedly annealed to keep it soft. Commercial door seals were installed and the door was backed with 1/2" impact glass to create a secure and maintenance-free front entrance to a waterfront residence. An antique bronze faux finish was added.

ArtsWork Unlimited. Aluminum doors fabricated using various techniques. The design was drawn on CAD, and then water jet cut from 1/2" thick plate. The three-dimensional leaves were formed from 1/8" aluminum sheet using custom dies and conventional repoussé tools, and repeatedly annealing the metal to keep it soft. Antique bronze faux finish. *Photo, Kathleeen Ballard*

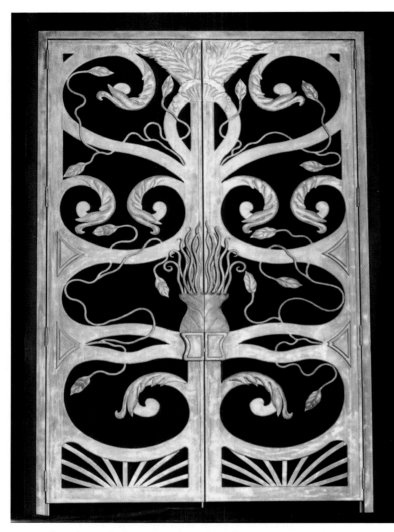

ArtsWork Unlimited. Aluminum doors, detail, show the routed edge finish, repoussé leaves, and door handles. *Photo, Kathleen Ballard*

Other doors and gates by ArtsWork Unlimited (Chapter 5) may be sinuous and flowing. Still others reflect their surroundings and the client's wishes and may include sunsets, flamingos, swamp plants, and other native flora and fauna.

A modern custom door by Corrina Rising Moon Mensoff was designed and created in collaboration with Charlie Smith. The door has a solid core and is laminated with forged, textured, and patinated copper, brass, and stainless steel.

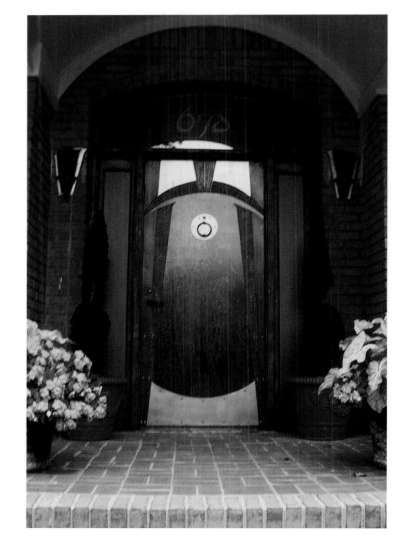

Corrina Rising Moon Mensoff with Charlie Smith. "Modern archaic" door. The door has a solid wood core laminated with forged, textured, and patinated copper, naval brass, and stainless steel, all mechanically fastened. *Photo, Jill Buckner*

The infinite variety possible with applied door decoration is shown in several examples. The shop door with grape vines is for a restaurant that sells wines in Szentendre, Hungary. The forged steel design shows when the door is opened to the street in an outdoor tourist shopping area.

Scott Lankton's grape vine door grilles are used to secure a door to a wine cellar. Grape clusters, vines, and leaves are a standard motif used throughout the ages but they are all used a little differently and bear the uniqueness of the blacksmith who created them.

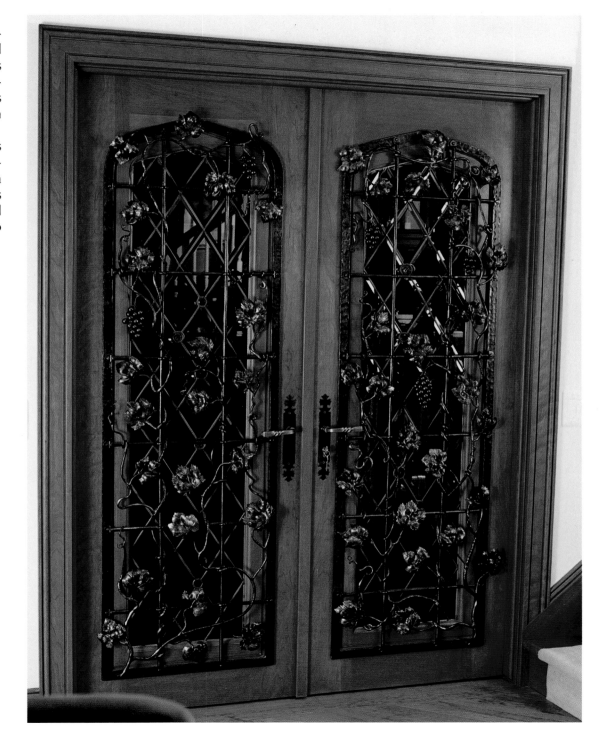

Scott Lankton. Wine cellar door grilles with grape vines, leaves, and grape clusters on a frame of horizontals and verticals. The frames are symmetrical but the designs are not. *Photo, artist*

Walt Hull's scroll insets enhance a plain door. Jim Hubbell creates a scene in an Art Nouveau design that overlays a single panel door.

Perhaps the ultimate overlaid designs are on the intricately Moorish patterned doors from Morocco. The handles that carry out the design of the door are probably cast iron. A Baroque decoration on a residential door in Budapest has glass in the central panel that serves as a peephole to see who is requesting entry.

The hinge-like decorative ironwork floral appliqué on a church door in Monaco is non-functional. Steve Lopes decorative strap hinges with a plant pattern extends over part of a door and is decorative and functional. Dan Nauman offers an elegant enhancement of a plain door with traditionally designed strap hinges.

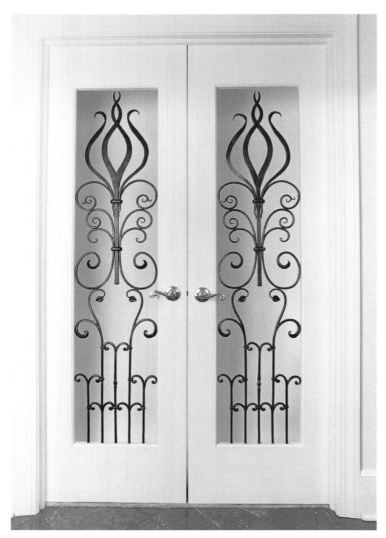

Walt Hull. Interior doors with varied scrolls and curved elements. *Photo, Wally Emerson*

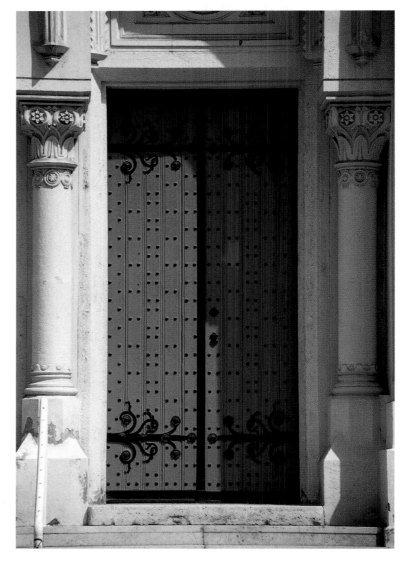

Iron hinges combine with iron nail heads in a decorative arrangement for an attractive door embellishment that raises it out of the ordinary. *Photo, author*

64

Hasp decoration (it doesn't function as a hasp or hinge) on a church door. Monaco. *Photo, author*

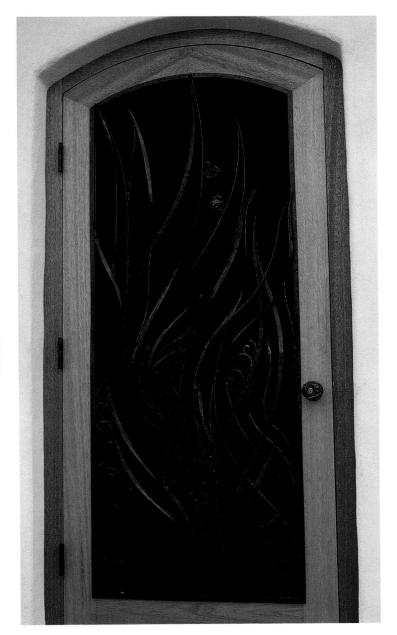

James Hubbell. Iron and screen in a stylized flower design with scrolls and curving lines. The iron becomes the surface decoration. *Photo, artist*

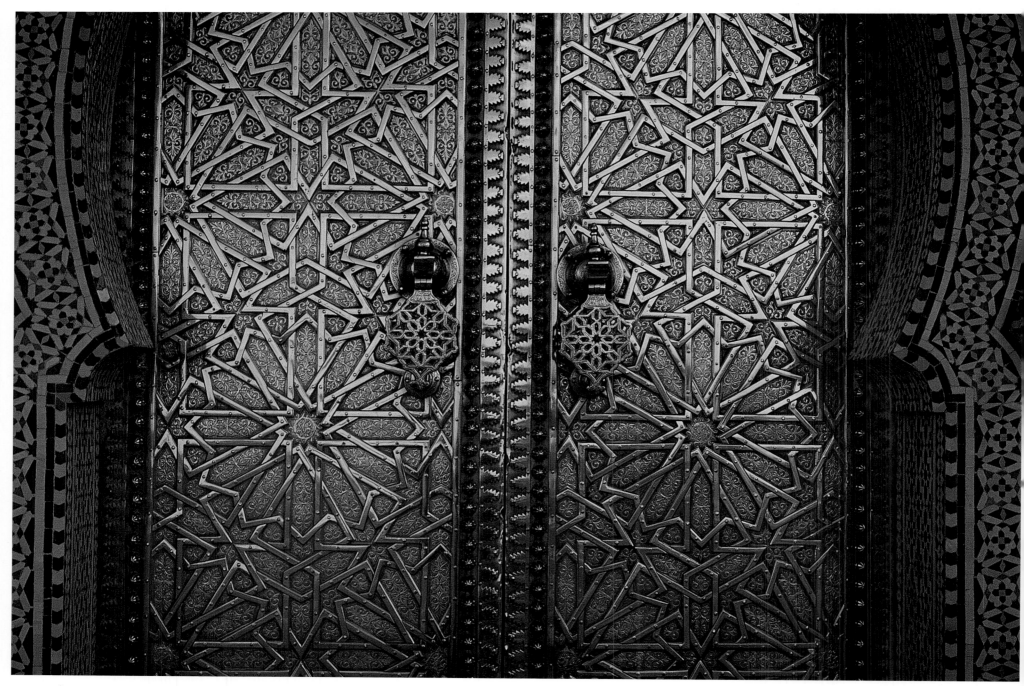

Rabat, Morocco. Metal overlaid on wood has an intricate Moorish design. Matching
handles and rosettes are probably cast iron. *Photo, author*

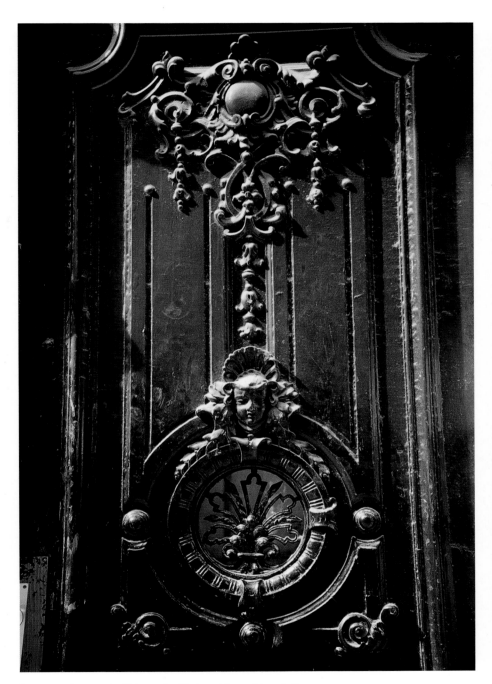

Baroque door embellishment with hand forged head. Budapest, Hungary. *Photo, author*

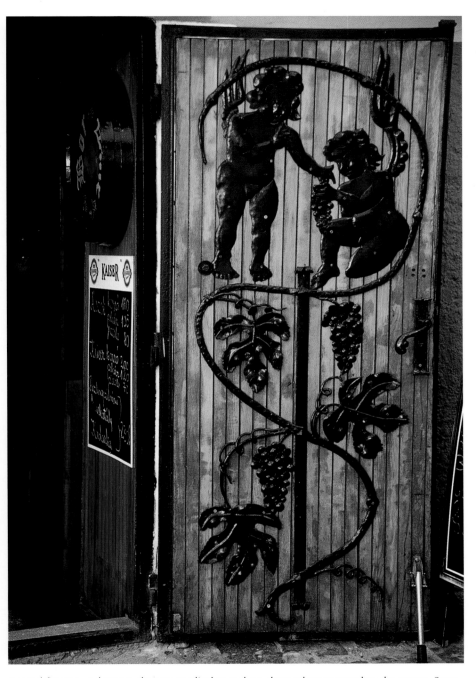

Forged figures and grape clusters applied to a shop door when opened to the street. Szentendre, Hungary. *Photo, author*

Latches, Locks, Handles, and Hinges

Several examples of custom hardware latches, levers, and other door hardware are shown. They are varied and only a sampling of the vast variety that can be created with a little imagination for individualizing an entry. They offer an alternative to the production types of hardware on the market. Often the locks, hinges, hasps, and doorknockers are coordinated for a consistent and coordinated effect. In business establishments, the gates, logos, mailboxes, and lighting fixtures might be designed for a unifying statement.

The escutcheon, or back plate, for door locks, knobs, levers, and handles, gives the metalworker an area for additional creative design by adding different shapes, textures, and imprints such as Steve Lopes' fossil plates. Russell Jaqua uses a technique called "ferra betute" which is an Italian term for "heavily beaten" for his door handles. It is used for heavy and irregular texturing done by a hammer. Jaqua cites as his influence the work by Italy's Antonio Benetton.

Dan Nauman. Strap hinge studies. The purpose was to utilize hot cutting methods and minor filing to retain the natural bevel produced by the cutting chisels. Veining was accomplished with chisels on the cold metal. Mild steel. 22" long. *Photo, George Lottermoser*

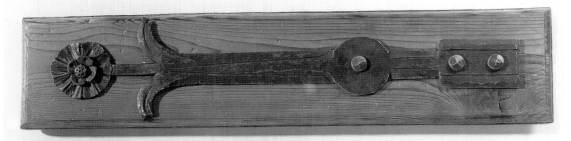

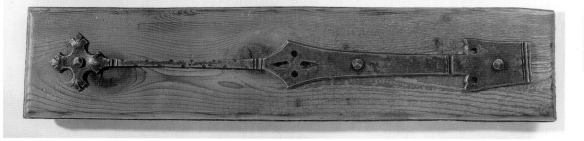

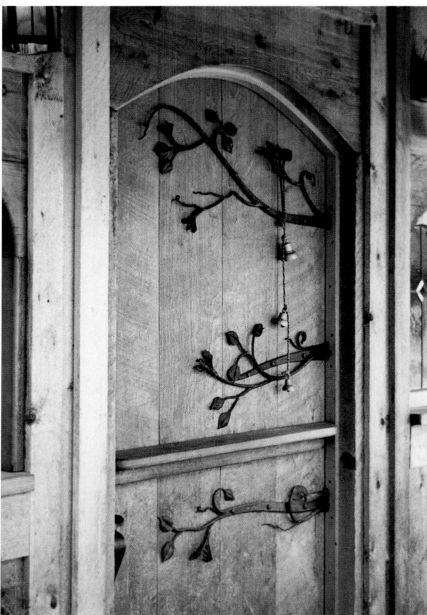

Steve Lopes. Strap hinges as branches and leaves. *Photo, artist*

68

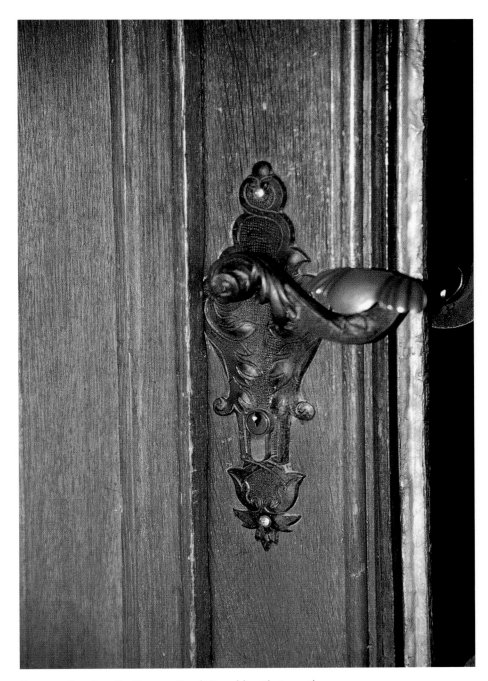

Baroque door handle. Prague, Czech Republic. *Photo, author*

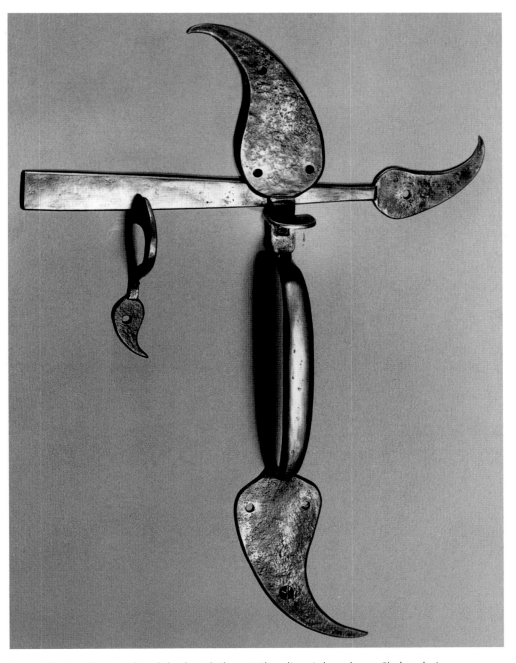

Lance Cloutier. Exterior thumb latch with the rattail endings is based on a Shaker design. Forged iron. 11" high. *Courtesy, artist*

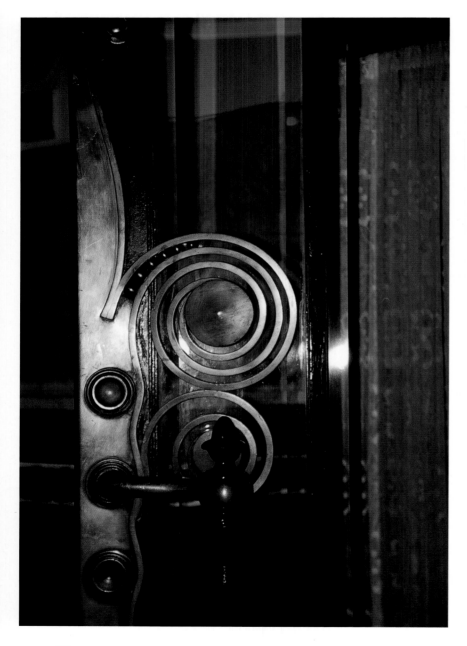

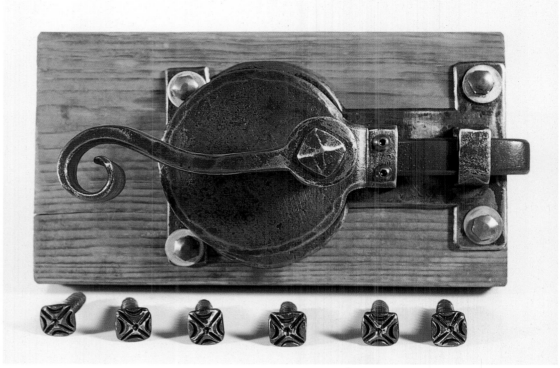

Frederic A. Crist. Spring latch. *Photo, artist*

Hotel Europa. Art Nouveau handle and escutcheon.
Brass. Prague, Czech Republic. *Photo, author*

Corrina Rising Moon Mensoff. Handle and backing for a restroom door. Forged copper and stainless steel. Whimble Designs. *Photo, Jill Buckner*

Tom Latané. Exposed interior of a lock/latch. Swaged and filed mild steel. A key functions from the outside; from the inside the tumbler can be lifted by hand to allow the bolt to be drawn. *Photo, Catherine Latané*

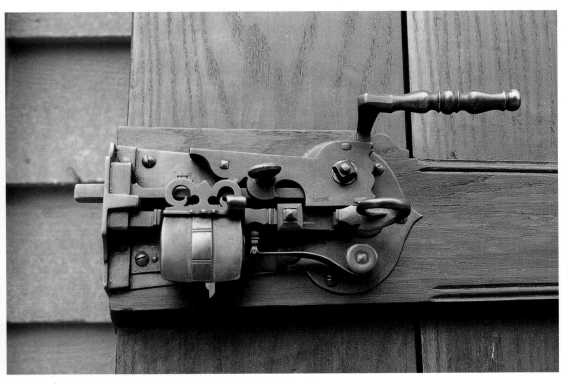

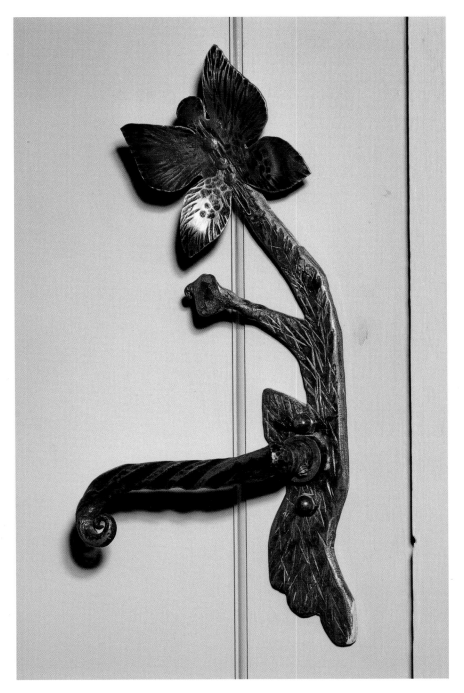

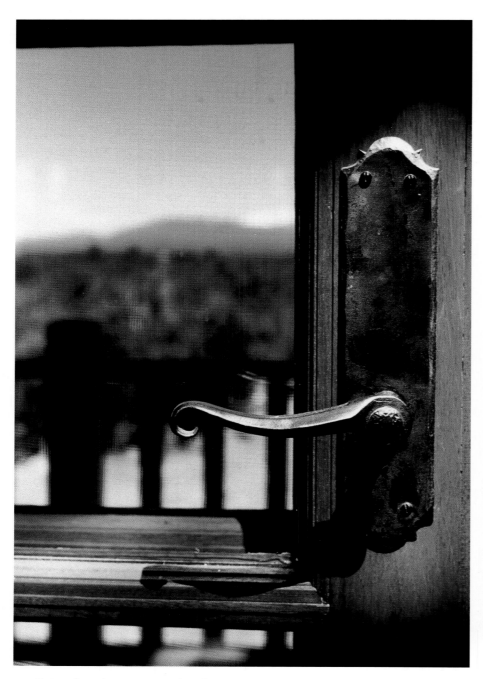

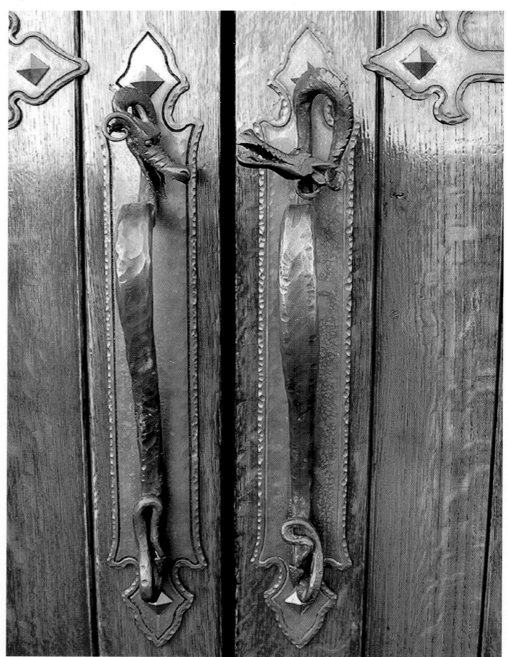

Christopher Thomson. Lever handle and escutcheon. *Courtesy, artist*

Tom McClane. Hand forged dragon handles of solid copper and hinges on 14-foot solid oak front doors. The buildings replicate a medieval castle. Each handle is 2' high and weighs 50 pounds. *Shakespeare's Restaurant & Pub, Ellwood City, Pennsylvania. Photo, Claudeen Chisholm*

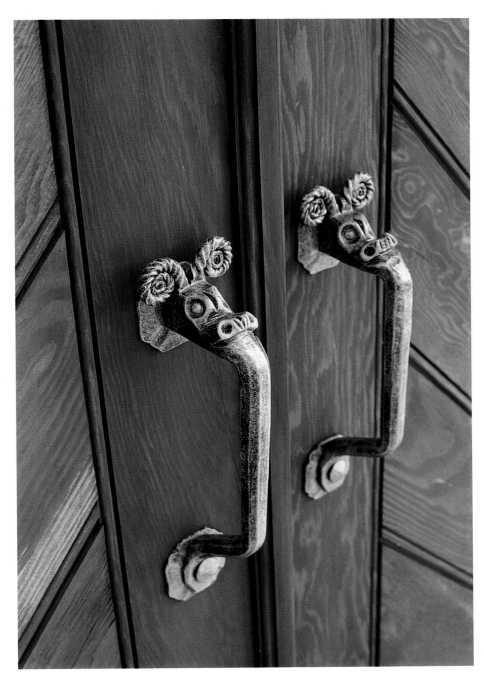

Frederic A. Crist. Door pulls with animal heads. *Photo, artist*

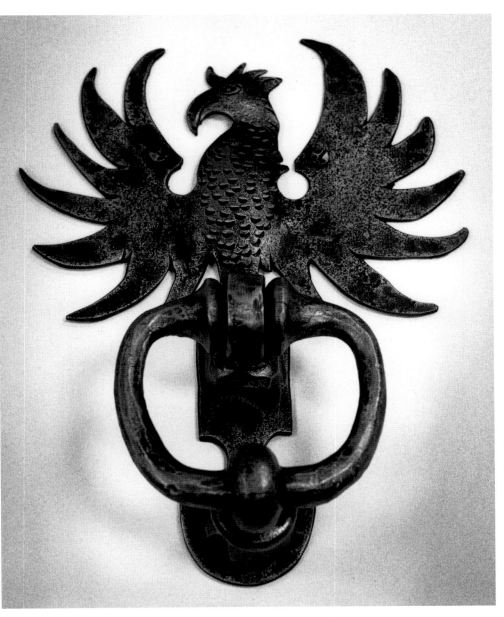

Frederic A. Crist. Eagle doorknocker. Forged steel. 6" high, 5" wide, 2" deep. *Photo, artist*

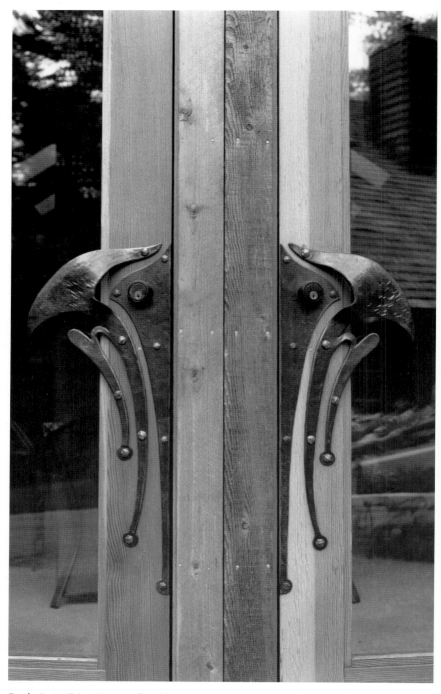

Frederic A. Crist. Door pulls with a contemporary design. Each 2.5' high. 1' wide, 2" deep. *Photo, artist*

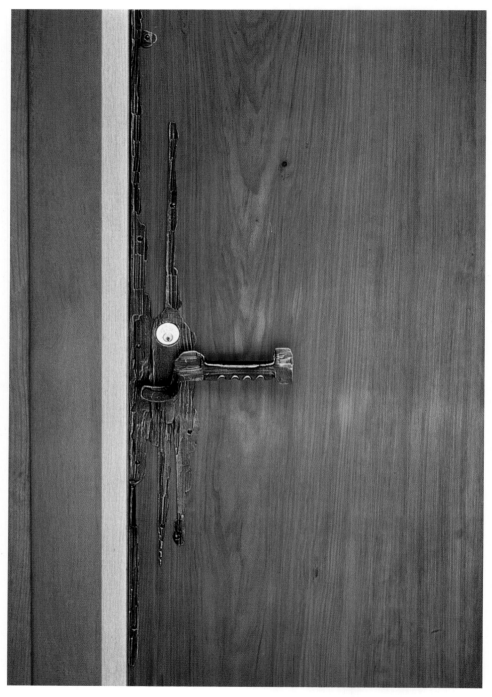

Stephen Bondi. Long, textured escutcheon of mild steel. *Photo, artist*

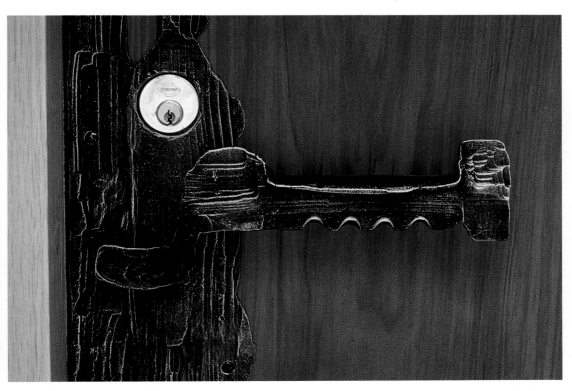

Stephen Bondi. Detail of door handle. When iron is red-hot it can be shaped so it appears soft after it has hardened. *Photo, artist*

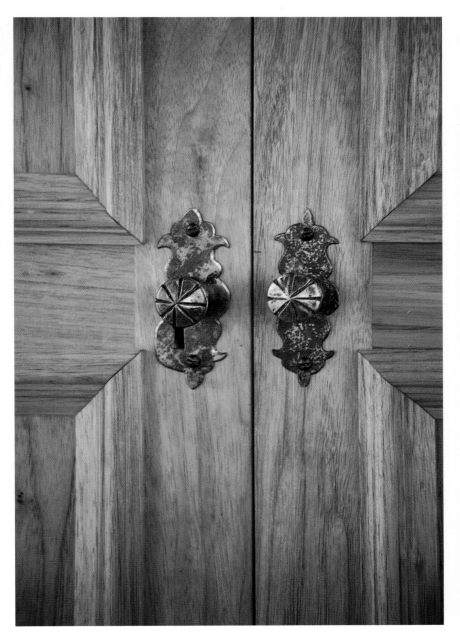

Frederic A. Crist. Cabinet door pulls. *Photo, artist*

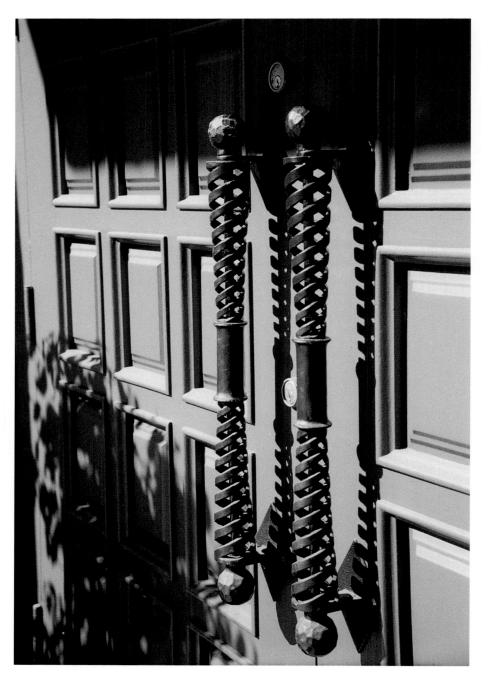

Spiral door handles for a bank. These are made similarly to the basket motif. *Photo, author*

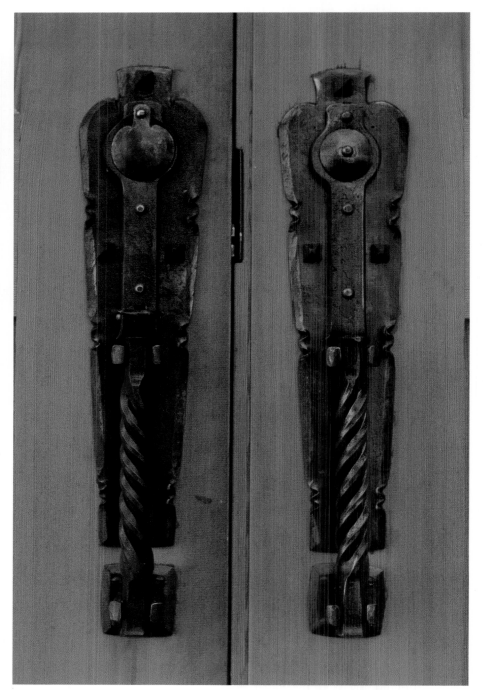

Steve Lopes. Spiral door handles. The ball-like protrusion on the left handle swings over and covers the key lock beneath. 16" high, 2.5" wide. *Courtesy, artist*

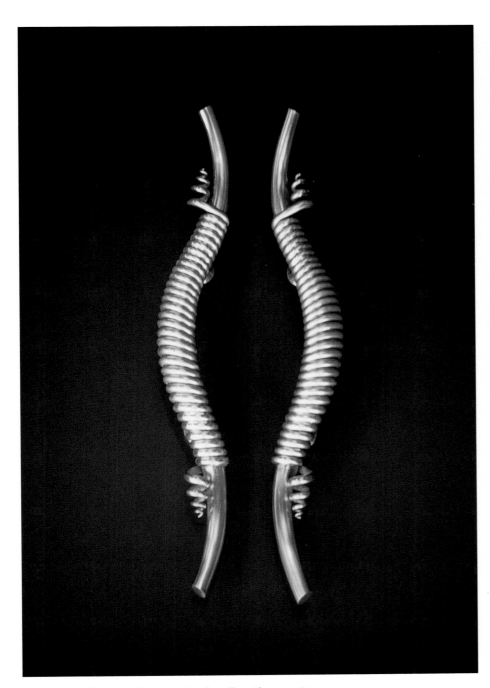

Michael Bondi. Forged bronze door handles. *Photo, artist*

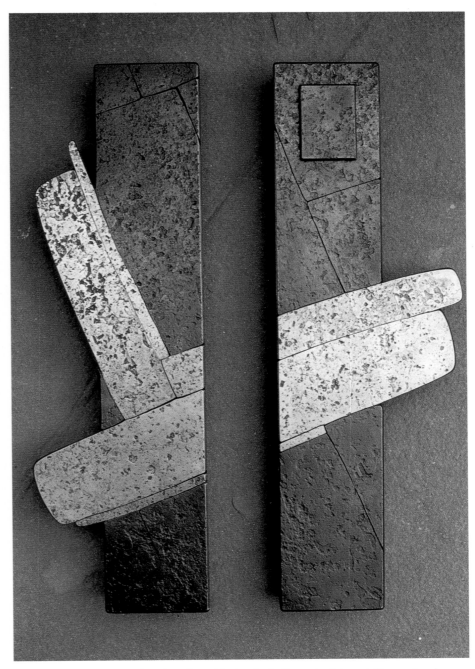

Tom Joyce. Pieced plate door handles with deadbolt. Forged mild steel. The rectangle on the top of the right handle swings sideways to reveal the key lock mechanism. *Photo, artist*

77

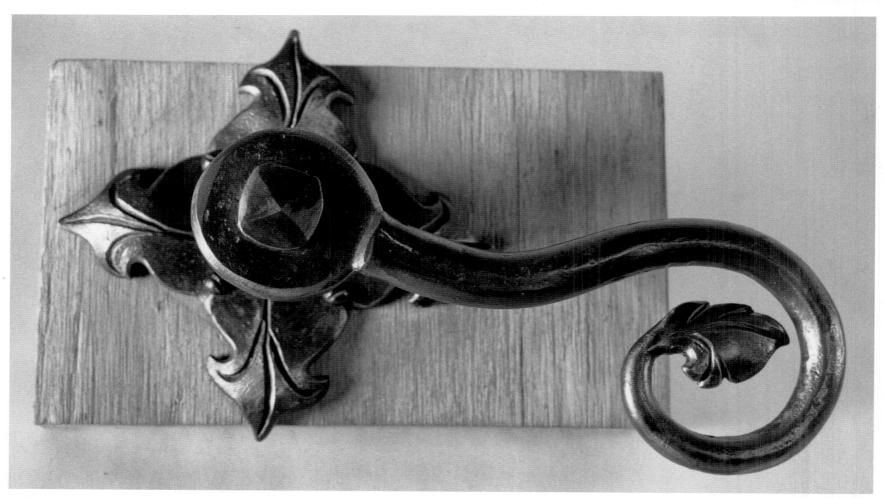

Frederic A. Crist and David W. Munn. Door handle and escutcheon with
leaves. 3" high, 7" long, 2" deep. *Photo, Frederic A. Crist*

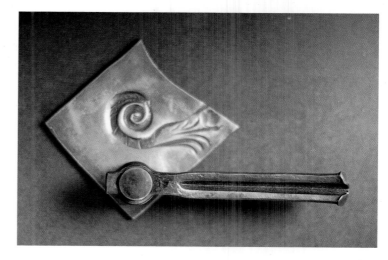

Steve Lopes and Dean Mook. Lever door handle with
copper "fossil" nautilus escutcheon. *Photo, artist*

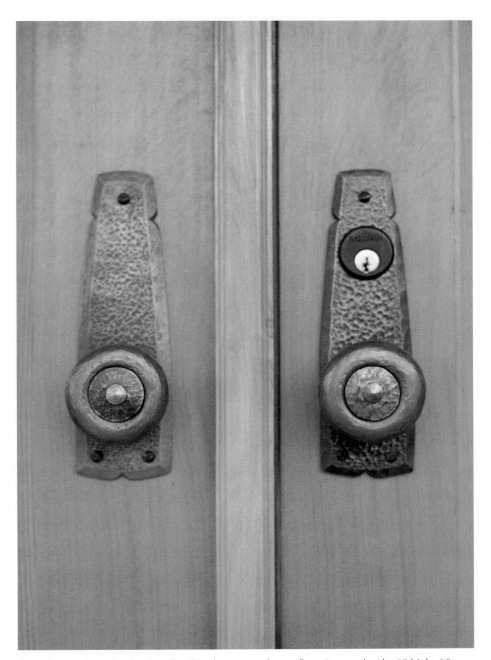

Steve Lopes. Doorknob with "fossilized" copper dragonflies. Bronze knob. 6" high, 3" wide. *Photo, artist*

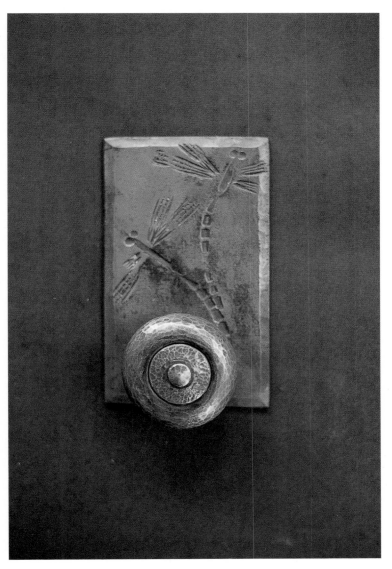

Steve Lopes. Craftsman style inspired knobs and escutcheons. Copper and bronze. 7" high, 2.4" wide. *Photo, artist*

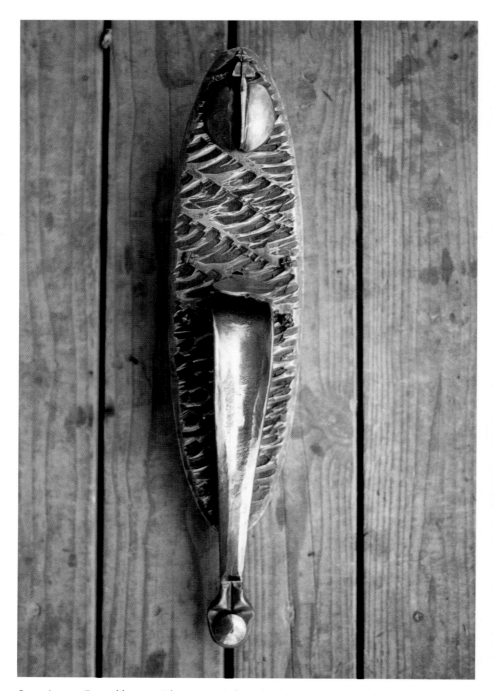

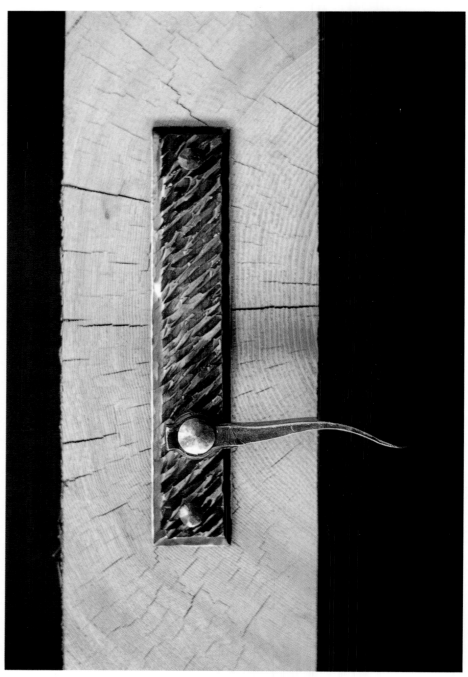

Steve Lopes. Forged bronze. The texture is based on a Japanese woodcut, "Views of Mt. Fuji From the Sea". *Photo, artist*

Steve Lopes. Lever and escutcheon; another shape inspired by the texture from the Japanese wood cut, "Views of Mt. Fuji From the Sea". *Photo, artist*

80

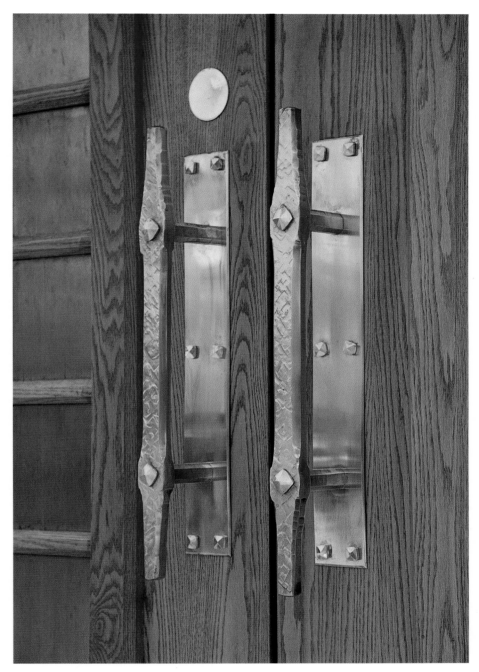

Russell Jaqua. Door handles. Naval bronze forged, punched, and riveted. The handles themselves show the heavy texture of the "ferra betute" (heavily textured) style as a contrast to the smooth, reflecting plates backing them. Two of four handles, each 20" high, 4" wide, 4" deep. *St. Francis of Cabrini Catholic Church, Tacoma, Washington. Photo, Frank Ross*

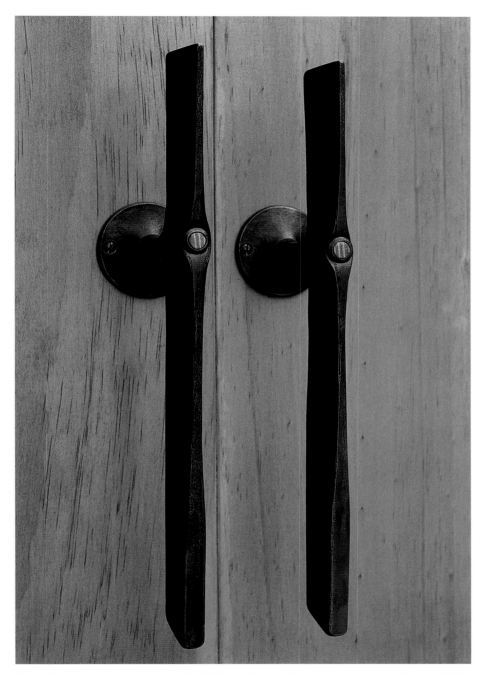

Marc Maiorana. Door pull study #1. Mild steel, wrought iron, and wood. 12" high, 1/2" wide, 1" deep. *Photo, artist*

Signage

Signage offers another area for the blacksmith's art. In Scandinavia almost every merchant has a sign that indicates his trade, such as the ironmonger, the fishmonger, the butcher, the baker, the candlestick maker. Making signs in such countries is an ongoing, never ending business and it is getting that way in the United States, too, as the popularity of iron signage increases.

Transfer Co., Kotaro Kurata and Goro Hatanaka. Forged French café sign and bracket in mild steel; the pot is fabricated of copper in actual design and size. 5.6" high, 5' wide. *Courtesy, artists*

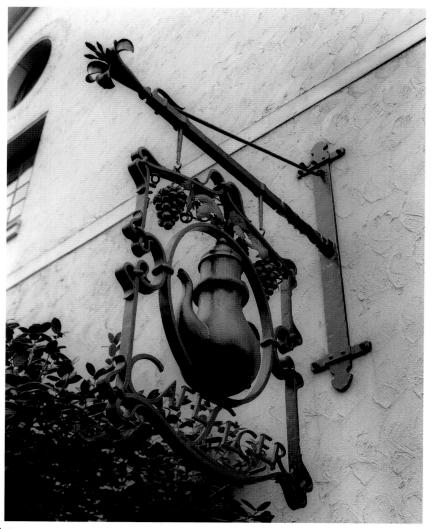

The blacksmith may have to compete with neon tubing fabricators, but there are plenty of people who want the old world charm of ironwork signage. As you travel, be aware of ironwork signage and you'll be amazed at its variety and creativity. Look at the poles and holders for the signs as well as the signs themselves for often they exhibit the blacksmith's fertile imagination and sure hands.

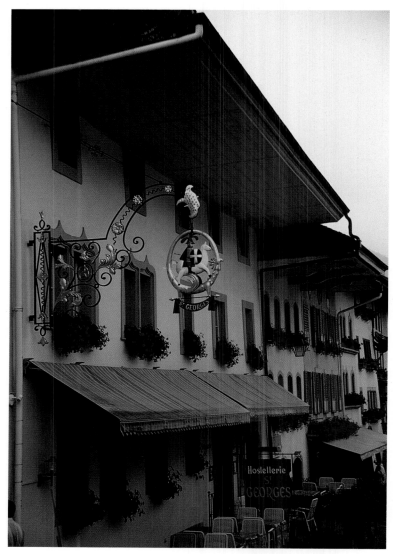

Hostelry St. George, Gruyere, Switzerland. Black with gold accents and a white horse. *Photo, author*

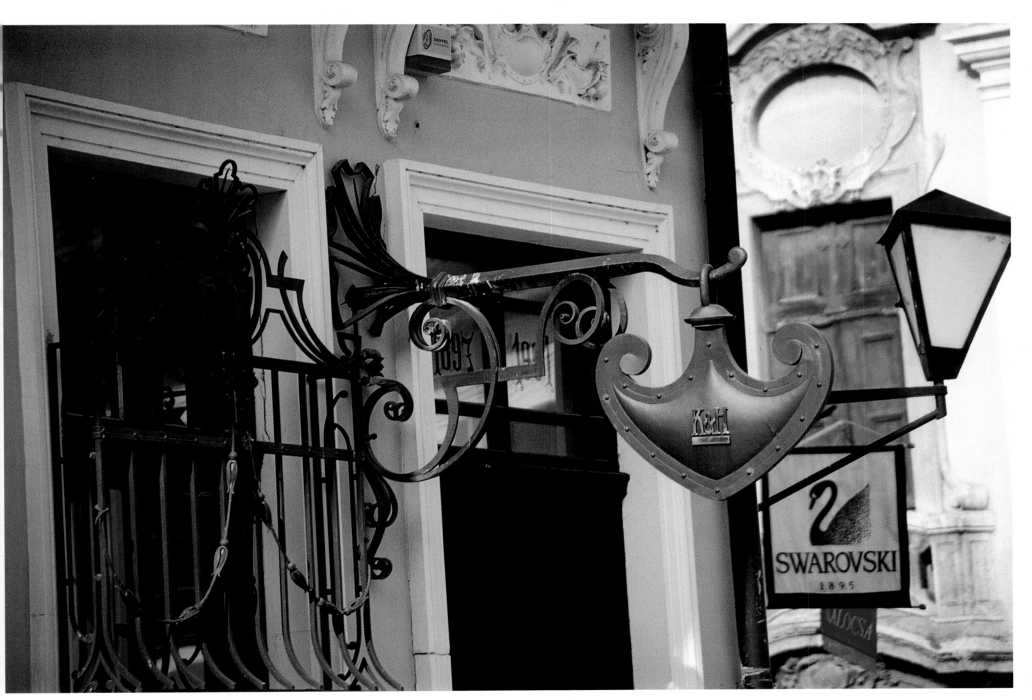

Signage and window grille. The sign displays the Swarovski Glass Co. insignia. Budapest, Hungary. *Photo, author*

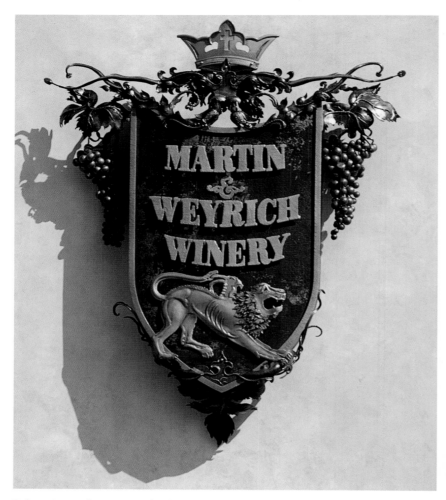

Robert C. Bentley. Signage for the Martin & Weyrich Winery has grapes and other symbols representing the company's logo and background. *Photo, Bruce Wood-worth*

Right: Craig Kaviar. A sign should have some indication of the type of business it represents. Here, the European tradition of signage inspired the idea of the spectacles. Kaviar forged the iron and carved the redwood panels. Letters have been gold-leafed for easy reading. *Photo, artist*

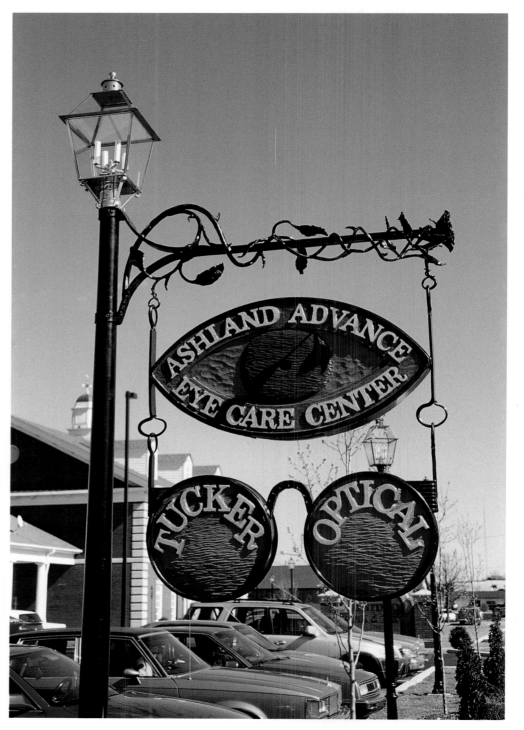

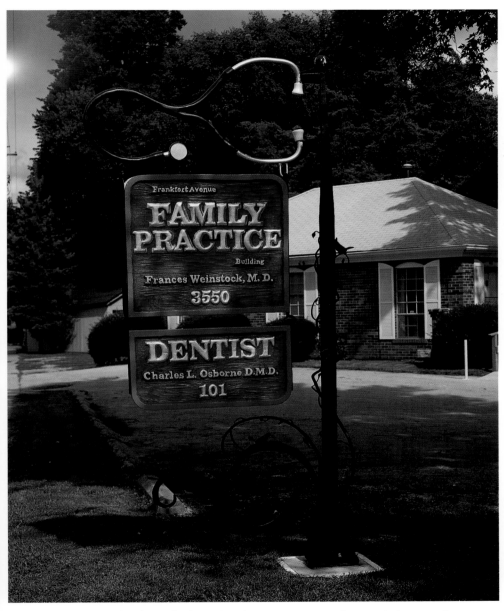

Craig Kaviar. A family medical practice sign uses an appropriate symbol … a stethoscope. Kaviar says, "I was thinking of Claes Oldenberg's sculpture when I enlarged the stethoscope for the sign bracket." *Photo, artist*

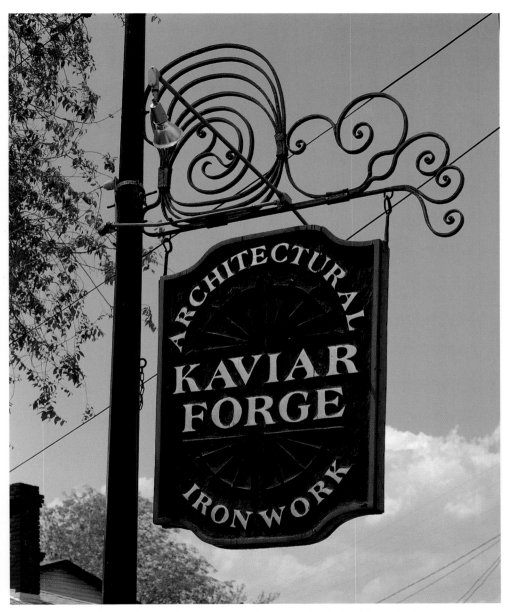

Craig Kaviar. For the smith's own business, near downtown Louisville, Kentucky, Kaviar made this sign of forged iron and carved redwood, with gold leafed lettering. *Photo, artist*

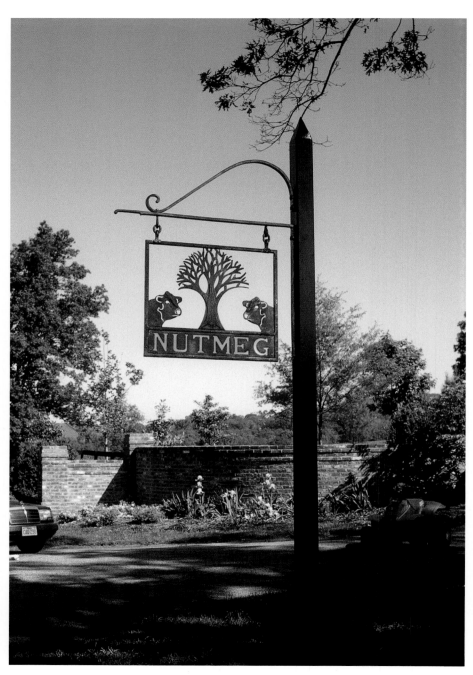

Frederic A. Crist and David W. Munn. Signage with a tree, cows, and negative areas, resembles a linoleum block print. *Photo, artists*

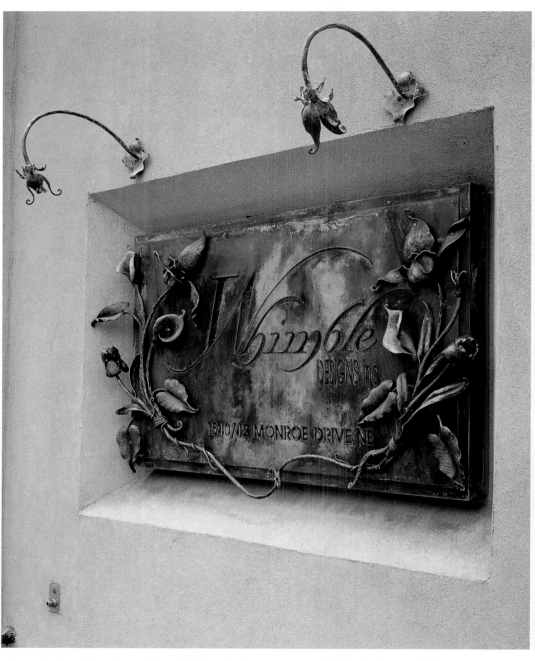

Corrina Rising Moon Mensoff. Whimble Design sign consists of a back plate with lettering, forged flowers and leaves, with an antique patina finish. The lighting is designed to match the sign rather than using ordinary industrial fixtures. *Photo, Jill Buchner*

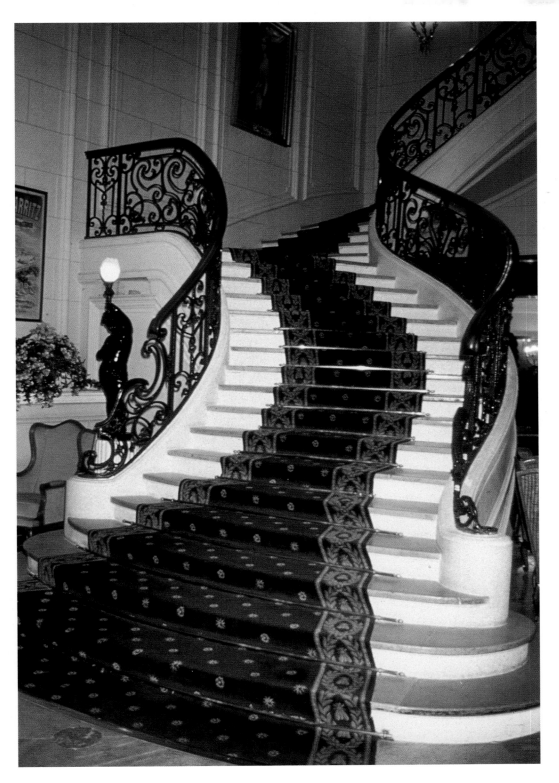

Chapter 3
Staircases

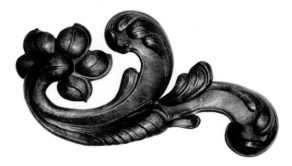

Anyone who has visited five-star hotels of the world, European palaces, and mansions, or taken a cruise on an ocean liner, would be hard-pressed to imagine that grand staircases that grace entry halls and ballroom floors never existed. Before the Renaissance, staircases were purely functional. Most likely they spiraled up a narrow, enclosed area like those in medieval castles, fortresses, and towers. Many had no handrails or, at best, the handrails were made of rope or wood. It was during the Renaissance that the grand ceremonial staircases evolved in the palaces of France and Italy and these had handrails on the closed sides.

The first open staircases with balustrades (uprights) supporting the handrails date from about 1550 in Florence, Italy, and 1688 in Versailles, France. It is boggling to realize that in America at that time, the Indian cultures were using rough steps hewn from rock or hard earth, with only finger holes dug in adjacent sidewalls to aid their ascent.

Edouard Niermans. Architect. Hotel Du Palais, Biarritz, France 1905. Art Nouveau grand staircase in the hotel's main lobby is an insight into French ironwork design at the turn of the 20th Century. *Courtesy, Hotel Du Palais, Biarritz, France*

The earliest and best-known iron staircase dates from 1637 in the Queen's House, Greenwich, England, designed by Inigo Jones. The gracefully curving elevation is still as breathtakingly beautiful now as it was then. Jones' circular staircase is composed of wavy lines, scrolls with abstract leaves, and tulips, and is called the "Tulip Staircase." It has no central support. The blue tulip balusters against white walls make a dramatic pattern as one looks up to the skylight in the roof. When a landing is reached, the repeat pattern changes only slightly; it mirrors itself and the bottoms of the balusters are rounded rather than pointed.

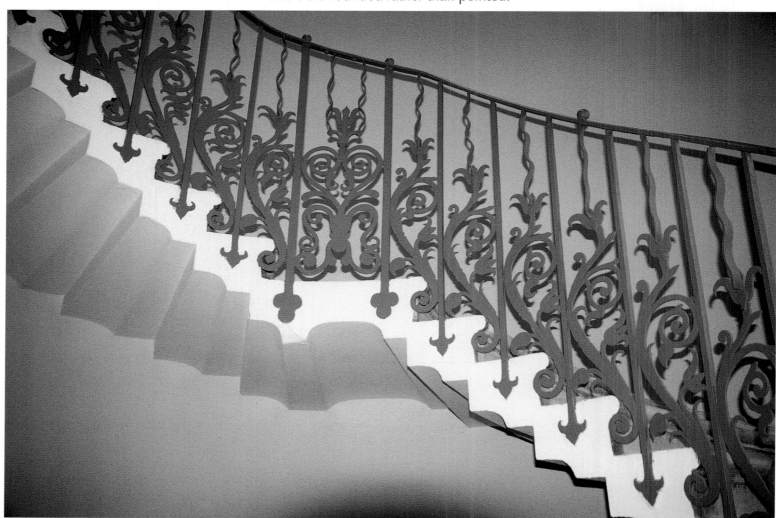

Inigo Jones. 1637. Queen's House, Greenwich, England. Named for the iron tulip shaped balustrade, the staircase became an inspiration for other architects who were building grand palaces and summer homes around London at the time. *Photo, author*

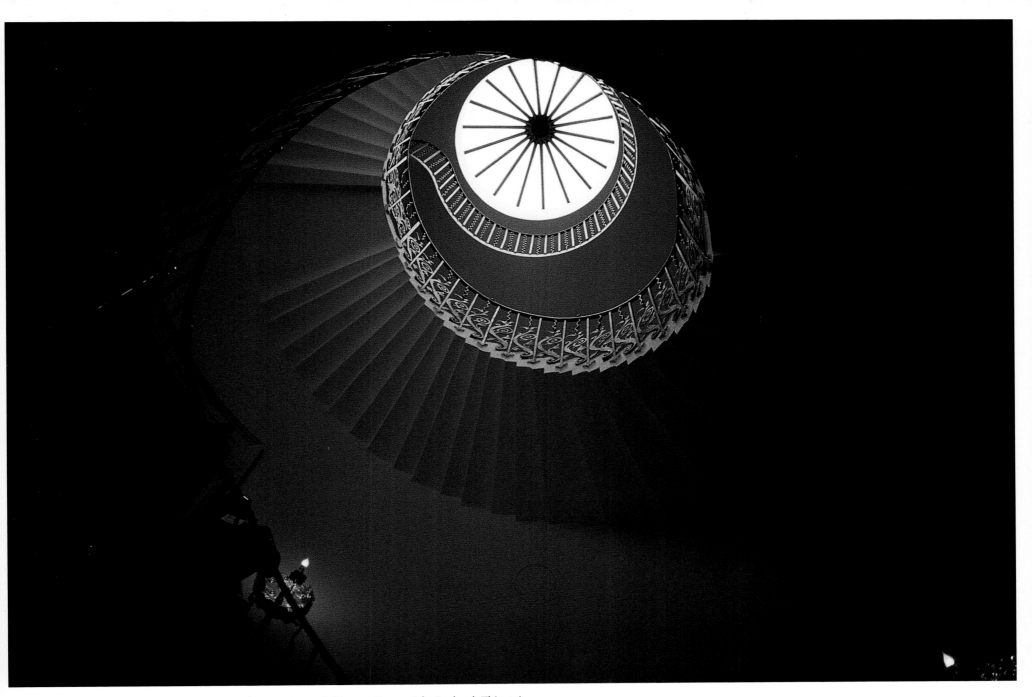

Inigo Jones. 1637. Tulip staircase. Wrought iron. Queen's House, Greenwich, England. This staircase, designed by the architect, curves sinuously upward to a dome. There is no central support. Inigo Jones is considered the father of English Renaissance architecture. *Photo, author*

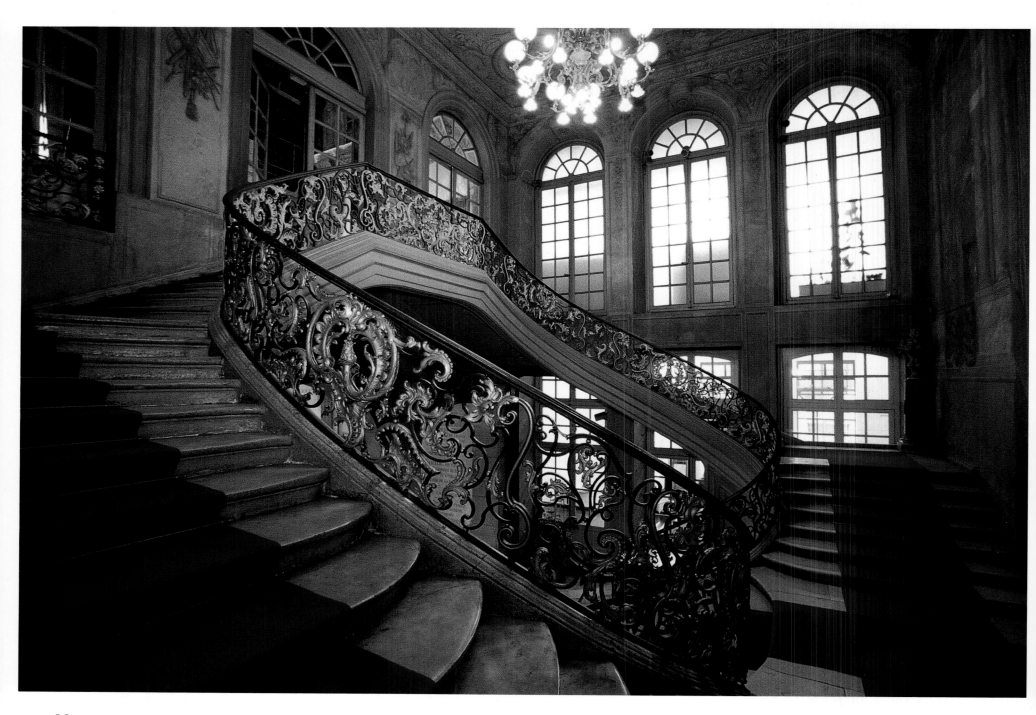

Several architects of grand houses in London emulated Jones's circular staircase into the late 1800s. Elsewhere on the continent, staircases came out of the closet, so to speak, and were soon more ornamented and opulent. The French Rococo grand staircase was elegant and spacious commanding the most important focal point of a lobby or foyer. Jean Lamour's two story staircase in the Hotel Ville de Nancy, in Stanislas Place, Nancy, France, exemplifies the style at his height. Lamour, who also did gates for Versailles, is one of the few designers of the times whose work is not anonymous.

In palaces, government buildings, hotels, and residences, the iron staircase, often encrusted with gold leafed details, could be the central dramatic feature for an imposing entry. As art styles changed from Renaissance, to Baroque, to Rococo, to Art Nouveau, and into the modern styles, staircase design followed the trends.

During the 19th Century, the need for repetitive balusters could be mass produced more quickly and cheaply by foundries than by hand forging. They could be shipped and fabricated on site, or before delivery, and installed as a unit.

The practice spread to the United States and was used with great success in office buildings and department stores by Louis Sullivan and Danmar Adler during the rebuilding of the Chicago's Loop between 1900-1910. Cast iron staircases could be fireproofed and they were used extensively in new mansions being built in the city's Southside.

Not surprisingly the blacksmith's work declined as cast iron became more popular on the continent. But it staged a comeback with the popularity of the Art Nouveau in Europe. The curving, freeform designs initiated by Victor Horta, (1861-1947), Louis Majorelle, (1859-1926), Henri van de Velde (1863-1958), and their followers in other countries, could only be accomplished by forging.

Whether one follows the history of the forged or the cast staircase in America, studies show that they differed by area of the country, by the heritage of the settlers, and by the style of the house. In New Orleans, the lacy scrollwork of the French style dominated. In the far West, a Spanish style was prominent, in the Southwest, a simple ranch style was appropriate to the adobe house, and so on.

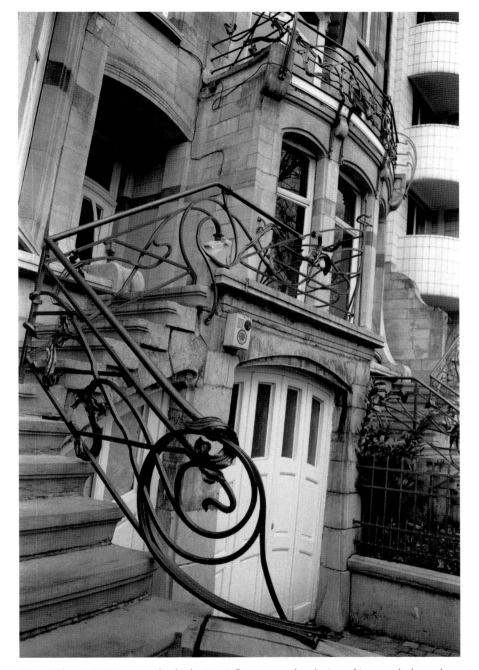

Ernest Blerot. Art Nouveau had a lasting influence on the design of ironwork throughout Europe. This example from the early 1900s in Brussels, Belgium, has free flowing, graceful curving forms that represent a break from the then popular ornate Rococo, Baroque, and Elizabethan styles. *Photo, Werner F. Bocqué*

Opposite page: Jean Lamour. Escalier stairs in French Rococo style in the Hotel de Ville, Nancy, France 1751-59. Compare this French Rococo staircase with its gilded embellishments and swirling forms with the Edouard Niermans' 1900 Art Nouveau staircase in the Hotel Du Palais (page 87). The stylistic differences become apparent. Niermans' staircase consists of simpler scrollwork with some horizontals and verticals. There are no plant forms, or gilded elements. *Courtesy, Office de Tourisme de Nancy, France*

Today, as people migrate everywhere from everyplace, as buildings become more eclectic, and as the world seems to shrink, it's not unusual to find all styles everywhere, especially in housing projects throughout the country. A series of French style houses with matching staircases could be developed in the middle of southern California and the Spanish style house could appeal to buyers in upper New York State. Fortunately, today's iron-workers are so versatile, they can create almost anything for anyone in any style, and they do.

Art historians refer to staircase styles by their country and historical deri-vation. That's a viable way to organize an art form. But the architect, the client, and the blacksmith understand that there's more to a staircase than its design. The space, the height to be ascended, and the type of staircase desired are all factors. Will the staircase be self-supported? Curving? Spiraled, with or without center poles? Will there be a landing between levels? Is the material chosen the best for the purpose? What shape will the banister be? After these issues are addressed, only then can the designer begin to think about the esthetics.

The client should also realize that a straight staircase is probably the least costly compared to one that curves or winds. The banister, or cap, is another consideration. A round or flat metal cap that proceeds up a straight staircase is the most economical. A simple curve or any contour caps isn't just a curved length of iron titled up on an angle, it must go up, twist, and curve at all points simultaneously. The blacksmith can negotiate these problems readily, but a curved or angled staircase requires much more work and set up time and becomes more costly than a straight unit.

A staircase, like other ironwork projects, is composed of basic construc-tion elements shown in the accompanying diagrams and photo. The draw-ing and photo also illustrate different design elements. In the drawing, John Medwedeff uses scrolls and acanthus leaves for the balustrade. In Robert Bentley's stair ending, the uprights and newel post are twists, straight bars, bushings and basket elements. Today, as people migrate everywhere from everyplace, as buildings become more eclectic, and as the world seems to shrink, it's not unusual to find all styles everywhere, especially in housing projects throughout the country. A series of French style houses with match-ing staircases could be developed in the middle of southern California and the Spanish style house could appeal to buyers in upper New York State. Fortunately, today's ironworkers are so versatile, they can create almost anything for anyone in any style, and they do.

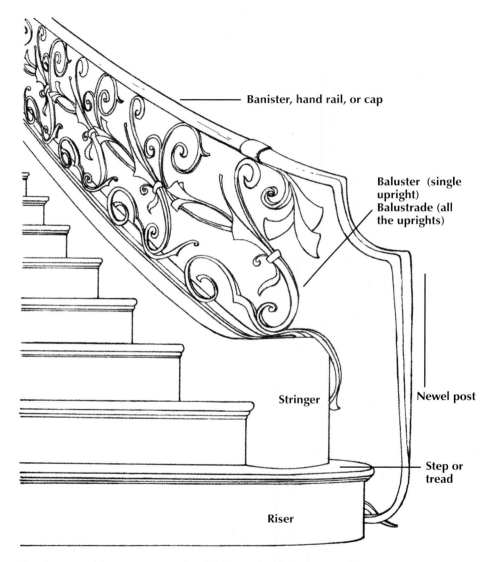

Banister, hand rail, or cap

Baluster (single upright)
Balustrade (all the uprights)

Stringer

Newel post

Step or tread

Riser

A staircase and its components. In addition to the elements noted, a decorative finial (not shown on this illustration) may be added on top of the newel post. *Drawing, John Medwedeff*

Reading from the bottom up, they are:

Riser - The vertical component of a step that supports the treads.

Tread or step - The horizontal component of a step upon which one walks.

Stringer - (Also called an apron). A supporting board or other material that runs the length of the stairway and supports the balusters.

Newel post - The major support for the balustrade located at the bottom and top of a stairway or at a turn in the handrail.

Finial - The "final" top ending of the newel post.

Baluster - A vertical member that helps support the handrail.

Balustrade - refers to all the balusters.

Banister or handrail or cap - A member that runs the length of the staircase over the stringers and newel post.

The following examples are organized by these elements and then loosely into historical periods. However, in today's milieu of ethnic mixture and eclecticism, it is sometimes difficult to put one staircase squarely in one design category rather than another. There is a great deal of overlap.

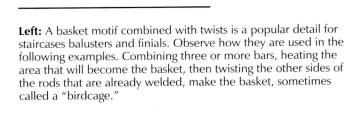

Left: A basket motif combined with twists is a popular detail for staircases balusters and finials. Observe how they are used in the following examples. Combining three or more bars, heating the area that will become the basket, then twisting the other sides of the rods that are already welded, make the basket, sometimes called a "birdcage."

Right: Robert C. Bentley. This staircase detail illustrates major stair construction members from the bottom up: riser, tread or step, stringer, newel post, finial, baluster, balustrade, and banister or handrail. It also has several design elements described: twists, C scrolls, bushings, and a basket pineapple for a finial. *Photo, Bruce Woodward*

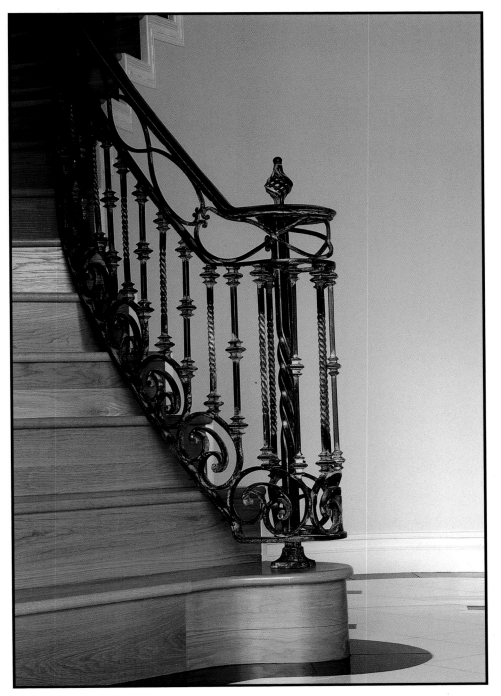

Scrolls, Curves, Arches

David Ponsler's staircases for clients in Southern Florida are based on French, Art Nouveau, and other historical references. But any one design may combine elements from one or more periods. He designs for the particular house and not for the historical period and strives to create a new look, a departure from tradition, yet retain traditional elements. Much depends on interviews with the client and understanding their visions for the commission. His stairways, gates, and fences are always rhythmical and varied in the design elements and how they are alternated.

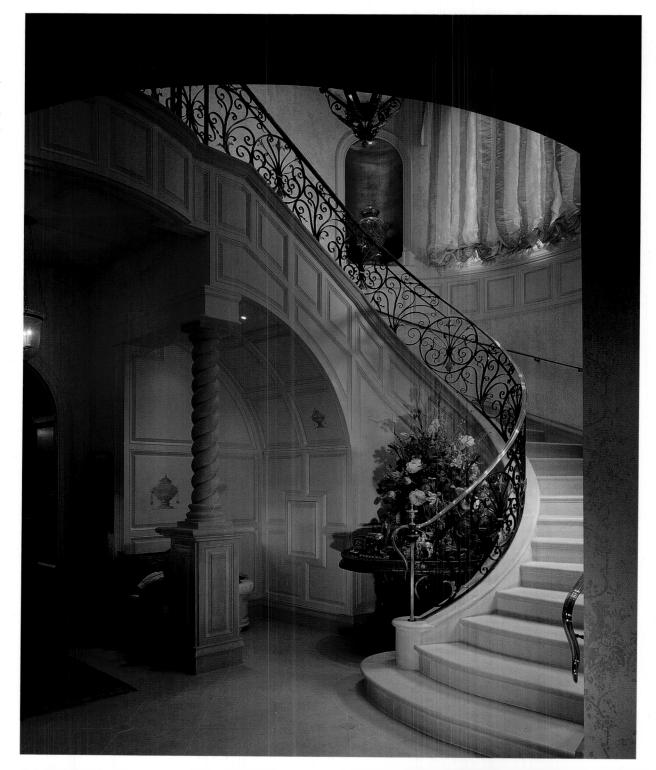

David A. Ponsler. A forged and fabricated steel railing for a private residence. Fan-like scrolls in two sizes alternate between those enclosed in a circle and those that are not. The circles reach to the cap and are alternately spaced. The theme is repeated but in a smaller scale and with a scroll that reverses its curve at each end. *Photo, Daryl J. Bunn*

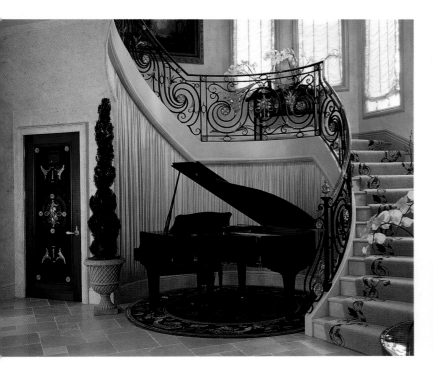

David A. Ponsler. Detail of above illustrating the intricate forging in the gold leafed floral pieces. *Photo, Daryl J. Bunn*

David A. Ponsler. French influence forged and fabricated steel railing for a private residence with scrolls, gold leaf rosettes, leaves, and floral arrangements. *Photo, Daryl J. Bunn*

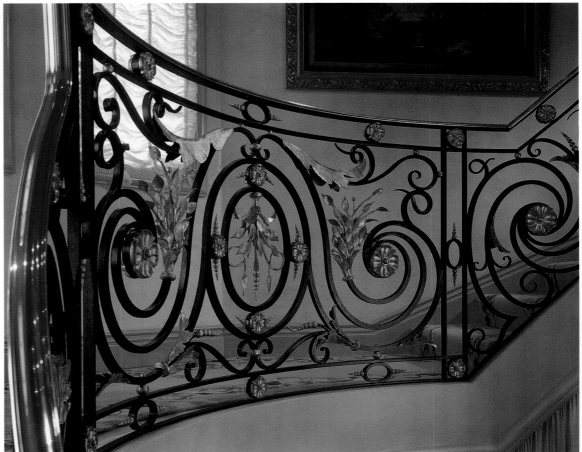

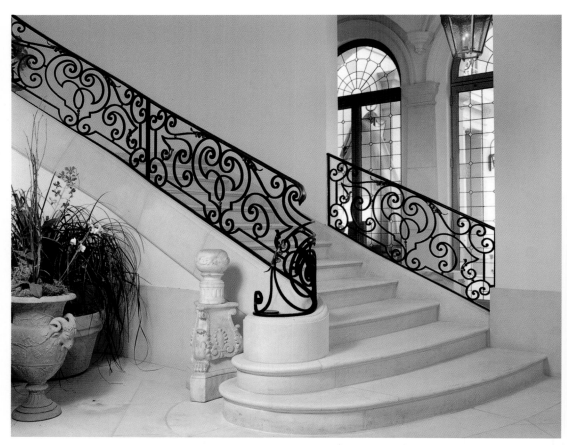

Michael P. Dillon. Traditional French style rail. The iron is painted a dull black with gold leaf accents, and has a natural hand rubbed steel cap. Stair Rail is 63' long with an additional 55' continuous rail and two 4' balconies. *Photo, Max Birnkamer*

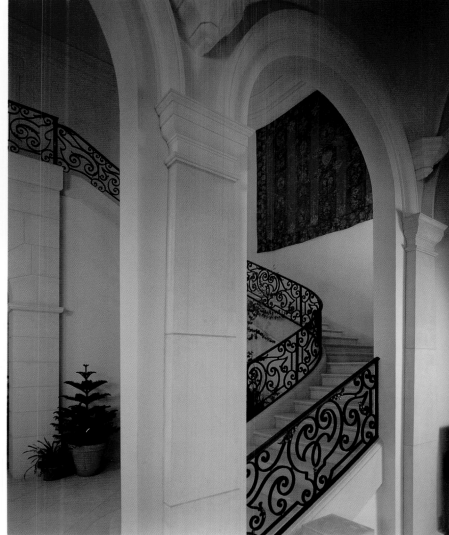

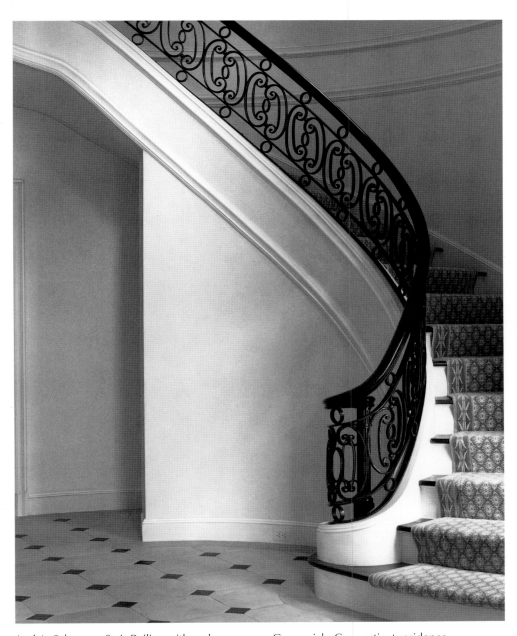

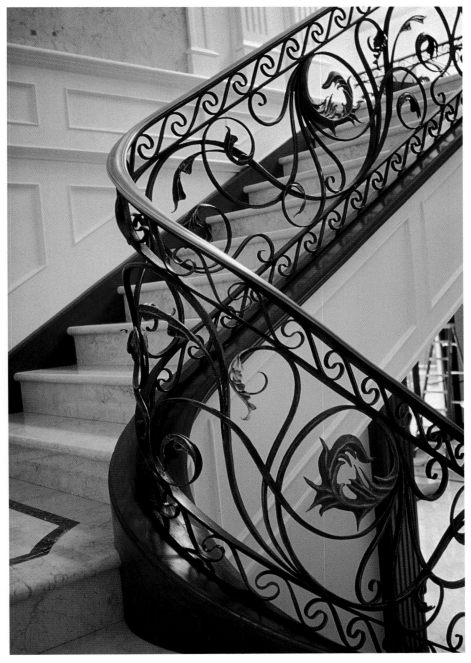

Joel A. Schwartz. Stair Railing with mahogany cap. Greenwich, Connecticut residence. Boris Baranovich, architect. *Courtesy, artist*

Michael Bondi. Forged steel stair rail with steel and bronze leaves, and bronze cap rails. A course of Vitruvian scrolls is along the top and bottom of the railing's length. Painted and patinated. Private residence, Atherton, California. *Courtesy, artist*

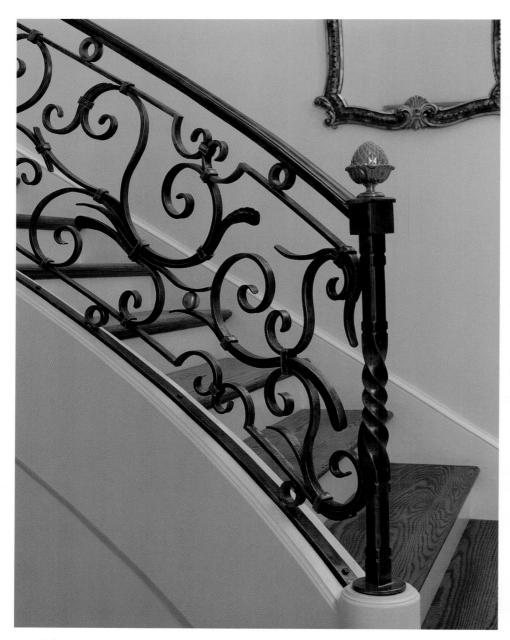

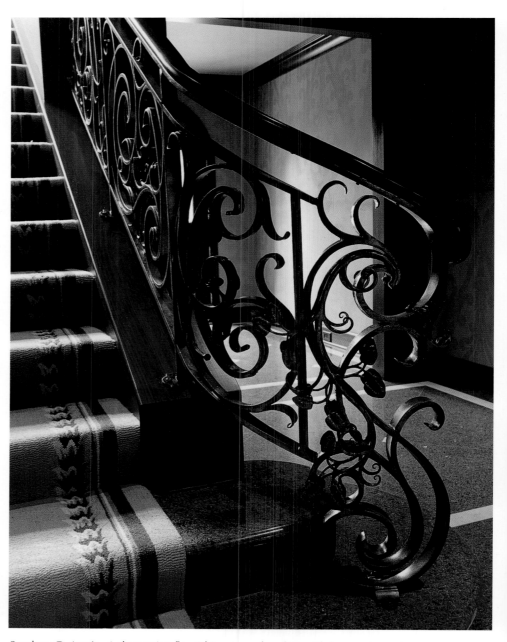

Robert Rotondo. A design based on a repeat curve. A pineapple finial tops the twist newel post. Mounting methods are an important element of the design and construction. The iron base of the railing attaches to the base of the staircase. Design elements are scrolls, circles, and gold painted balls. Newport, RI. Residence. *Photo, Roger A. Birn*

Stephen G. Austin. A decorative flourishing curved ending with leaves gives a baroque look to this elegant staircase. The upright supporting posts are attached directly to the wood stair base at regular intervals. *Courtesy, artist*

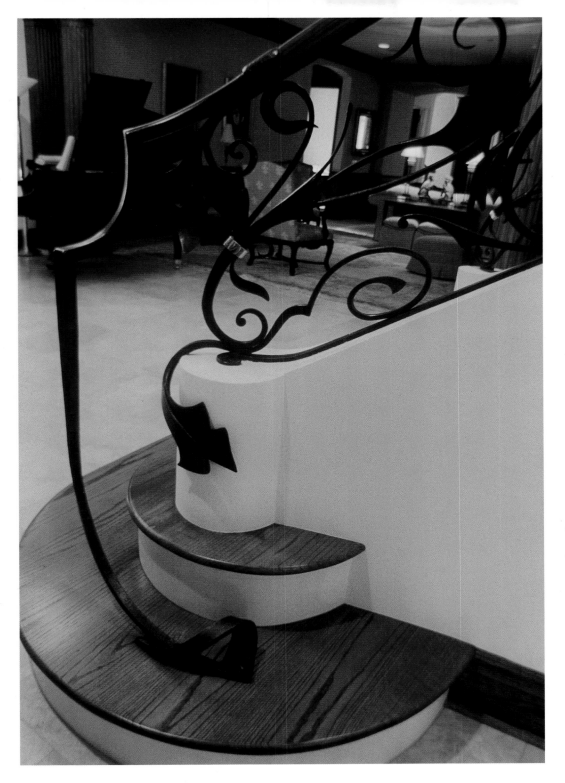

John Medwedeff. Grand staircase ending. Another solution for an elegant, yet simple staircase ending without using a traditional newel post. Scroll ends vary in design and a leaf wraps around the stair. Steel with bronze on an oak staircase. *Photo, artist*

The French influence is evident in the scrollwork, leaves and floral details of Scott Lankton's French design railings. All floral details are steel that has been brushed while hot with a bronze brush in a process known as mechanical or abrasion plating. They are finished in clear acrylic. Says Lankton, "This finish is more subtle (less gaudy) than gold leaf and gives more of an old world look." They are in perfect harmony with the buildings for which they are designed. This harmonious wedding of elements results when the architect, designer, and ironworker, cooperate to create a totally integrated statement.

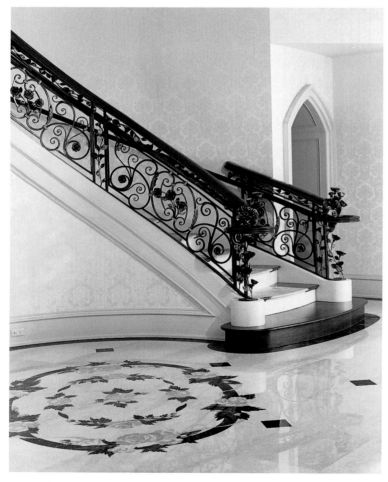

Scott Lankton. Serpentine Rose balcony railing is the perfect accompaniment for a French interior complete with ornate custom plaster moldings, gold leaf, and painted ceilings. (See details, Chapter 1.) 65' long. *Photo, artist*

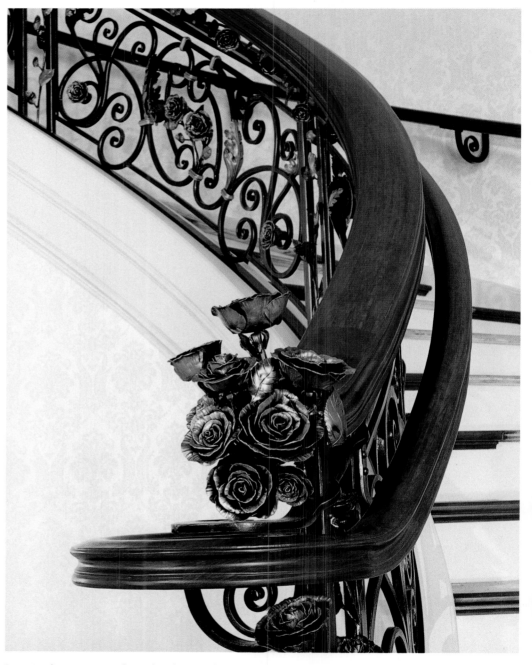

Scott Lankton. Rose Railing, detail. Roses by Brian Cook and Jim Roth are composed of layers of the steel, worked petal by petal, then assembled, joined, and bronze plated. A bouquet is used as the newel, but scores of other roses line this staircase, along with acanthus leaves, scrolls, and scrolls within scrolls. *Photo, Scott Lankton*

100

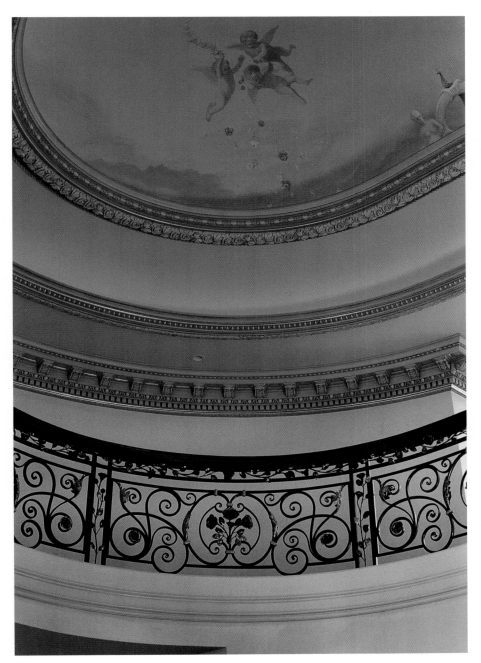

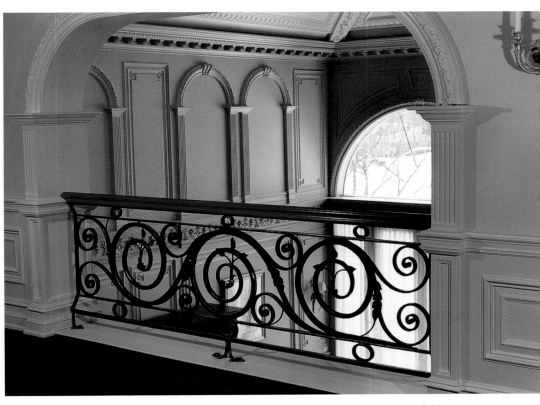

Scott Lankton. French style railing in black and gold enhances the French interior of this building and also becomes a strong contrast to the beige and gray interior. *Photo, artist*

Scott Lankton. Serpentine Rose balcony railing illustrates how the ironwork ties in with the ceiling design. Roses and acanthus leaves with heavy scrolls and circles are set between horizontals. Forged steel. Cherry wood cap. 3' high. 6.5' long. *Photo, artist*

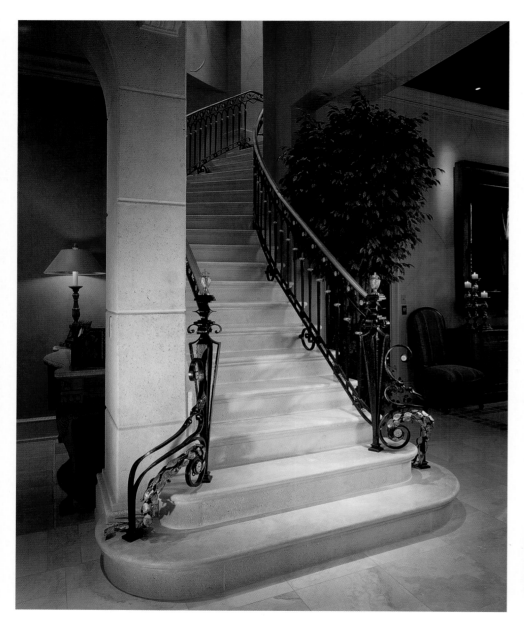

David A. Ponsler. Forged and fabricated steel railing for a private residence. Each single Vitruvian scroll has a gold leafed medallion within and a leaf between. Repeat rounded arches form the center of the railing with gold painted banding. The Vitruvian scroll and gold leaf center are repeated in a larger size at the end of the handsome newel. A gold finial at the top and gold leafed leaves at the bottom add to the richness of the design. *Photo, Daryl J. Bunn*

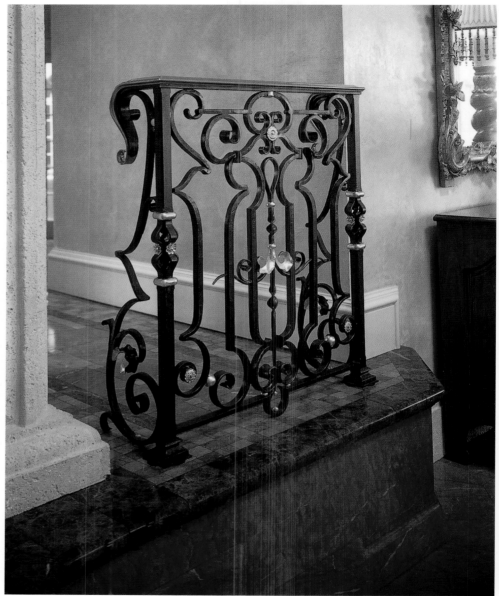

David A. Ponsler. Forged and fabricated steel railing for a private residence. Another example of the curve and rectangle as the basic geometric form. Different size fish tail scroll ends and the protruding leaf ends provide a third dimension to the railing. The unusual placement of the rail closes the space, yet gives an open feeling by not having the ends joined to the wall. Forged and painted with gold leaf. The same motif is repeated in staircases throughout the private residence plus an outdoor staircase. *Photo, Daryl J. Bunn*

Jean-Pierre Masbanji comes to his elegant French staircase designs by birthright and experience. Born in France in a family of blacksmith's he apprenticed at his father's side when he was only twelve years old. He later studied in France earning a diploma in the fine art of "repoussage" from "La Maison des Compagnons du Devoi," a technical institution. The staircases shown exhibit a delicacy that provide just the right weight and complement the rooms' interior. His staircases have won several awards from the National Ornamental & Miscellaneous Metal's Association (NOMMA).

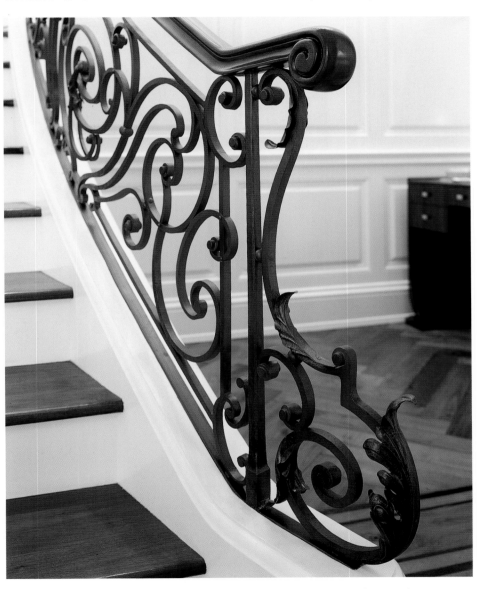

Jean-Pierre Masbanji. This hand forged staircase railing complements a French estate designed in the spirit of "Ile de France" architecture. The design features gold ended scrolls, notched and riveted details, and custom repoussé ornaments. Finished with a waxed oxide patina. *Photo, Terry Moore*

Jean-Pierre Masbanji. Newel post detail of "Ile de France" style newel showing the C scrolls, bolt ended scrolls, and acanthus leaves. *Photo, Terry Moore*

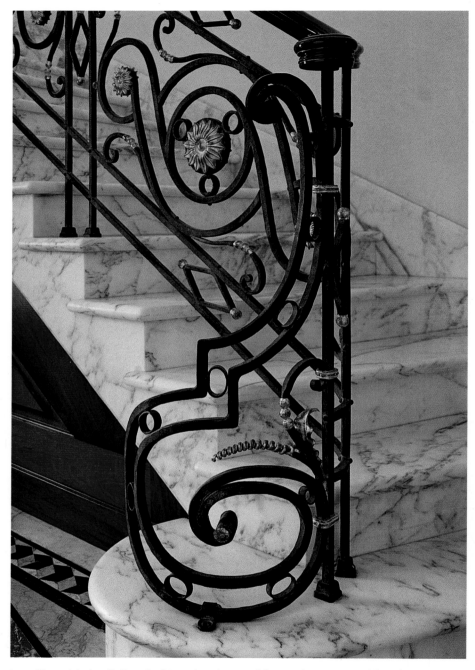

Jean-Pierre Masbanji. Detail of French style newel for a railing on a marble staircase. The scrolls, diamonds, circles, and gold leaf carry out the designs in the marble flooring. Vert-de-gris patina. *Photo, James Chen*

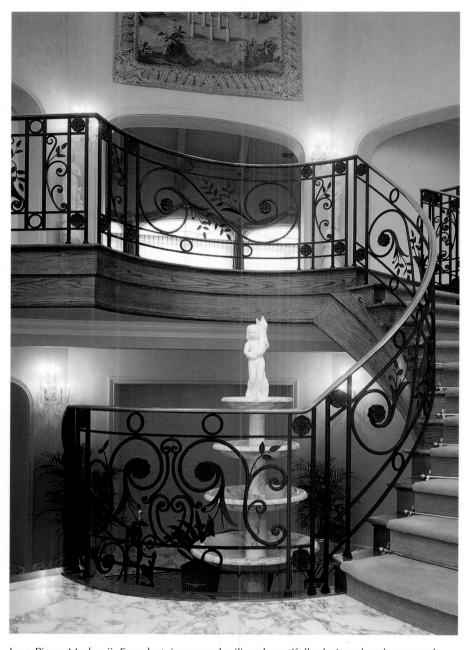

Jean-Pierre Masbanji. French staircase and railings beautifully designed and executed (see cover photo). A hand raised cornucopia, centered on the railing at the top, is a surprise detail for this light, airy, formal staircase for a California residence. All scrolls and acanthus leaves are hand forged. The polished bronze cap is a contrast for the black enameled ironwork. *Photo, Mario Quintana*

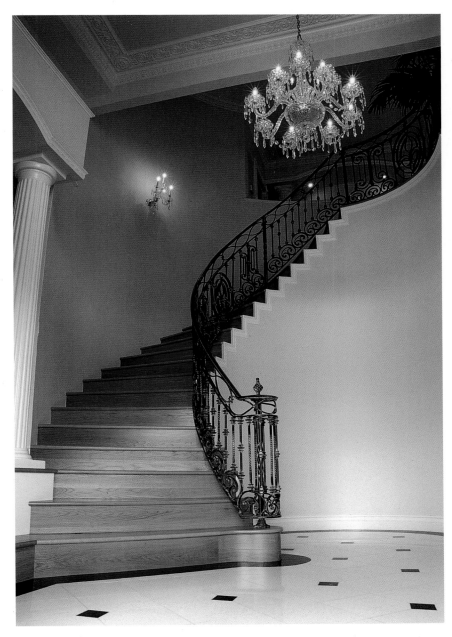

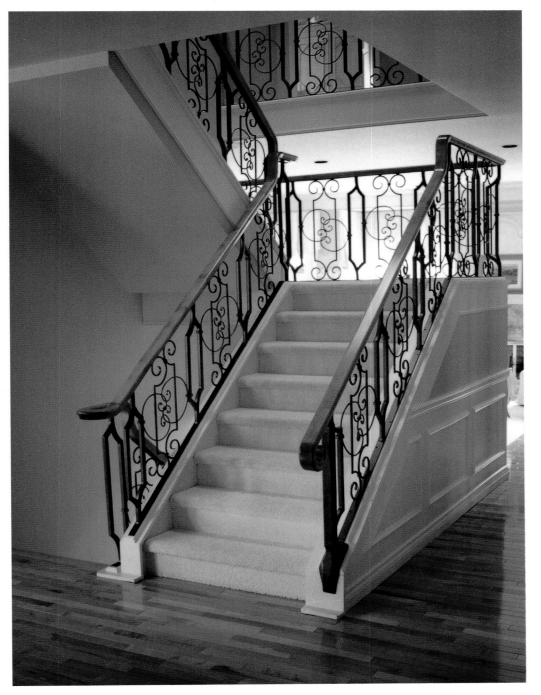

Robert C. Bentley. The varying placement of the elements gives this staircase variety and movement. The circle with the 3-leaf design is only at the curved part of the stair and railing. The upright scrolls, too, vary in their placement so that the staircase is not completely symmetrical, yet all the elements repeat to form a harmonious unity. A basket motif finial is a fitting ending for the banister. *Photo, Bruce Woodworth*

John Monteath. Residential staircase. A combination of scrolls and rectangles with a triple band joining each scroll overlap. The handrail is maple wood. *Photo, artist*

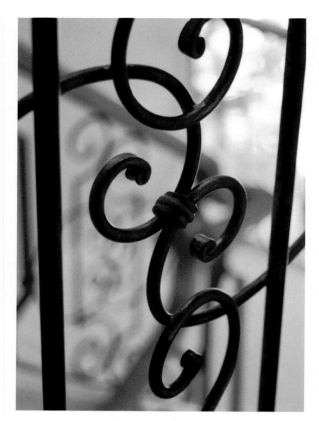

John Monteath. Detail of a triple wrap. Note the closed scroll end. Different treatments for the scroll end can change the look of a railing from modern to baroque. *Photo, artist*

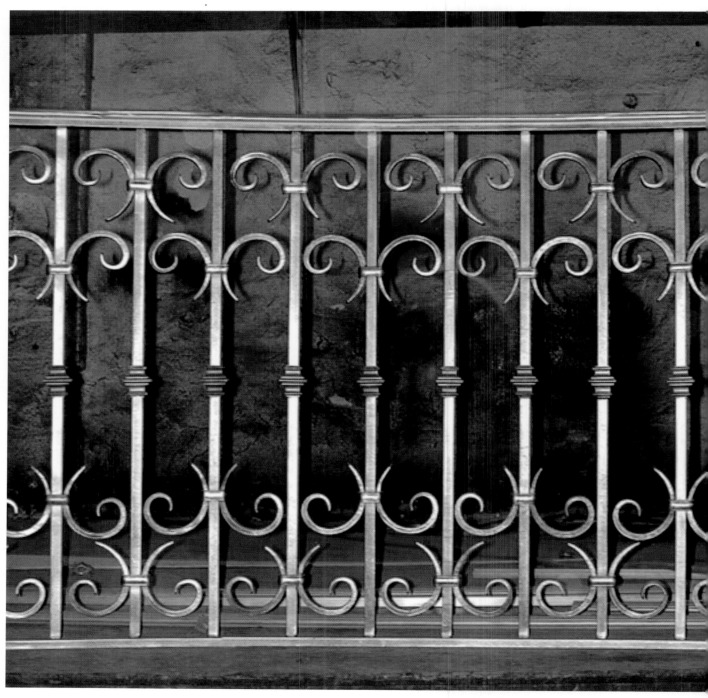

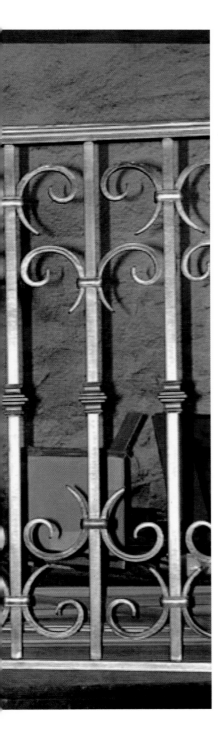

Left: Robert Rotondo. Railing (in progress). Repetitive C curves in opposing positions are collared to the balusters for an effective use of basic forms. A square baluster collar along the center of each upright adds to the rhythm of the repetitive theme. *Courtesy, artist*

Right: Joel A. Schwartz. Design by Joel Schwartz, glass accents by Laurel Herter and Josh Simpson. Stair balustrade with glass inserts. Scrolls, circles, textured verticals, and round balls. Glass panels are in the central circle of alternating balustrades and a glass ball is the finial. South Carolina Residence. *Photo, Ron Blunt*

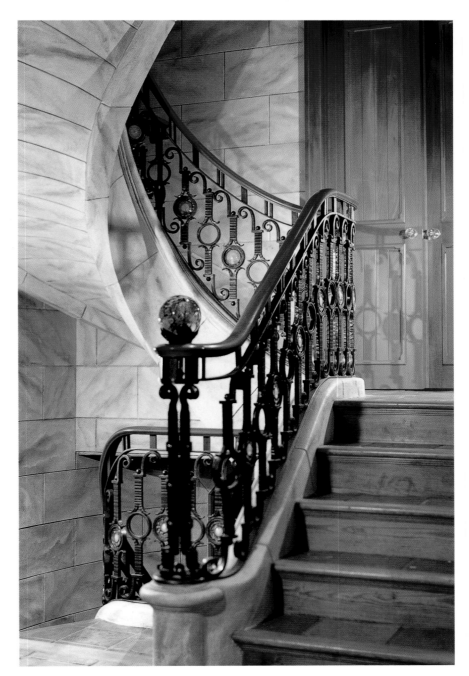

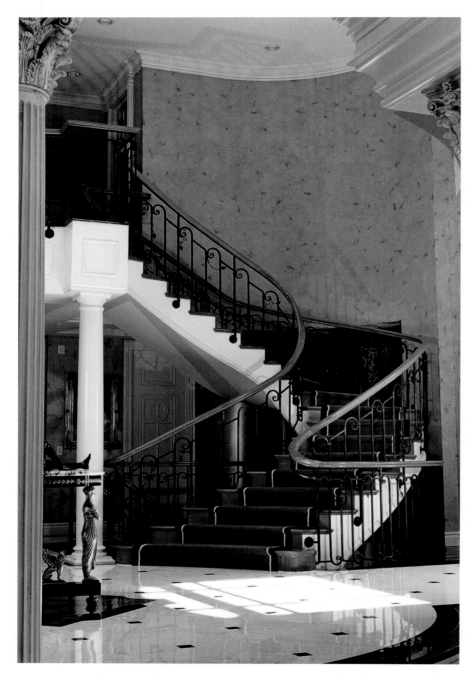

Scott Lankton. Elegant detailing on a curved staircase using scrolls with straight bars continuing to the railings on the landing. Medallions are used to attach the balusters to the staircase stringboard allowing a wider passage. Leaves are randomly wound into the balustrade. Cherry wood cap. *Photo, artist*

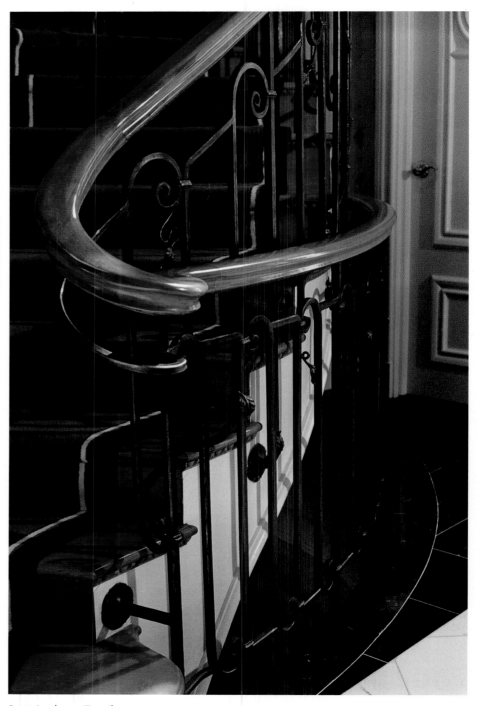

Scott Lankton. Detail

Plant Forms

Michael Dillon's French style staircase uses S curves in reverse positions to create an inverted heart shape with extra scrollwork within each large shape. The gold acanthus leaves are a French motif but the staircase also has a "slight lean towards Gothic," says Dillon. After the drawings were accepted, a wood template was made by a master stair builder to aid the stone carver in his construction of the limestone curb and layout of the treads. Dillon explains, "I was able to use this template to bend my top and bottom rails. These frames were built on site and brought back to the shop to fill in the design. Some areas of the design are floating attached by 3/4" balls." The newel panel consists of eleven bars arranged in the vertical plane and a decorative "D" for the name of the house. Two four-foot balconies and seven panels are mechanically fastened together to complete the rail. The finish is painted dull black with gold leaf accents and the steel cap is natural hand rubbed. The project took six months and over 500 hours to complete.

Joel Schwartz's stair railing has a heavier look than Dillon's French style staircase. Tightly controlled shapes give it a classic look. The simple repeat design is based on circles and an elongated C shape sandwiched between horizontals.

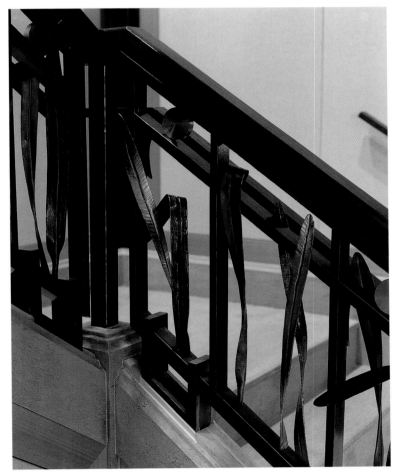

Joel A. Schwartz. Stair balustrade (detail) with forged leaf work. Monel, steel, Cupro nickel, and stainless steel. The same artist can work with very delicate or with more substantial shapes. Each leaf is individually and differently textured. Gensler & Assoc. Architects. *Courtesy, artist*

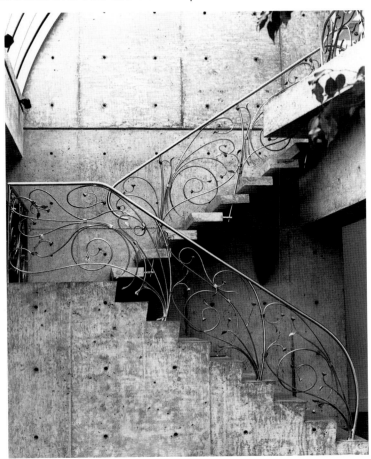

Joel A. Schwartz. Stair railing with scrolls, leaves, and a curved ending without a newel post. Perfect for a garden area. Stainless steel. There is a matching pair of entry doors. *Courtesy, artist*

Michael Bondi combines steel with bronze leaves and a cap rail, rather than the more traditional gold leaves. The acanthus leaf, popular in classic work, has continued to permeate ironwork in all periods, and is often included in Victorian and Art Nouveau designs. Bondi uses an exaggerated leaf shape to add interest and dimension to ends of graceful curving elements.

Fruit, different plant forms, gargoyles, balls, grape clusters, basket shapes, flowers spires, and a variety of objects may be used for the finial on a newel post such as a pineapple on the newel post of Robert Rotondo's staircase.

Finials and other details may be hand forged in the blacksmith's shop, or purchased from a company that specializes in making such items, and then assembled to the post. Some are cast from a mold. When one considers including such an item both the client and the blacksmith should specify the type to be used. Hand forged pieces are generally more costly than those that are cast.

A newel post doesn't have to be a post. It can be replaced by a more decorative ending as in the staircase by Stephen Austin. Austin carries the leaf idea further and adds an entwined vine to the flourishing stair ending. Austin's uprights are secured to a wooden base of the staircase while Rotondo's has a metal plate along the staircase side that is secured to the base. Rotondo avoids the need for regular uprights. Instead he fashions the banded curving elements as supports that also become the balustrade.

Joel Schwartz's geometric staircase has a repoussé tree for one newel post and a tree trunk for the other. Another of his staircases has glass inserts and a glass finial with heavily textured elements that contrast smooth with rough, and shiny with dull.

French designs tend to have controlled curves and arcs, and a general feeling of movement. The examples shown have some plant details such as leaves, acanthus, vines, and so forth. But many staircases rely almost completely on plant forms for their design, leaving the arcs and curves almost as an afterthought. The balustrade for Joel Schwartz's staircase is essentially plant forms.

Contemporary staircases often are inspired by late Art Nouveau designs. Lines are curved, or sinuous, or randomly shaped, but not as unrestrained and wild as those of the Belgian artists of the early 1900's. Perfect examples are the staircases by Scott Lankton, who can easily move from French to Art Nouveau, Art Deco, and modern, as the commission dictates. Because many of today's smiths have degrees in art and design their results reverberate with their backgrounds in art history.

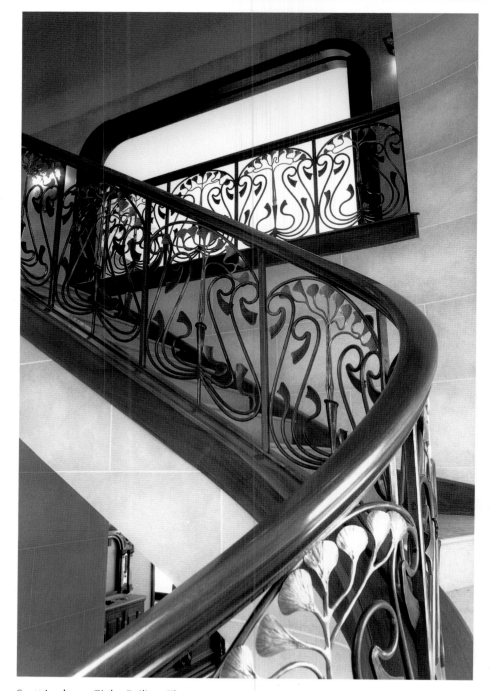

Scott Lankton. Ginko Railing. The Art Nouveau movement inspired the use of abstract plant forms in a series of curves. Forged steel and bronze. Mahogany cap rail. 40' long. *Photo*, artist

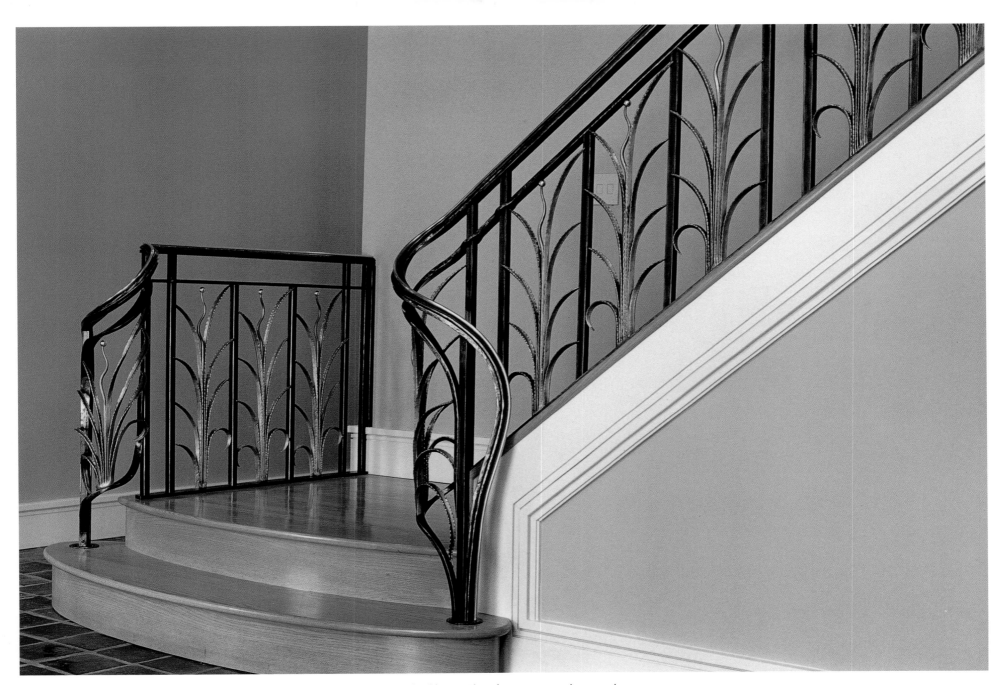

Scott Lankton. Deco Railing. Forged steel, angle iron, bronze and brushed brass. Plant forms are evenly spaced between balusters. A graceful curving banister reaches to the bottom of the front step. Plant elements are TIG-welded together rather than using traditional banding. The vertical balusters pierce the slit and drifted horizontal elements creating a beautiful solution to the joinery. *Photo, artist*

Think of the problems one might incur creating a staircase for a three floor townhouse in Manhattan and you'll have an idea of the design dilemma faced by Dimitri Gerakaris for his free form composition in iron. Each floor is slightly different, the banisters had to be shaped and sizing was a headache. But the results show Gerakaris' virtuosity in iron.

Kirsten Reese faced a different challenge when she was commissioned to create her "Circle Railing" for a craft Design center in Stowe, Vermont. She says, "The magic happened when I gathered my 1500-pounds of materials. I started to see shape and pattern instead of function and part. From the scrap yard grave of Vermont's rural farm and small industry cast-offs I found new life, movement and pupose."

John Boyd Smith's Iris staircase and Acorn and Oak Leaf railing, with their use of plants and curving balustrades, are inspired by Art Nouveau. Smith's plant shapes most likely represent geographical fauna of the client's environment.

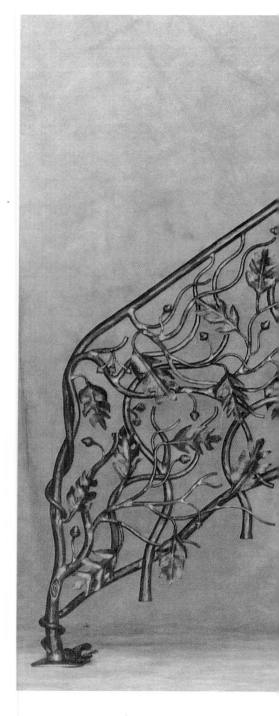

John Boyd Smith. Iris railing. Forged steel polished and sealed with boiled linseed oil and clear varnish. Inspired by an Art Nouveau design. Private residence in San Jose, California. Approx. 10' long. *Photo, Rhonda Nell Fleming*

Right: John Boyd Smith. Oak leaf and acorn railing. Forged steel polished and sealed with boiled linseed oil and clear varnish. The oak leaves and acorns depict realistic aspects of the red oak that is indigenous to the southern Virginia residence where the railing is installed. Approx. 14' long. *Photo, Rhonda Nell Fleming*

112

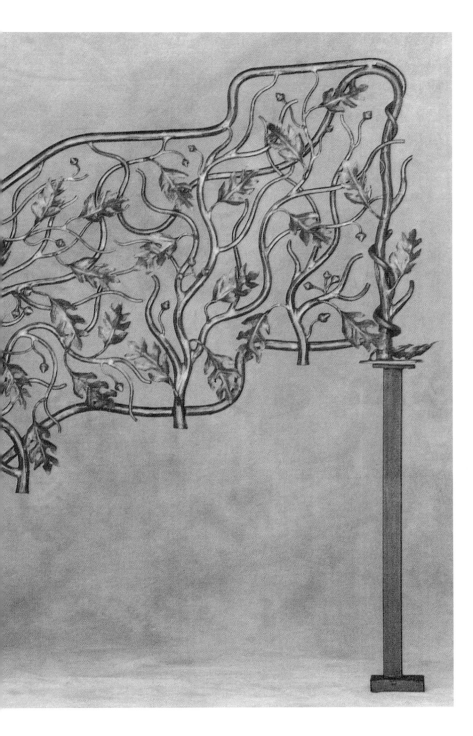

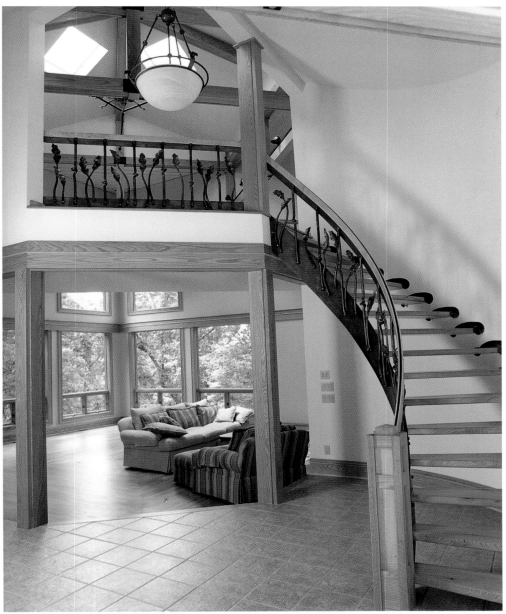

Jeff Fetty. Curving staircase with leaves alternating with crimped uprights. Instead of a flat stringboard along the wall each tread is supported by a cast iron support made by a sculptor. Omitting the risers gives the staircase an open airy feeling. The wood part of the cap is laminated to the steel top cap. The steel bottom plate is finished with a copper patina and coated with a clear acrylic sealer. Curved staircase is 14'; top rail is 8'. *Photo, Jurgen Lorenzen*

A double staircase often is used in Southern style homes but this impressive grand staircase is in a home in the Midwest. Says artist blacksmith Keith Johnson; "The architect sent me drawings of what was wanted and I made a couple of samples until we agreed on this one with the leaves. Then the architect asked that the back side of the leaves be textured as well as the front. He said, 'It will only take you another minute to do the back.' On 250 leaves, that 'other minute' amounted to about 10,000 extra hammer blows!" Johnson's wife cut out all the leaves on a Beverly shear. The balusters were assembled in pairs to sit on each stair and single balusters form the curve of the balcony. The oak handrail is mortised to fit over the top of the balusters.

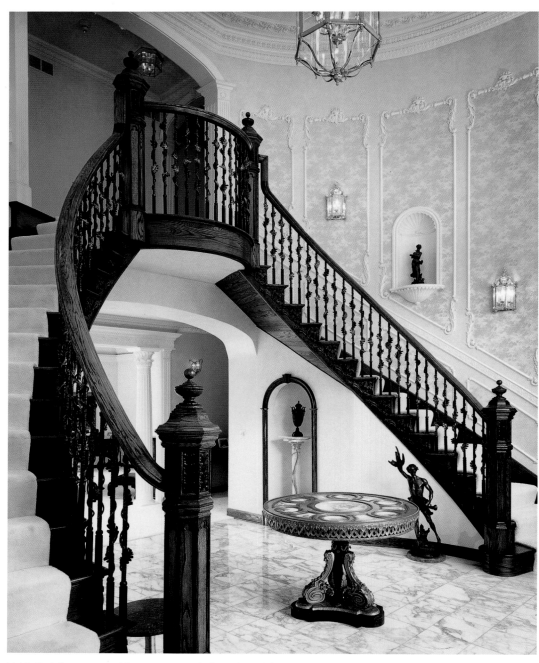

Keith R. Johnson. Double staircase with forged steel balusters and forged bronze vines winding around them. Oak cap. Arlington Heights, Illinois residence. *Photo, Courtesy, Architectural Impressions*

Keith R. Johnson. Detail of above showing the vines on the hammered textured uprights. It is this exquisite detailing that identifies hand forging and is not found in mass produced ironwork. *Photo, David Grondin*

114

Steve Lopes uses a different interpretation of growth by having the curving uprights form a Gothic-like arch, but they represent a plant and each tendril has a slightly different shape. The tendrils are placed randomly as in nature itself.

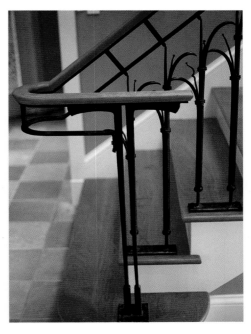

Steve Lopes. This ironwork continues around the landing and swings into a reverse curve. *Photo, artist*

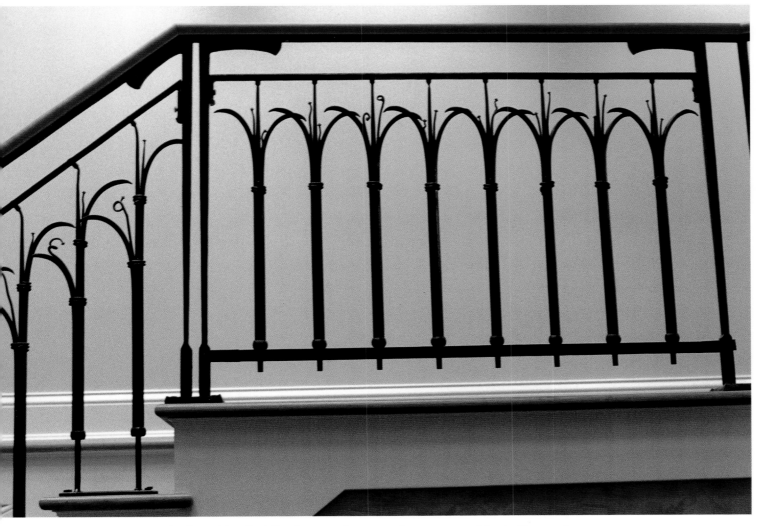

Steve Lopes. Staircase and railing with a disciplined repeat of curves at the top are combined with a random use of different shaped tendrils. Note the beautifully hand fashioned fittings at the bottom, and the one that joins the staircase and the landing railing under the banister at the top. The design on the staircase changes slightly from that on the railing because each stair supports two balusters. *Photo, artist*

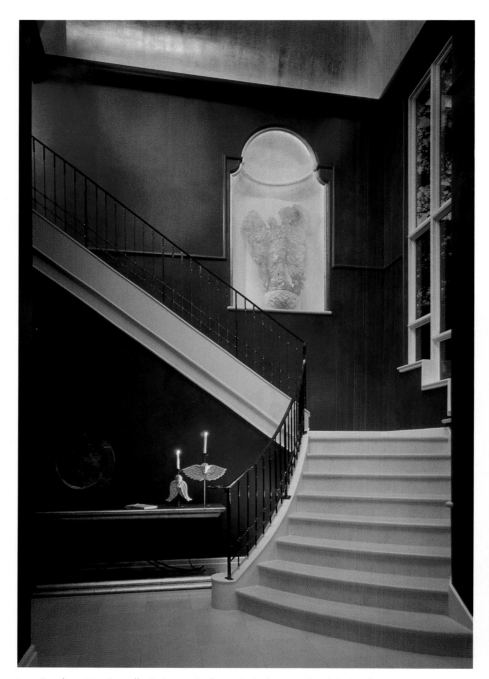

Geometric Shapes: Circles, Squares, Rectangles

Moving away from the French curves and nature, takes us to geometrical forms. Instead of the cone, the cylinder, and the cube the ironworker relies on straight lines, squares, and rectangles. Lars Stanley and L. Japheth Howard share a vision of simplicity in their staircases of iron. Handrails, too, lend themselves to this simplicity in the examples from John Medwedeff, Rick Smith, Frederic A. Crist, and David W. Munn.

Jack Brubaker's "Maria Staircase" is so named because it is based on the designs from the pots of pueblo potter Maria Martinez that are collected by the client. It is made of steel, with the "feather shapes" of copper and bronze. The top rail is formed of a cluster of flat stock and round tubes to suggest the round black shape in many of the Martinez pots.

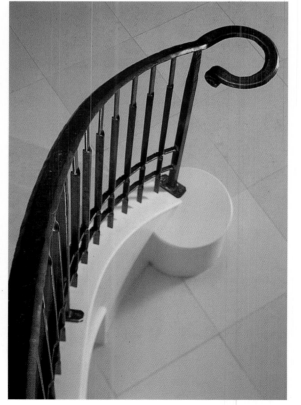

Lars Stanley, AIA Frucella Staircase (detail). Each upright is composed of flat bars with twisted and riveted intersections. The banister ends in a horseshoe shape with a tight scroll. *Photo, AtelierWong Photography*

Lars Stanley, AIA. Frucella Staircase is dramatic in its restrained design for a contemporary home. *Photo, AtelierWong Photography*

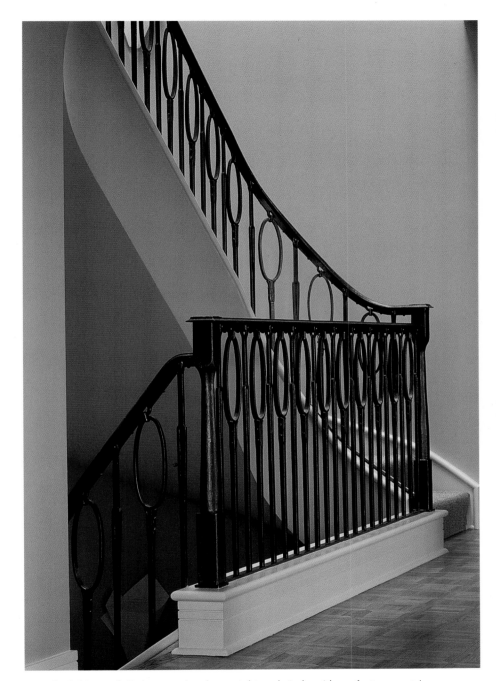

L. Japheth Howard. Staircase using the upright and circle with perfect geometric symmetry is beautiful in its simplicity. Detailing in the uprights and impeccable joinery lend to the rhythm of this staircase and railing. Private residence. Seattle, Washington. *Photo, Jay Dodson*

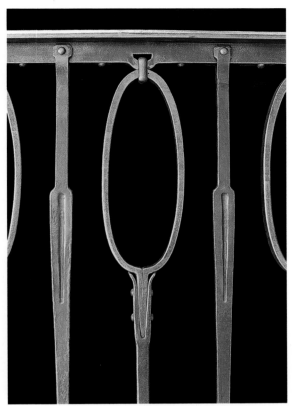

L. Japheth Howard. Every detail is thoroughly and magnificently executed to explore, and take advantage of, steel's inherent beauty. *Photo, Jay Dodson*

Below: L. Japheth Howard. Detail shows the joinery, texturing, and designs on each upright. *Photo, Jay Dodson*

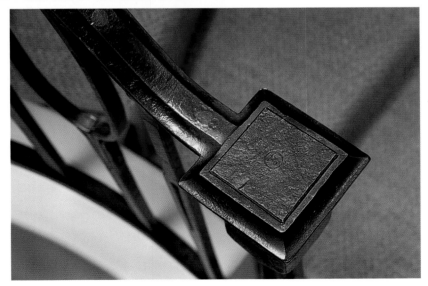

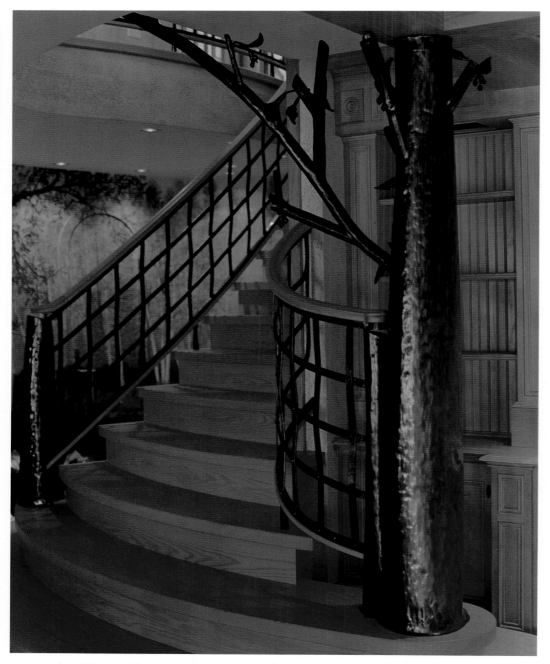

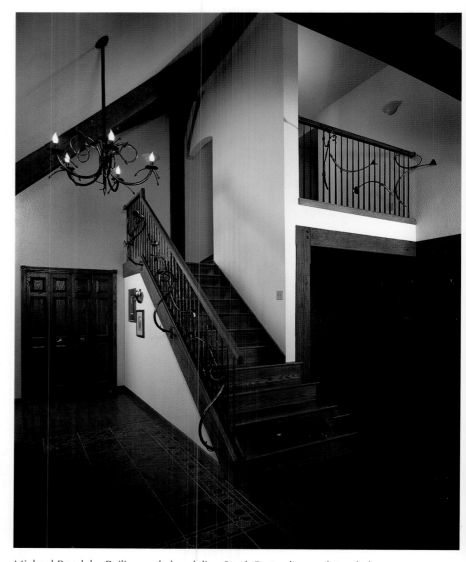

Michael Bendele. Railing and chandelier. Steel. Protruding sculptural elements support the subtly twisted uprights. The coordinated chandelier is also by the artist. *Photo, Jim King Royal Images*

Joel A. Schwartz. Banister with repoussé tree for one newel post and a tree trunk for the other. The riveted horizontal and vertical pieces are squares in a straight area changing to diamond shapes as the angle of the banister changes. Bolton Landing, New York. Interior design: Edmond DeRocker Associates. *Courtesy, artist*

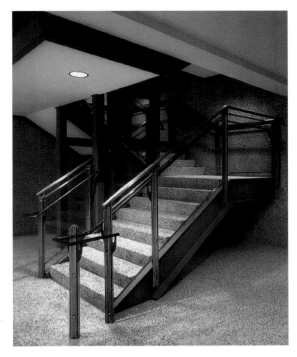

Lars Stanley, AIA. An I-beam for the base, steel banisters and balustrades, yield an industrial appearance. The jutting upright and handrail at the one side is a subliminal control of the direction people should take as they leave the stairway. *Photo, Paul Bardagjy*

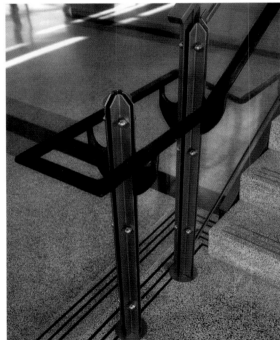

Lars Stanley, AIA. Detail of the uprights, hand railing, and joinery. The rivets become a decorative element. *Photo, Paul Bardagjy*

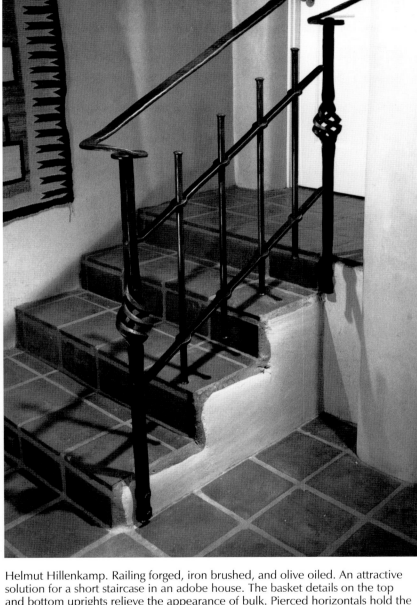

Helmut Hillenkamp. Railing forged, iron brushed, and olive oiled. An attractive solution for a short staircase in an adobe house. The basket details on the top and bottom uprights relieve the appearance of bulk. Pierced horizontals hold the uprights with just a simple upset top. The banisters have graceful bends and they curve so that the uprights can be attached to the staircase sides instead of on the treads. 5' high, 3' long. *Photo, artist*

Free Form

Then, as if straining beyond its boundaries, objecting to being confined to a simple shape, design, or dimension, the iron seems almost alive, as though it has a mind of its own. Nicholas Semenov's railing is one of many he created for a home in St. Petersburg, Russia, that includes banisters, porch railings, and other items. The beauty of his work is in the character that he gives to the metal. It has a wonderfully tactile quality that invites touching and fondling. It appears as soft as melted chocolate even though it is hard.

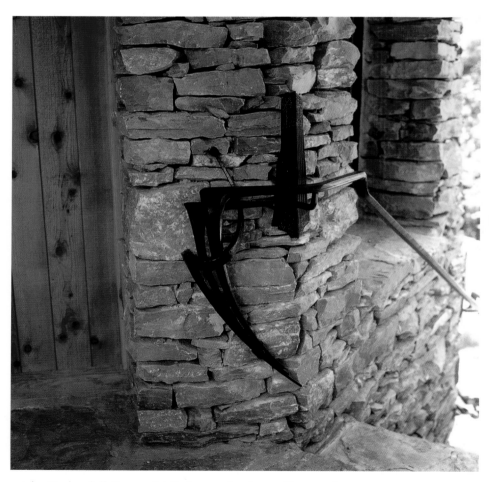

John Medwedeff. Corner detail of a grand staircase. *Photo, artist*

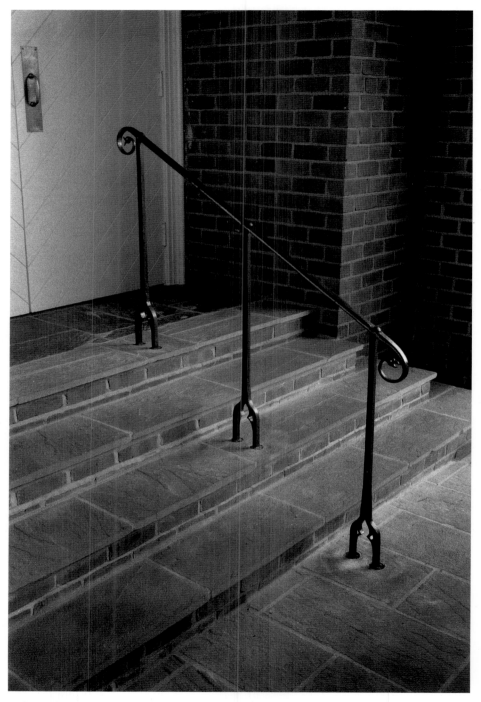

Rick Smith. Handrail. Penland School of Art, Penland, North Carolina. *Photo, artist*

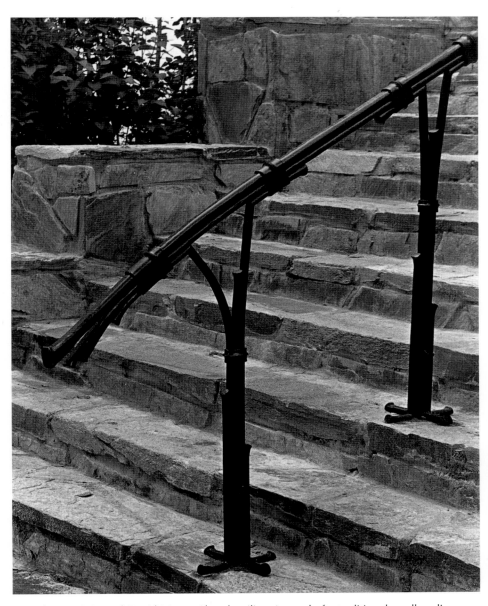

Frederic A Crist and David Munn. Church railing. Instead of a traditional scroll ending, a small animal head nests in the curve. An extra detail in the bottom repeats the curve in the church's windows. *Photo, artist*

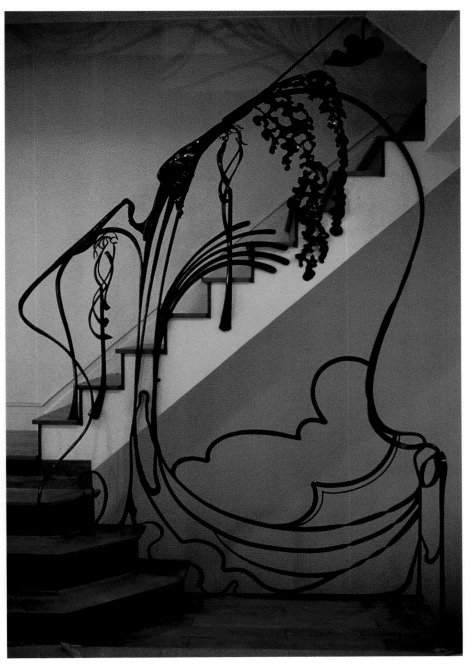

Enrique Vega. The Proctor residence railing includes this decorative abstract plant form at the corner of the landing. The plant motifs are used throughout the railings to accentuate the varied plants in this home. *Photo, artist*

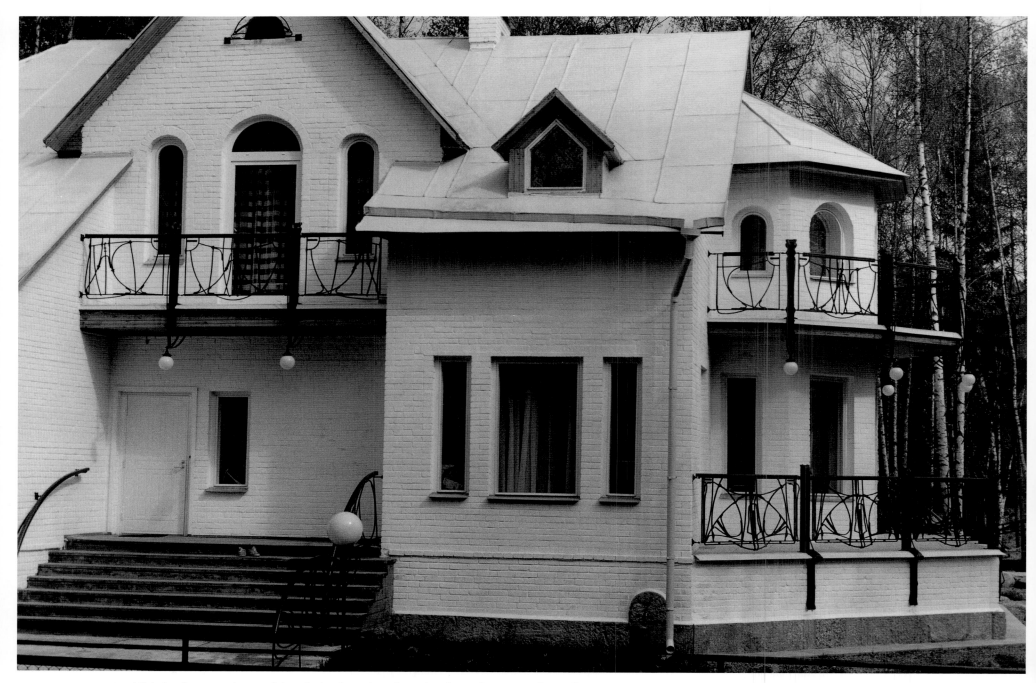

Nickolay Semenov. Ironwork installation for stair and porch railings, dormer window grilles, and coordinated light fixtures for a residence in Repino, a suburb of St. Petersburg, Russia. *Courtesy, artist*

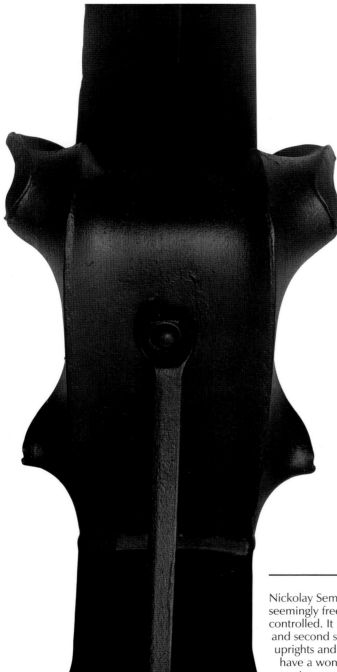

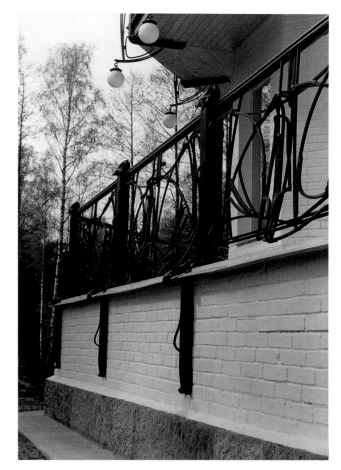

Nickolay Semenov. Detail of porch railing and joinery (page 122). The steel is so beautifully formed, its resemblance to soft clay invites touching. *Courtesy, artist*

Nickolay Semenov. Porch railing in a seemingly free form design is really very controlled. It is repeated in banisters and second story porch railings. The uprights and hardware attachments have a wonderful plasticity. *Courtesy, artist*

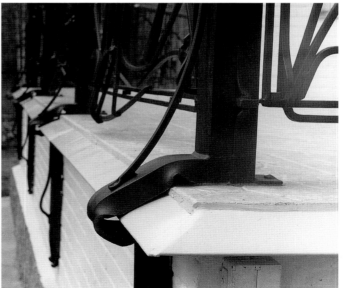

Nickolay Semenov. Closeup of the finish of the iron and its seemingly softness. *Courtesy, artist*

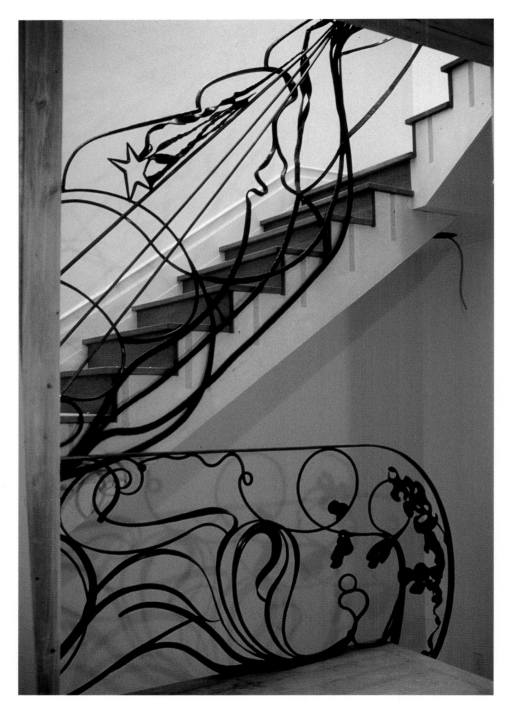

Dimitri Gerakaris. Multiple story railing for a Manhattan town house. Steel. *Photo, artist*

Dimitri Gerakaris. The staircase at a second level. Although the stair railing appears free form, every part of it is carefully worked out beforehand and made to a planned drawing. *Photo, artist*

Jack Brubaker. "Maria Staircase." This unusual staircase represents elements in the pots by Maria Martinez that the client collects. The "feather" shapes are copper and bronze. *Courtesy, artist*

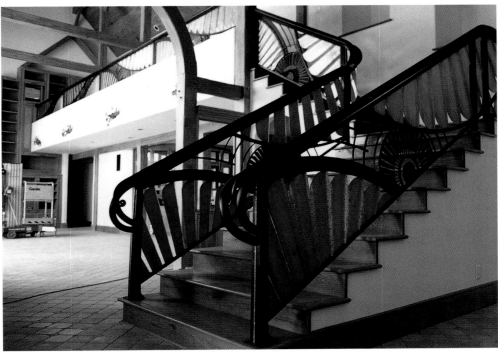

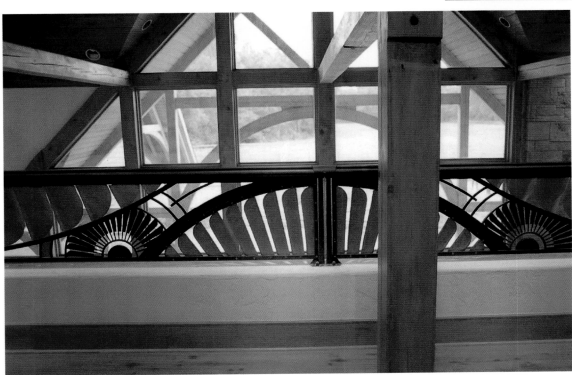

Kirsten Reese finds beauty in combining the formed bar with gears, wheels, and detritus from our mechanized society. Her staircase railing is carefully composed but has a seemingly random use of circular forms.

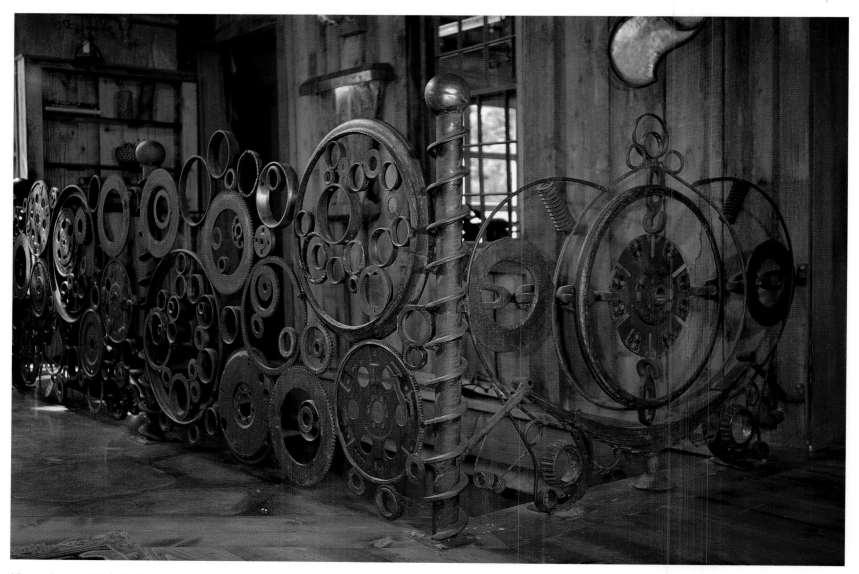

Kirsten Reese. "Circle Railing." Handrail of detritus from Vermont's rural farm and small industry. Found objects rescued from a scrap yard take on a new life and purpose when they are skillfully assembled with forged elements to unify them. *Rail for The Stowe Craft Design Center,* Stowe, Vermont. *Photo, artist*

John Boyd Smith's Egret rail is astounding in the workmanship and the complexity of the forms. It takes courage, experience, and an understanding client, for a blacksmith to venture into creating seemingly free form shapes though he is always in control of every bend and nuance of the metal.

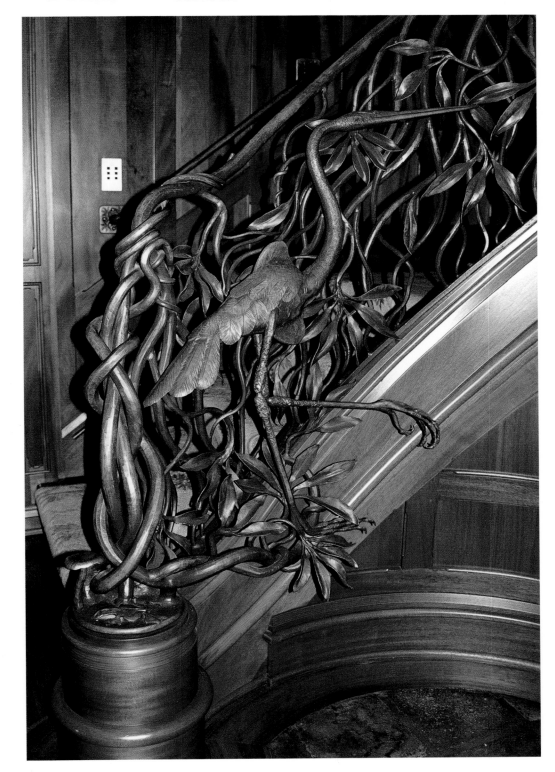

John Boyd Smith. Egret staircase depicts the birds among mangroves, palmettos, and various grasses with small animals. The railing of forged mild steel with a faux-bronze patina weighs about two tons and is installed in a private residence in Hilton Head, South Carolina. *Photo, Rhonda Nell Fleming*

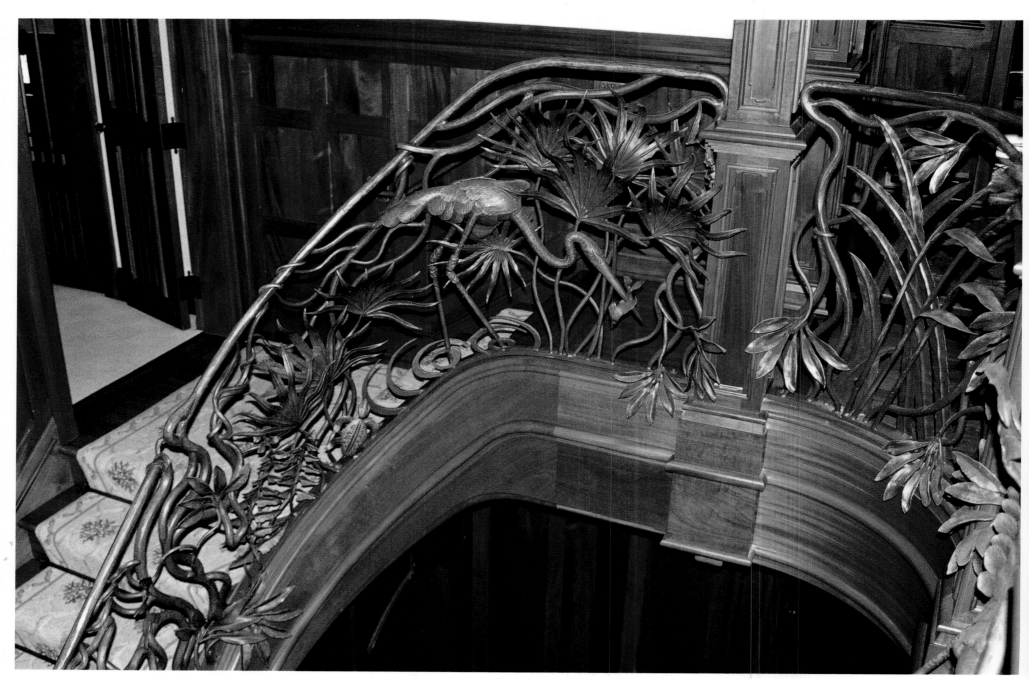

John Boyd Smith. Detail of page 127. *Photo, Rhonda Nell Fleming*

128

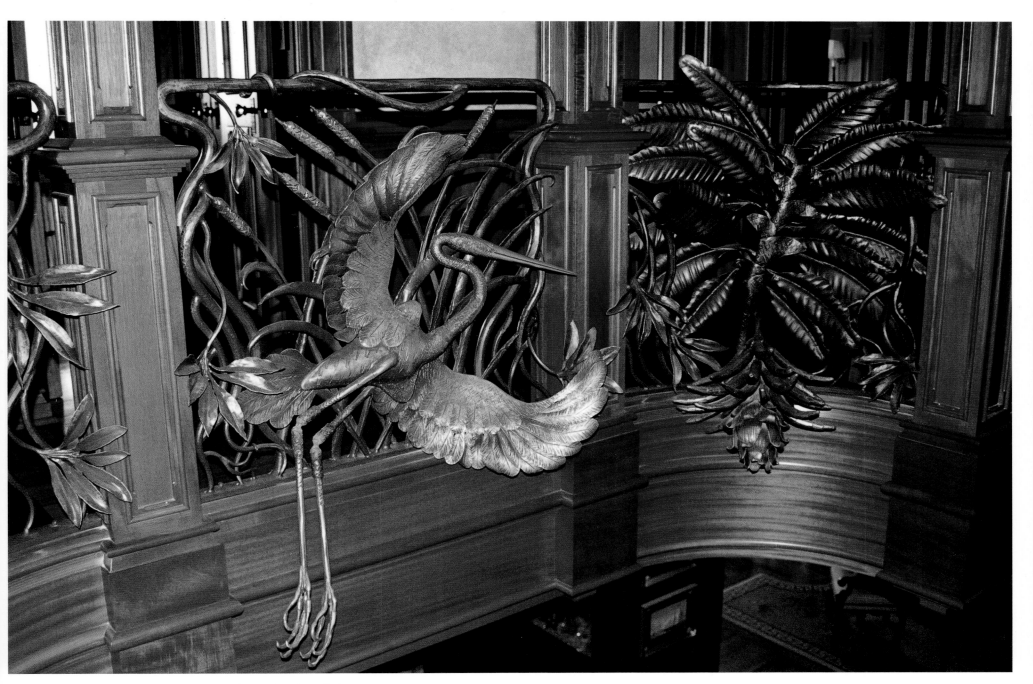

John Boyd Smith. Detail of page 127. *Photo, Rhonda Nell Fleming*

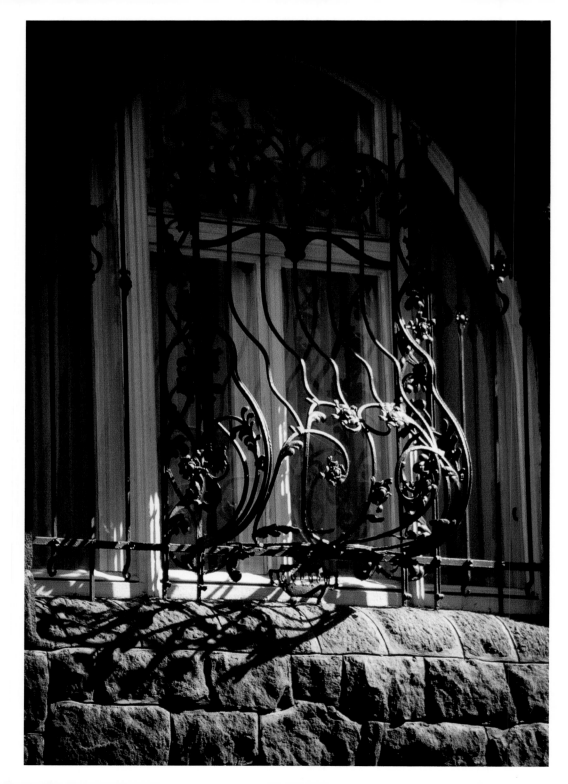

Window grille. Most grilles are two-dimensional; this one protrudes into space for a three dimensional treatment in an Art Nouveau style. Budapest, Hungary. *Photo, author*

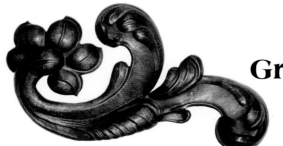

Chapter 4
Grilles, Screens, Railings, and Balconies

Railings, screens, and grilles have multiple applications. Examples of their use appear in architecture throughout history. Regardless of the commission and its size, the techniques, design, and construction problems for these items are similar. Exterior railings exposed to weathering must have finishes that will withstand different environments. National and local building codes may dictate conditions such as height, materials, spacing between horizontal and vertical bars, and other factors. Some artist blacksmiths feel stifled by these codes. Others look at special conditions as a test and a challenge to their creativity.

Some railings could easily double as fences. Indoor railings could fall into the stair chapter. If you're looking at railings for a specific purpose and design, study railings and fences to see how they might cross over and serve your needs.

As in any other art form, it is revealing to observe the ironwork designs that reflect the period in which they probably were made. It's also revealing to see how artists use historical references to create new designs. Not surprising, grilles, screens, and balconies created during the

Art Nouveau period continue to inspire today's blacksmiths. The designs remain universally and infinitely appealing. The excesses of Baroque, the delicacy of French Rococo, the minimal approach of the Bauhaus School and the restraint of modern design can be seen in this microcosm of ironwork illustrated with examples from many countries.

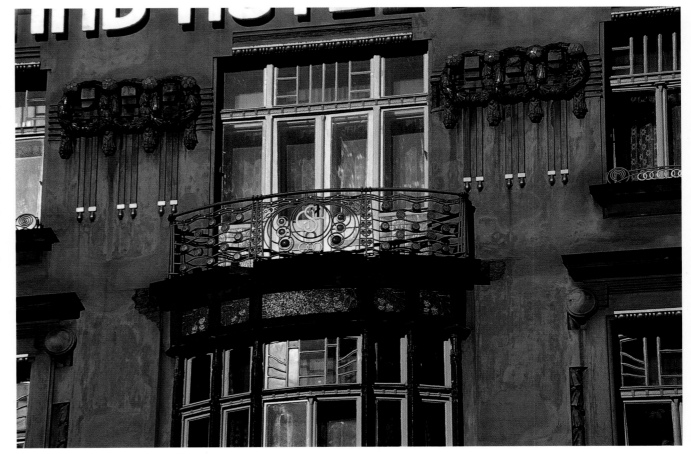

Hotel Europa. Prague, Czech Republic. The Hotel Europa, built in 1905, is a prime example of Art Nouveau. From door hardware to exterior decorations, the ironwork is a fully integrated element of the building. The balcony ironwork is based on the wavy line with circle repeats in gold. *Photo, author*

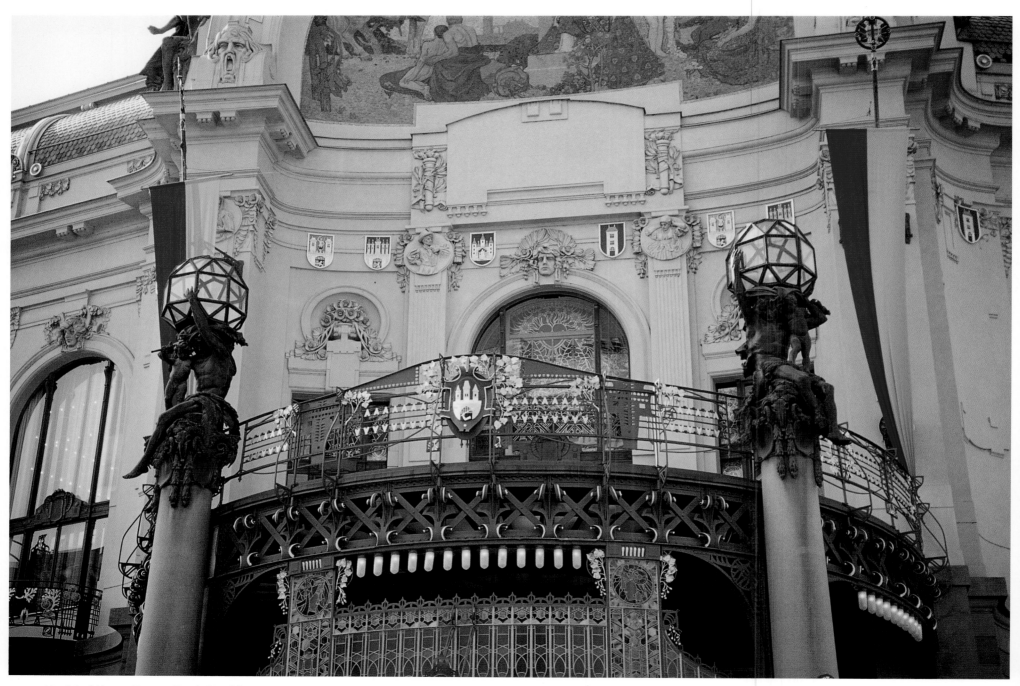

Municipal House. Prague, Czech Republic. Prague's most prominent Art Nouveau building, designed by Antonín Balšánek, replaced a former Royal Court in 1905-11. The ironwork is used structurally and decoratively. *Photo, author*

Underscoring all ironwork is the importance of wedding the design to the building. A free form exterior porch railing, for example, would look out of kilter on a traditional Cape Cod or Southern Plantation style home.

The Japanese Pavilion. Brussels, Belgium. The repeat squares in the railings of this building show the varying styles that can be achieved and are indigenous to a national style. These railings are made of wood, but they illustrate railing design diversity. Only in the past 25 to 30 years have Japanese architects begun using iron architecturally. *Photo, author*

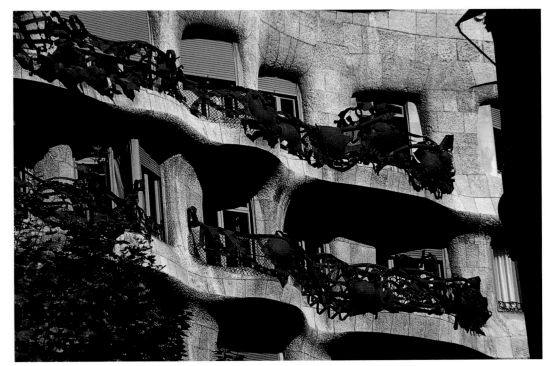

Antoni Gaudí. Barcelona, Spain. No discussion of ornamental ironwork would be complete without credit to Gaudí's unique interpretation of Art Nouveau in the early 1900s. The free form balconies on his Casa Milá (1905) illustrate the inventive use of iron at a time when Art Nouveau was already well entrenched in other European countries. *Photo, author*

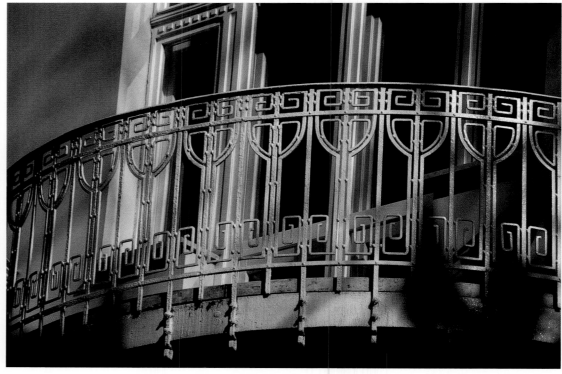

Balcony railing. Art Nouveau design using the Greek key motif at the top and bottom in two different shapes. Painted white for a light look against a light building. Budapest, Hungary. *Photo, author*

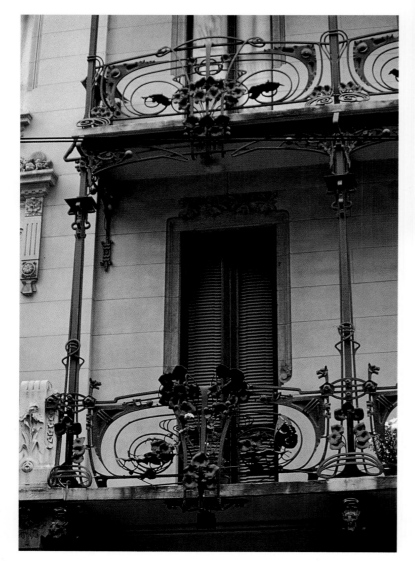

Allesandro Mazzucotelli. Italy. Detail of the Casa Ferrario balconies. The railings extend around the entire support and overhead areas and integrate with the architecture. They give the façade a decorative, lacy look. *Photo, Stephen Bondi*

Grilles:
Security and Decoration

The efficacy of, and our preoccupation with, security devices are not new. Consider the ironwork used in medieval and Renaissance architecture and you can almost hear the clunk of a drop gate at the entry to a palace, a fortress, or a dungeon. When grille work is developed for maximum security, a crowbar, saw, or heavy metal cutter could easily bend or sever a thin bar, while thicker, heavier bars can thwart a thief who must work quickly and undetected.

Grilles and dividers are an integral part of religious architecture. Ironwork screens, often heavily gold encrusted, were used extensively in the cathedrals of Europe. The screen in the choir aisle of St. Paul's Cathedral, London, England, by Jean Tijou is noted in many art history books. Tijou, who worked under the model plan of the Cathedral by Christopher Wren, designed pieces that are light and lacy looking. (See bibliography for an illustrated Internet Site.)

The French, the English, and German balconies and grillwork remain the influence for ornate ironwork used in churches and traditional buildings today. But it is the Art Nouveau ironwork that exerts the greatest inspiration and influence on today's ironworkers. Allesandro Mazzucotelli's ironwork breaks from it traditional ornamental implications. The façade of his Casa Ferrario is part of the building's architecture not just a decorative addition. The total design becomes a sculptural composition that begins with more dense ironwork on the lower levels graduating to laciness on the top floors.

It is Spain's Antoni Gaudì that artists look to when they don't want to be bound by conventional structure. His balconies, though they border on challenging the practical, are imaginative and vigorous.

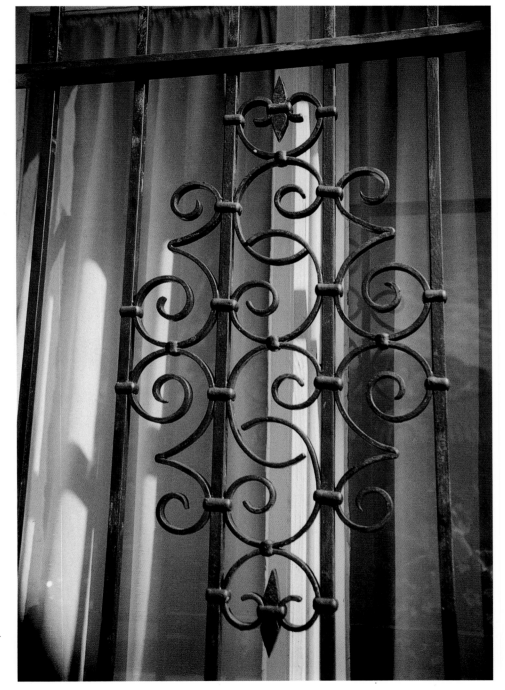

William Requa. Window grille (detail). About 1925. In America, William Requa was influenced by ironwork he saw during a trip to Andalusia, Spain. The result was the California Mission style. In this ground level security screen detail he used C curves in interlocking relationships banded to the verticals. *Photo, author*

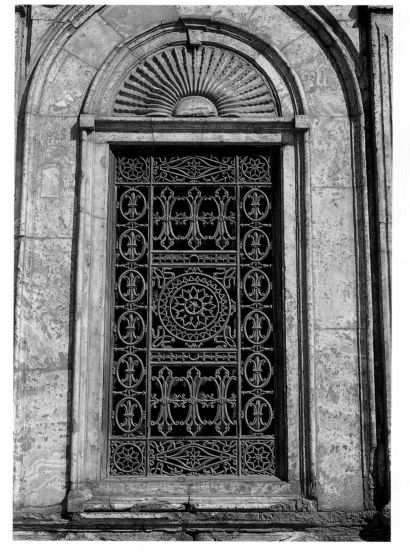

Window grille. Turkey. Old world cast iron grilles contain design elements that are used today but in different relationships. *Photo, artist*

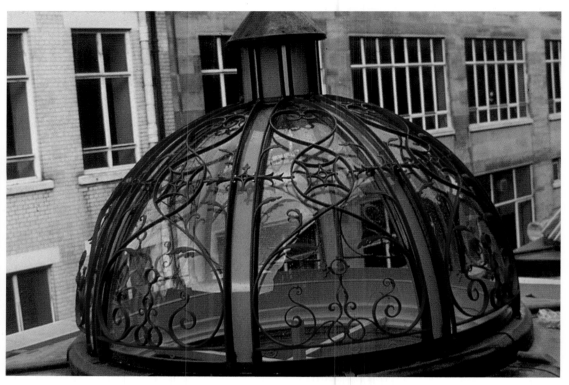

James Horrobin. By designing and shaping the panels for the curve, the artist created a dome shaped grille for a glass skylight over an area of the Sir John Soane's Museum, London, England. *Photo, artist*

A grille can be designed to frame a window or obliterate views to the outside. The best designs are attractive from both inside and outside the building. They should relate to the pattern of the window or door and not introduce a new series of lines. They can be flat or bellied out. They should enhance a building's inherent beauty, not detract from it. When grilles are poorly designed, they can be a hodge-podge from inside and out, and reduce a property's value.

Grilles today have many purposes, but most are for security. Darryl Nelson's grille is for a cashier's cage. Helmut Hillenkamp's grille is for a jewelry store window. Dimitri Gerakris's fish grille for an aquarium entrance certainly fulfills its security function. It relates to the business within, and is attractive and fun. Eric Cuper's grilles rely heavily on negative space for their decoration and serve more as a suggested barrier than security designed to conform to code restrictions.

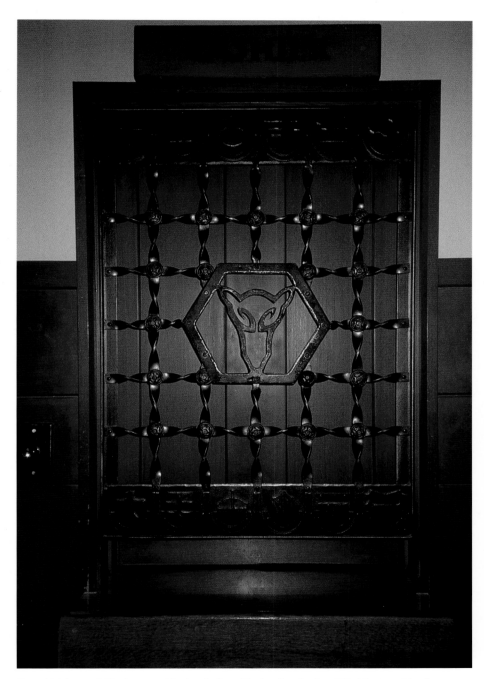

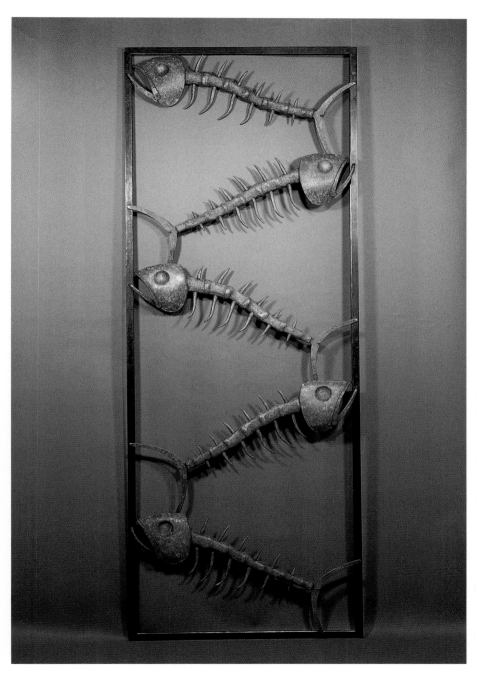

Darryl Nelson. Grille for a cashier's window. Timberline Lodge, Washington. Northwest Coast Cascadian Style. 2.5' high, 1.5' wide. *Photo, artist*

Eric K. Cuper. Skeletal fish grille. Steel. 3.7' high, 2' wide. *Courtesy, artist*

Lars Stanley created a latticework enclosure for a tower at the University of Texas, Austin, Texas. Built in 1937, the 28-story building's tower had been closed for 25 years. It had been the site of student leaps and a sniper assault in 1966 so a stigma was attached to it. Until then it had been one of central Texas's biggest tourist attractions affording sweeping, unobstructed views of the campus, the state Capitol, and downtown Austin. Says Stanley; "I remember

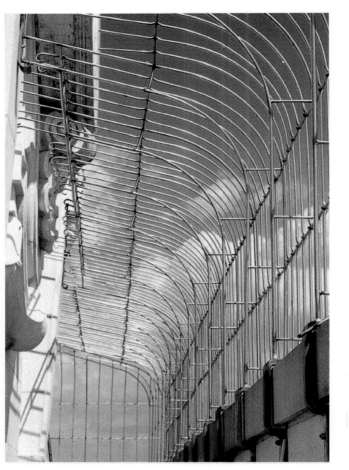

when I went to architecture school there, how the tower was a brooding presence on campus, always seeming a bit menacing and mysterious since it was inaccessible. After it was reopened, it seemed as though a veil had been lifted and the community had reclaimed an important part of its past."

Lars Stanley, AIA. A large curved latticework grille encloses the tower observation deck at the University of Texas tourist attraction, Austin, Texas. *Photo, Paul Bardagj*

Lars Stanley, AIA. The University of Texas tower grille from the inside looking out shows the construction and the forged brackets that attach it to the stonework. *Photo, artist*

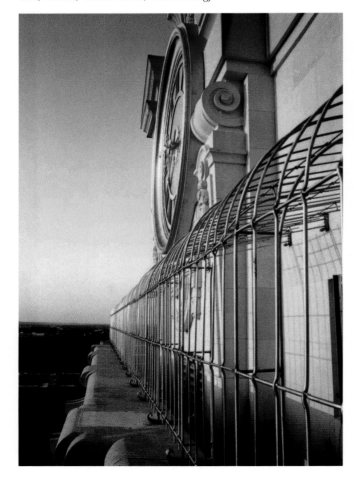

Below: Lars Stanley, AIA. The grille, during construction and installation, looks small from a distance, but it was a huge, complicated project with many problems to solve. *Photo, M. Miller*

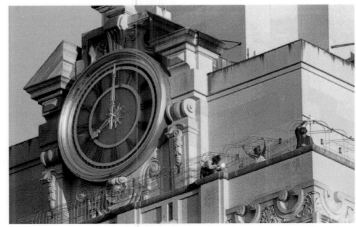

Stanley's steel enclosure wraps around the entire tower. Its details are lost from a distance, but there are many small subtleties. The idea was to avoid making it appear as a cage, but to keep it as light and unobtrusive as possible. Each intersection of the bars is forged into an offset which helps create a subtle pattern and softens the overall effect. Several forged scroll details at the attachment points repeat, or pick up on, the building's carved limestone scrolls. The pieces are all stainless steel that gleam lightly in the sunlight reflecting the changing color of the clouds and sky. Stanley notes that, "From a distance, this subtle lattice glows like a crown on the proud tower. I never suspected there could be such grace and beneficial energy associated with a small bit of metalwork."

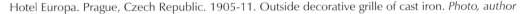

Hotel Europa. Prague, Czech Republic. 1905-11. Outside decorative grille of cast iron. *Photo, author*

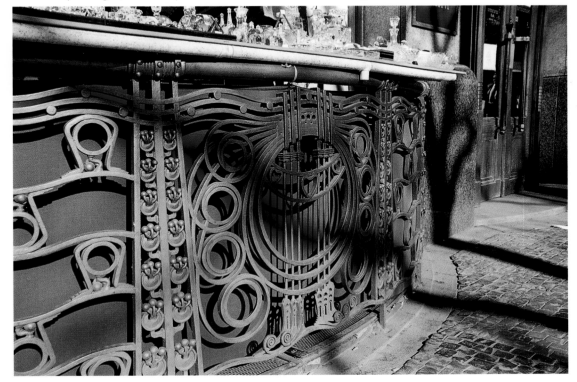

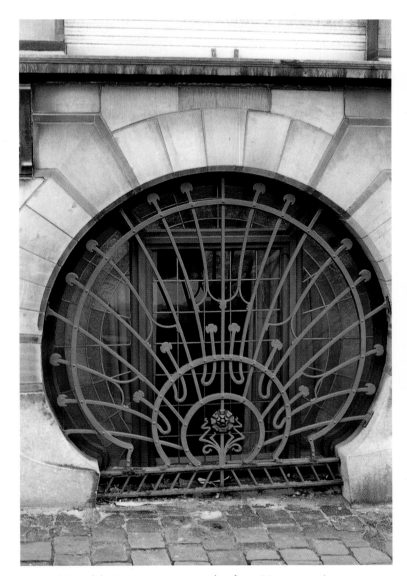

Gaspard Devalck. Art Nouveau example of a cuisine-cave window; a type of security grille used in Belgian homes in the late 18th and early 19th Centuries. *Photo, Werner F. Bocqué*

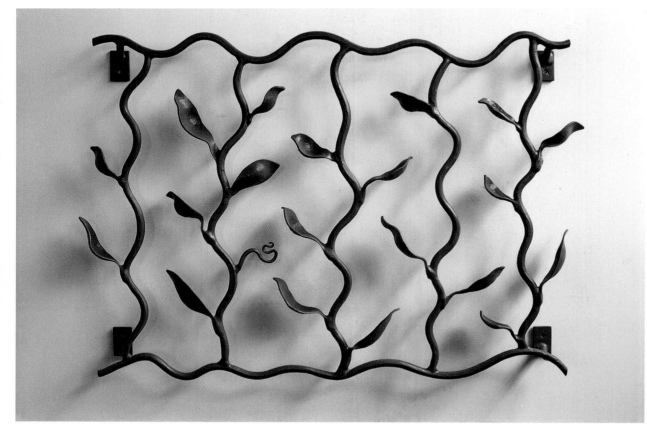

Jean Whitesavage and Nick Lyle. Leaf grille with wavy lines representing branches. *Courtesy, artists*

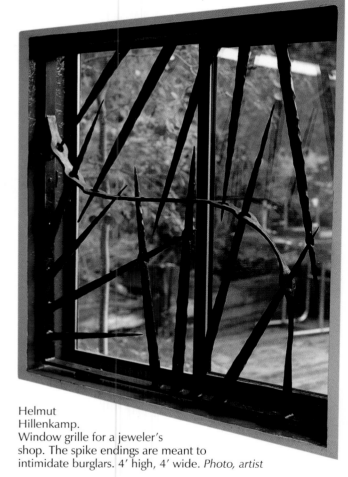

Helmut
Hillenkamp.
Window grille for a jeweler's
shop. The spike endings are meant to
intimidate burglars. 4' high, 4' wide. *Photo, artist*

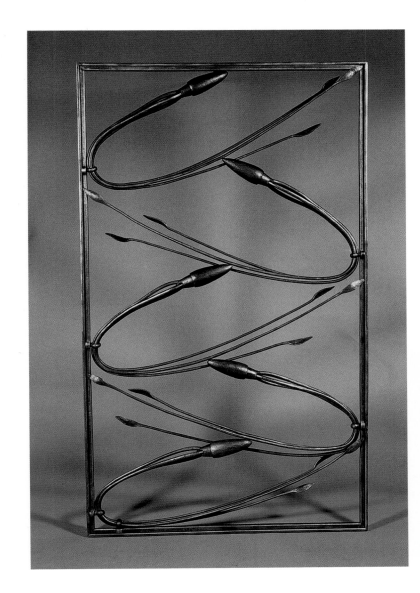

Eric K. Cuper. Squid grille. Steel. 6.2' high, 3' wide *Courtesy, artist*

Dimitri Gerakaris. Fish Grille for the entrance to an aquarium. Forged and color-galvanized steel. 4' high, 5' wide, .5" deep. *Photo, artist*

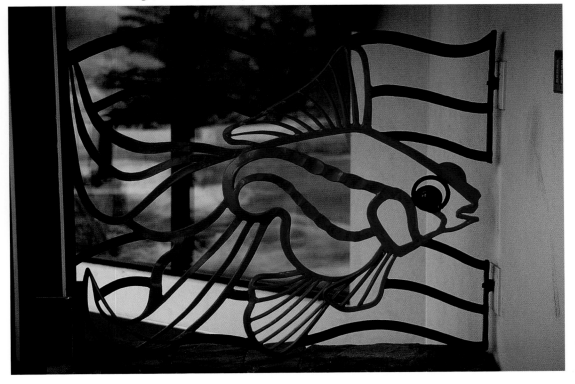

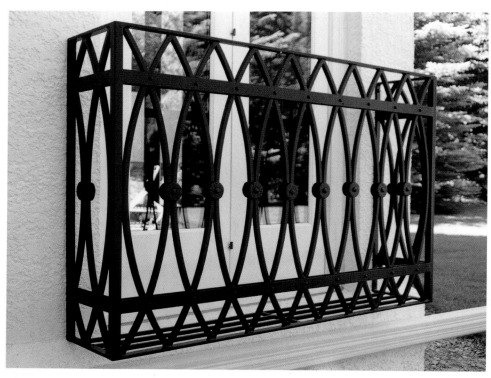

John Monteath. Door grille with ovals and medallions. *Courtesy, artist*

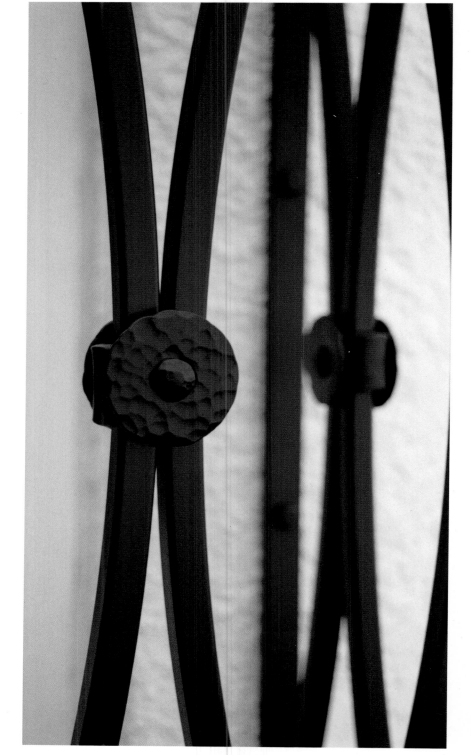

John Monteath. Detail of forged medallions with rivets set into the collar. Rivets used to attach the horizontal top and bottom are part of the repeat design. *Courtesy, artist*

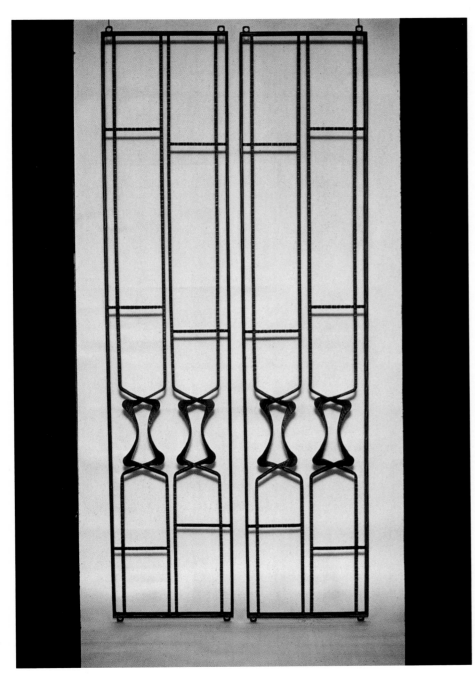

Stephen Bondi. Security door grille, pair. Detail. Each, 6.8' high, 1.5' wide. *Photo, artist*

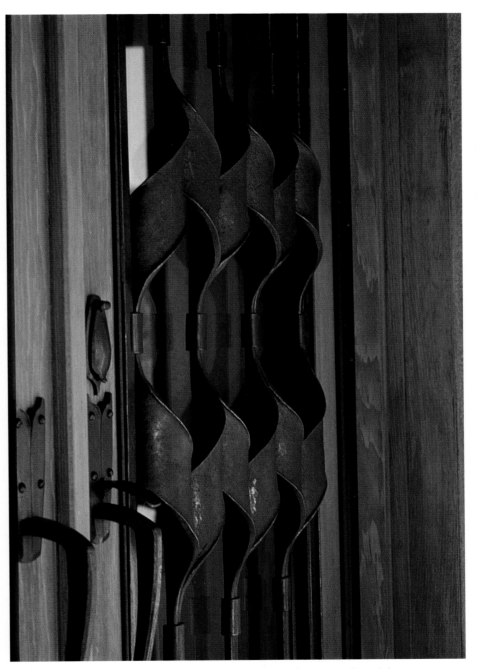

Tom Joyce. Door grille. Detail. The repeat curving three-dimensional steel shapes are a unique treatment for a grille. The handle with thumb latch and lock picks up the same curve and shape as in the grille. *Photo, Anthony Richardson*

Screens, Railings, and Balconies

Screens can serve several functions. They define a space, but are higher than a railing. They may be light and airy or dense. The ironwork screen can be used to camouflage an area, or as a backdrop in a room where it is also a divider. They are popular in restaurants, hotel lobbies, shopping areas, churches, and synagogues. They may be permanent or, if they are portable, they can be moved to redefine areas as needed.

Enrique Vega helps decorate the space and bring the high ceiling to a human level using three screens on a raised area in an Asheville, North Carolina, shopping mall. These "Blue Ridge Habitats" screens also prevent people from getting too close to the water fountain and children from jumping up into the area.

Enrique Vega. "Blue Screen Habitat" consists of three screens each with a different theme, installed in a raised landscape area in a shopping mall, Asheville, North Carolina. Forged steel and brass. *Photo, artist*

144

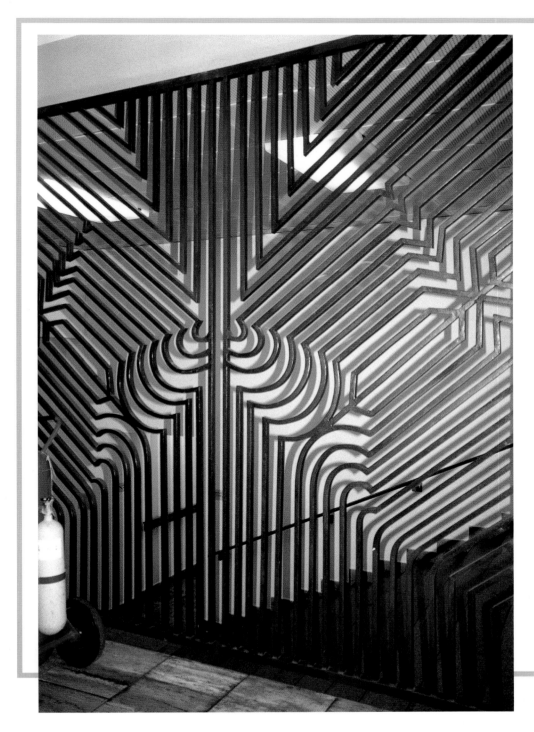

Czech Republic. A screen divider in a museum separates two floor levels and defines the upper level space. The linear design is like a Victor Vasarely painting, only in iron. *Photo, author*

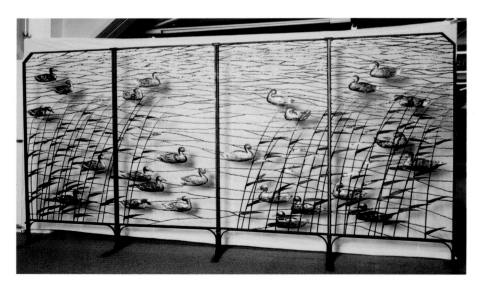

The screens by Hiroshi Minamizawa are examples of a variety of screens and their functions. The Czech Republic screen is installed on a raised area of an art museum to indicate a step and divide the space's functions.

Hiroshi Minamizawa. Waterfront Screen divider. *Courtesy, artist*

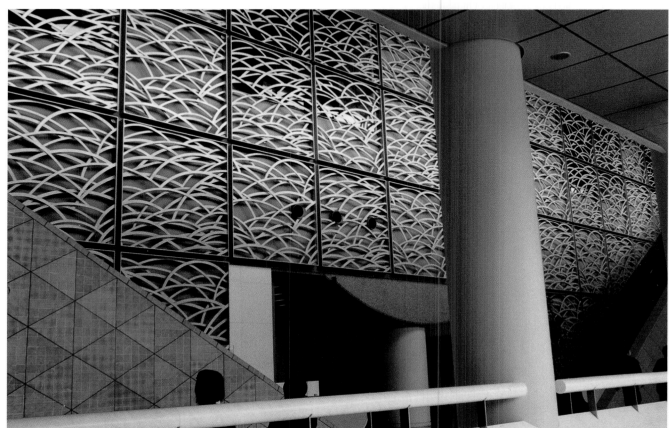

Hiroshi Minamizawa. Screen wall of the Kyoto Exhibition Center. *Courtesy, artist*

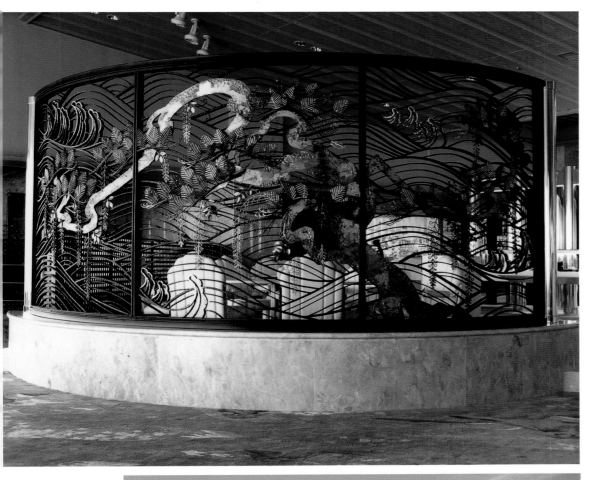

Hiroshi Minamizawa. Screen in a hotel lobby has traditional Japanese themes. Sendai City, Japan. *Courtesy, artist*

Railings are designed to keep people in or out and may have a safety application as well. Railings may be at ground level or along landings. They suggest something to hold on to, lean against, and they also define a space.

A balcony is designed to keep people in. It is essentially a safety structure. Balconies are platforms projecting from the wall of an upper floor and enclosed by railings. The balcony railing provides an opportunity for enhancing a structure. When several balconies appear on a structure, they can add a visual rhythm and may be the only design relief to a plain building. Traditionally, the ironwork railing was black but today they may be painted any color.

Balcony railings serve their safety function while being decorative and diverse. Focusing on exterior balcony designs in an older city can reveal a feast of historical design styles. Exterior balconies are the most obvious. But there are a surprising number of decorative railings used within contemporary buildings; the more public the space, the more decorative the railings are apt to be. Find them in hotel lobbies, office building lobbies, theaters, and department stores. They may or may not be extensions of staircases.

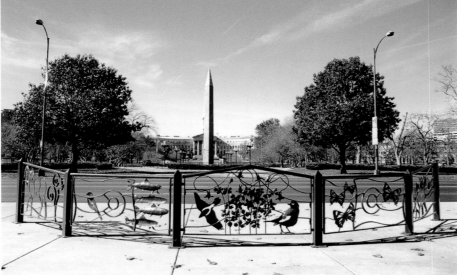

Rafe Ropek. "Colorado Symbols Rail." Sited in front of the Denver, Colorado State Capitol. It represents all the State's symbols, including the flag, flora, and fauna. *Courtesy, artist*

147

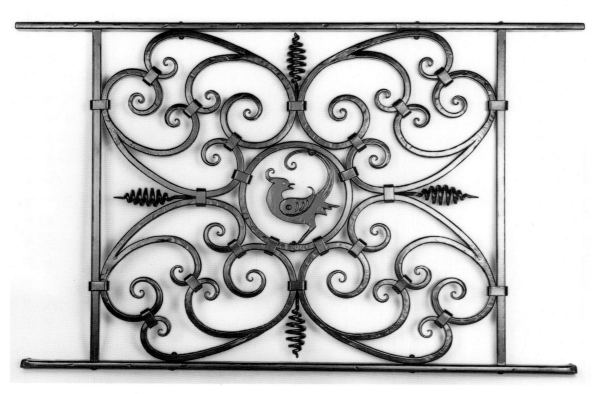

Dan Nauman. Railing section. A railing, symmetrical and geometrical, and with feelings of lightness and movement. The "distelfink" (German for "thistle finch") bird in the center, and the use of ribbon end scrolls, give this railing a fanciful appearance. *Photo, John Cumming*

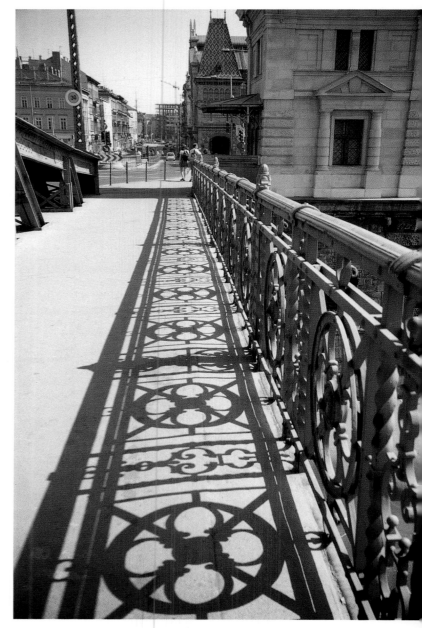

Bridge Rail. Circles with quatrefoils within create an interesting shadow on this iron bridge railing in Prague, Czech Republic. *Photo, author*

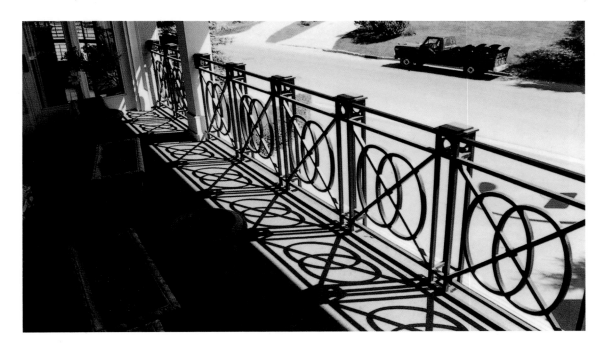

John Monteath. Balcony railing illustrates another use of circles, and the importance of the cast shadow to the design. *Photo, artist*

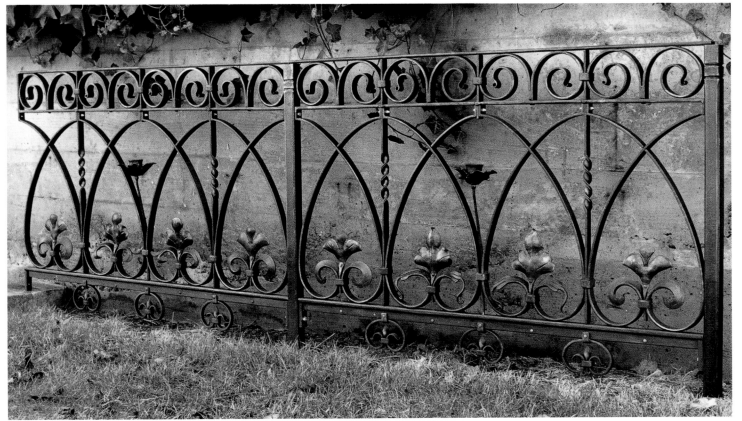

Steve Lopes. Exterior railing with intersecting arcs that result in reverse heart shapes. Each flower shape at the bottom is different, and has a candleholder. One 8' section of 32'. *Photo, artist*

149

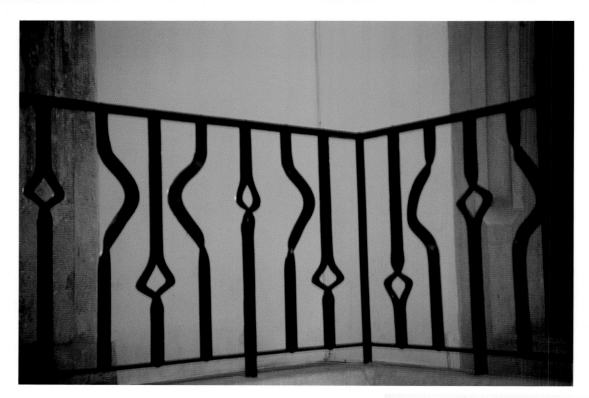

Interior railing. Twisted and curved uprights add a dimension to the railing. Double rods are separated at the point where the diamond shape occurs. The uprights are twisted and bent. *Photo, author*

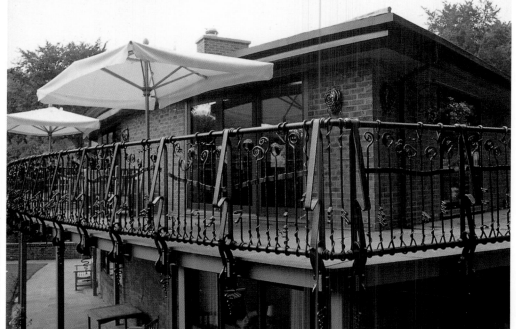

Terrence Clark. Exterior porch railing. Rich detailing in unusual arrangements with sculptural support brackets. A horizontal bar looks like it is woven through the verticals. Wildwoods Farm. Surry, England. *Courtesy, artist*

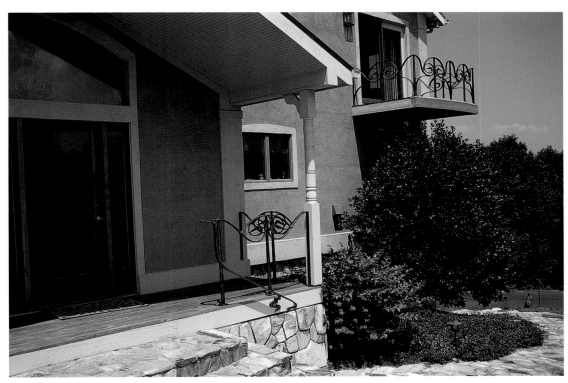

Frederic A. Crist and David W. Munn. Leigh porch railing
and balcony rail. Courtesy, *artists*

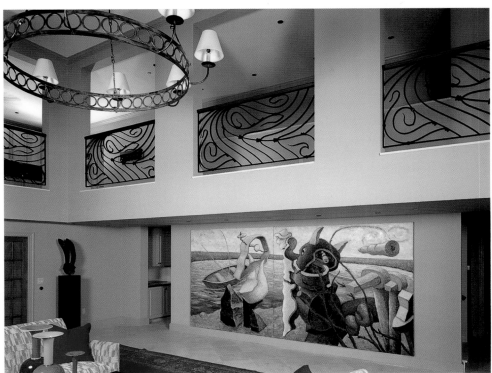

Michael P. Dillon. Nouveau Rails. Four iron panels for the
second floor landing of a private residence. Each panel, 6' long.
Photo, Max Birnkamer

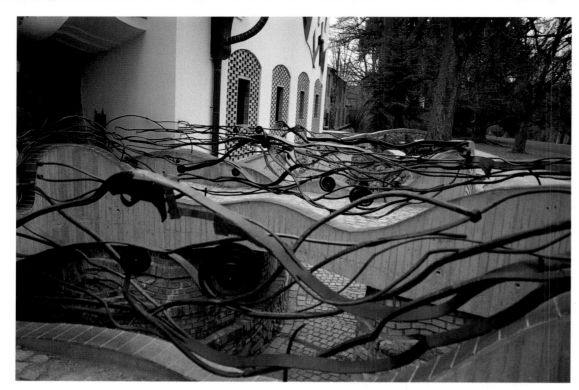

Free form forged railing. An abstract, flowing, free form railing overlooks a fountain in front of a convention meeting building. Stirin Palace, Czech Republic. *Photos, author*

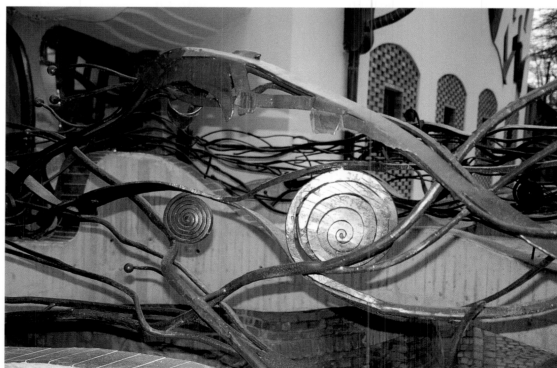

Detail of free form forged railing. Stirin Palace. There's little doubt that Gaudí's Casa Milá railings influenced this artist.

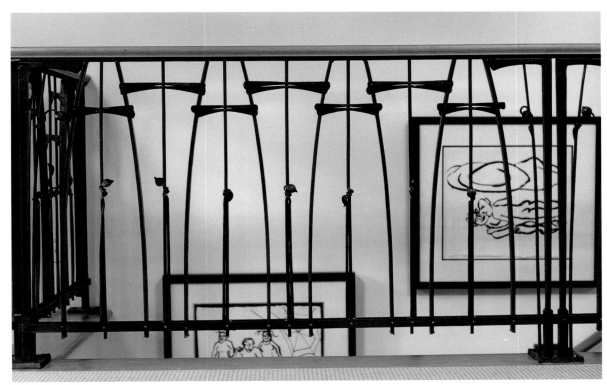

Steve Lopes assisted by Josh Jones. Dragon Fly railing. The interplay of negative and positive space provides exciting visual interest. *Photo, artist*

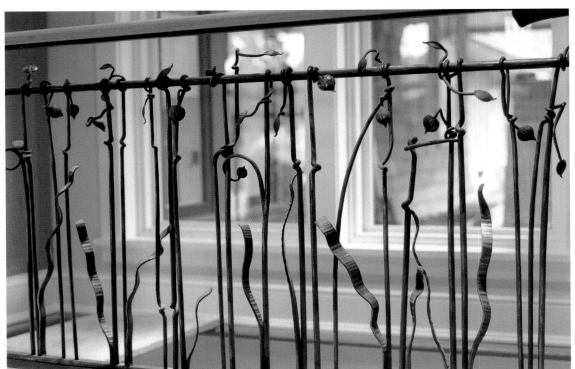

Steve Lopes. Vine Railing with leaves and shoots. The seemingly random formed round bars in wide and narrow widths, and with odd bends, appear as in nature. Wavy abstract leaves seem to grow from the base. *Photo, artist*

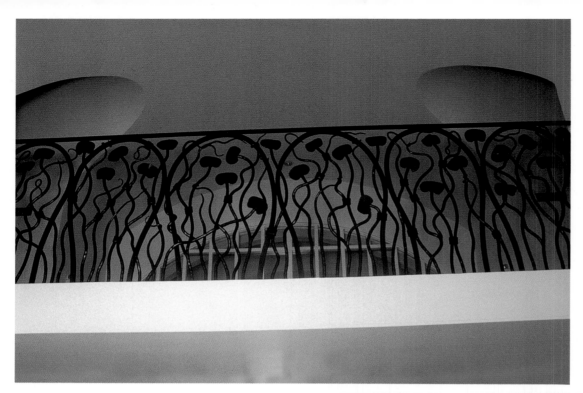

Adam Piper Booth. Railing, House of Formartine, Aberdeen, Scotland. *Photo, artist*

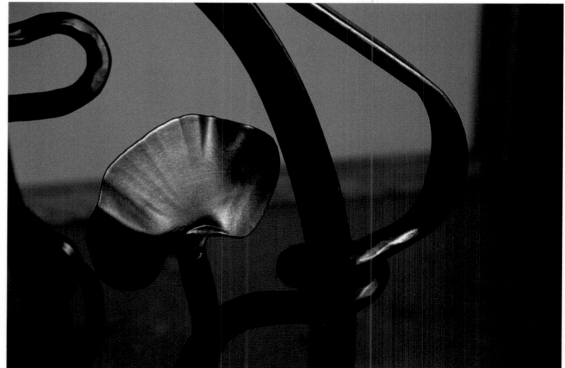

Adam Piper Booth. Detail of leaf and wrap showing the texturing and shaping. 3' high, 10' wide. *Photo, artist*

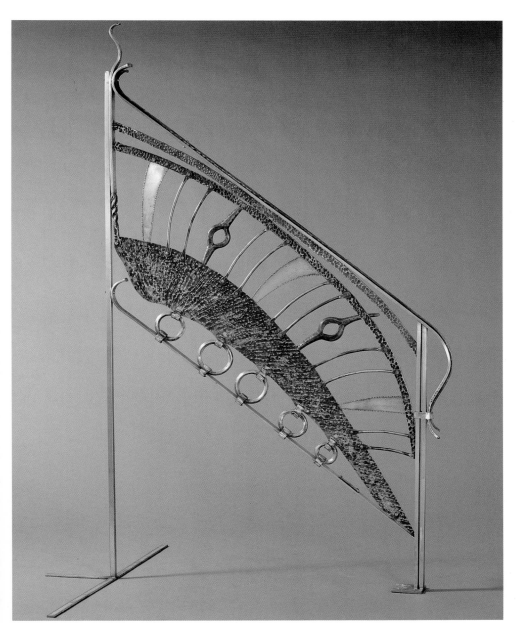

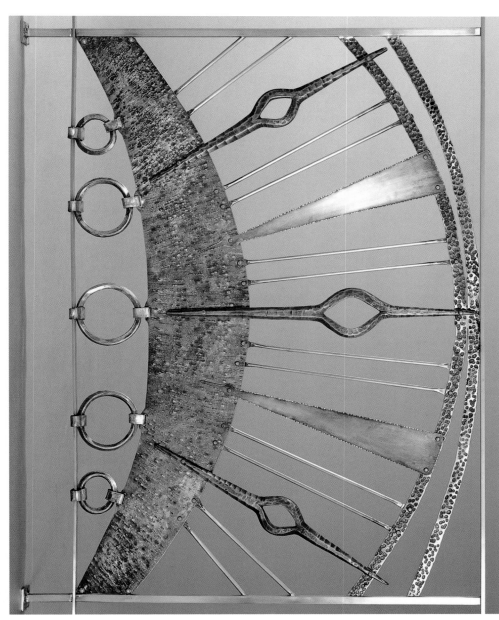

Corrina Rising Moon Mensoff. Modern Archaic. The 35' of handrail includes an accompanying staircase and balcony section in a combination of old and new design and technique, hence called "Modern Archaic". Stainless steel fabricated with forged 1-1/2" round copper elements. The brass arcs at the bottom, and the runners along the top, are manipulated and textured using hand and power hammers. *Photo, Jill Buckner*

Corrina Rising Moon Mensoff. Modern Archaic balcony railing sections. There are an accompanying door and wall sconces. Each panel is 3.75' high, 4.5' wide. *Photo, Jill Buckner*

155

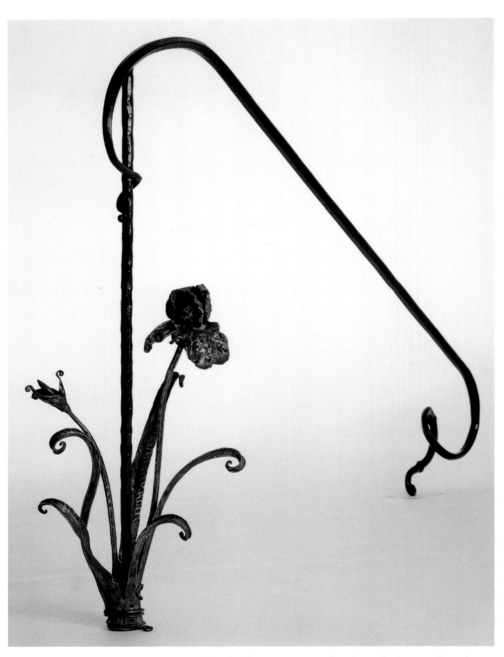

Corrina Rising Moon Mensoff. Iris hand railing. Exterior grab rail, made from 1" forged iron with a copper iris. 4' high, 5.5' long. *Photo, Jill Buckner*

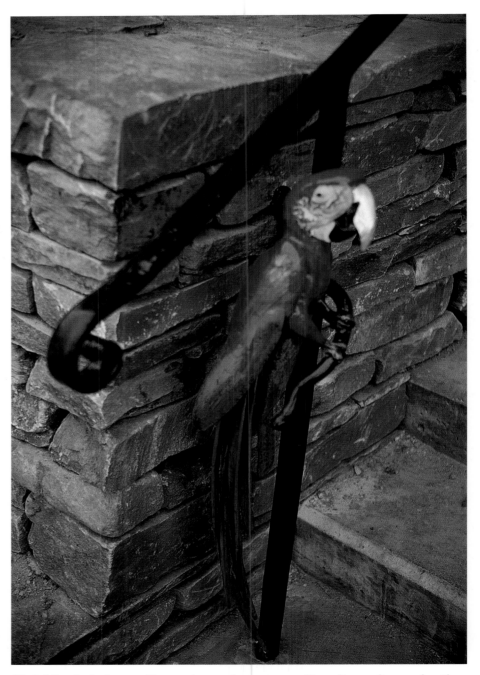

Dimitri Gerakaris. Parrot railings at the pet shop entrance. One of two railings each with a parrot positioned differently. The parrots were forged of separate sections, and then fabricated, along with the railing. Color-galvanized. *Photo, artist*

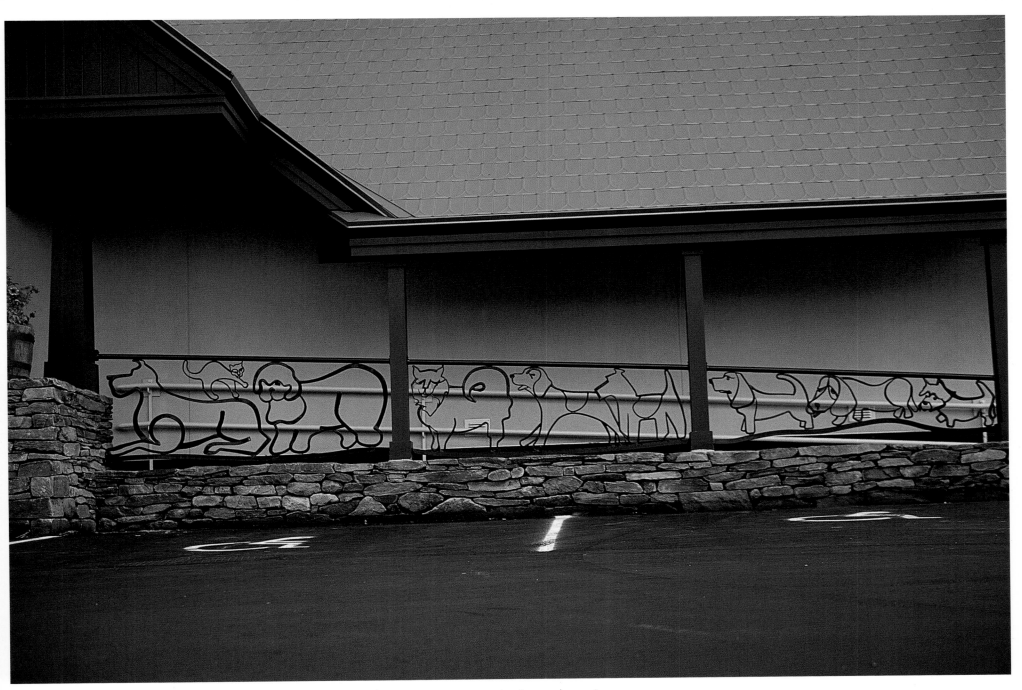

Dimitri Gerakaris. "Procession of the Canines Railing" is installed along a ramp access to a pet shop and aquarium. Various dog breeds are shown in ascending height, along with a solitary cat, which seems to be in ultimate command. Forged and color-galvanized steel. 36' long. *Photo, artist*

A modern version of Art Nouveau with waves and scrolls, by Alber De Matteis, is perfectly suited to the porch of a modern residence overlooking the Pacific Ocean on a beach in La Jolla, California.

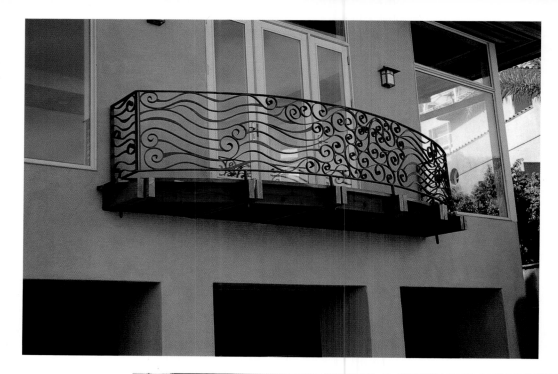

Alber De Matteis. Sea form balcony railing. Waves and scrolls in differing lengths and sizes form the balcony rails overlooking the ocean in a residence in La Jolla, California. *Photo, artist*

Alber De Matteis. View looking out through the porch rails. *Photo, artist*

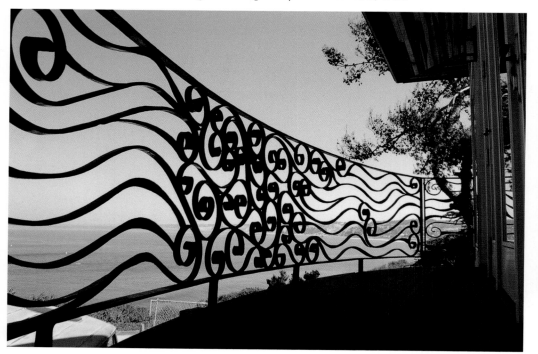

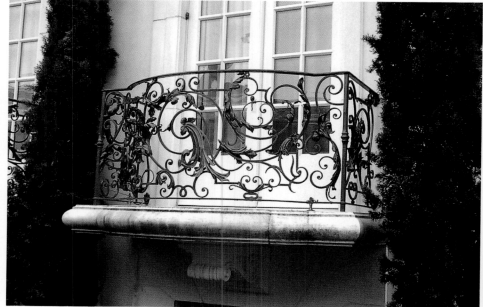

Eric Clausen. A pair of French doors open onto a French style balcony. The client wanted her house to be like Versailles, so Clausen based this asymmetrical design on the 18th Century French style. *Photo, artist*

The balcony photos from Budapest, Hungary, show dynamic applications of Art Nouveau styles. Many were taken in an area where large homes and embassies exist. But a number were from ordinary apartment buildings that were given this architectural fillip instead of plain horizontal and vertical bars. Often, that extra decoration made an ordinary building extraordinary. Is it possible that this attention to cosmetics and function made a difference in the tenant's perception of the building and justified higher rents?

Potpourri of balcony railings from Prague and Budapest. Both cities are like a museum of ironwork. Most examples are of late 19th and early 20th Century buildings in the Art Nouveau style. Many buildings also exhibit Renaissance, Baroque, and Neo Classic styles. Some appear so modern, they might have been created today. *Photos, author*

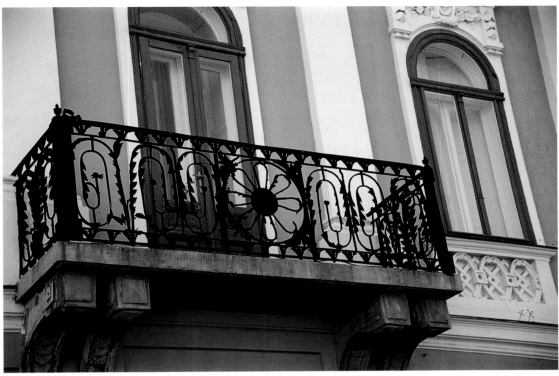

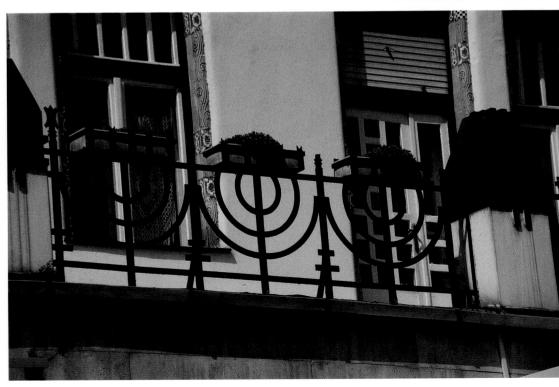

159

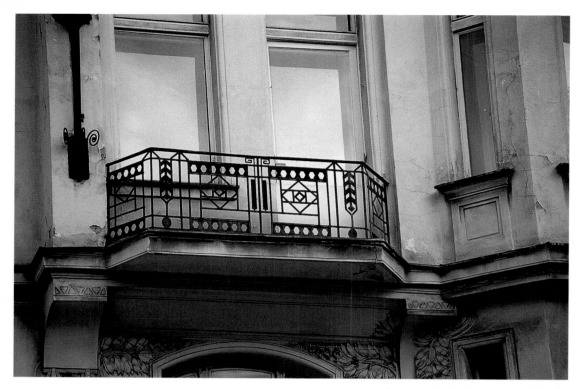

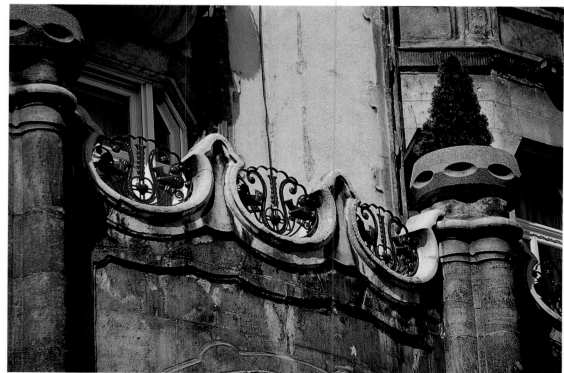

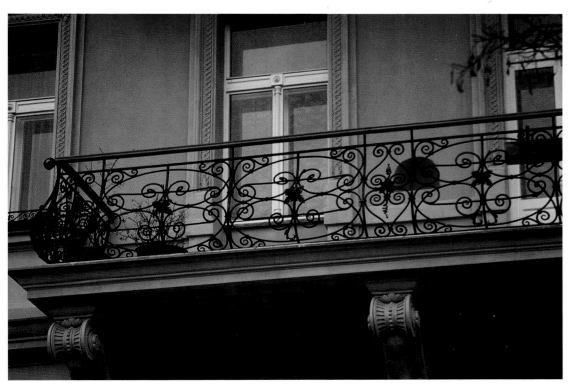
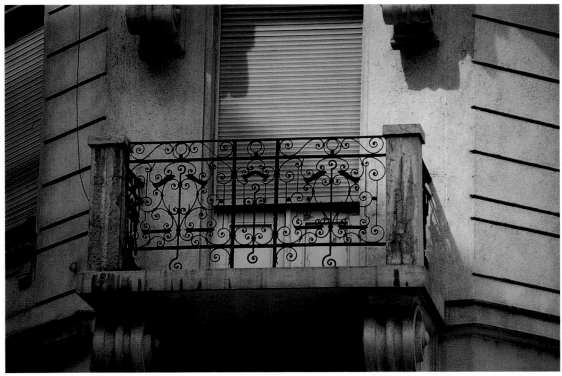

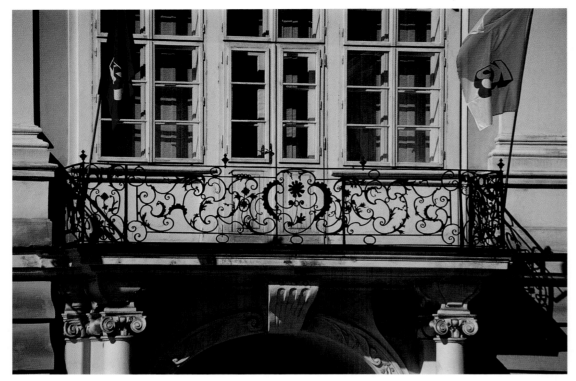

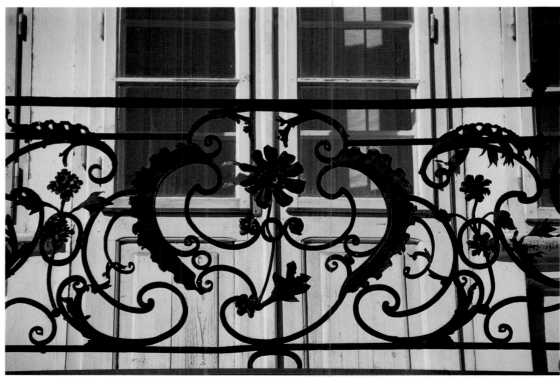

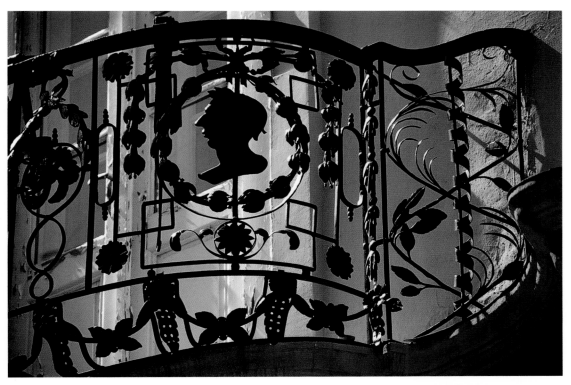
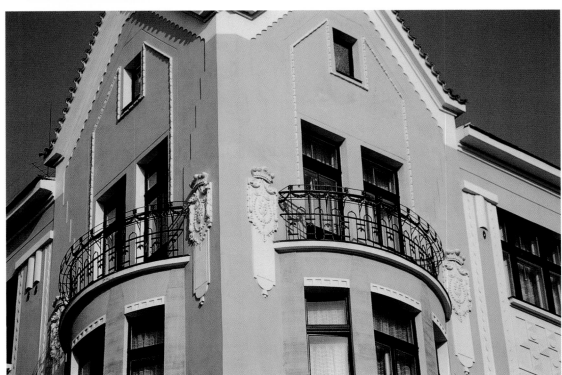

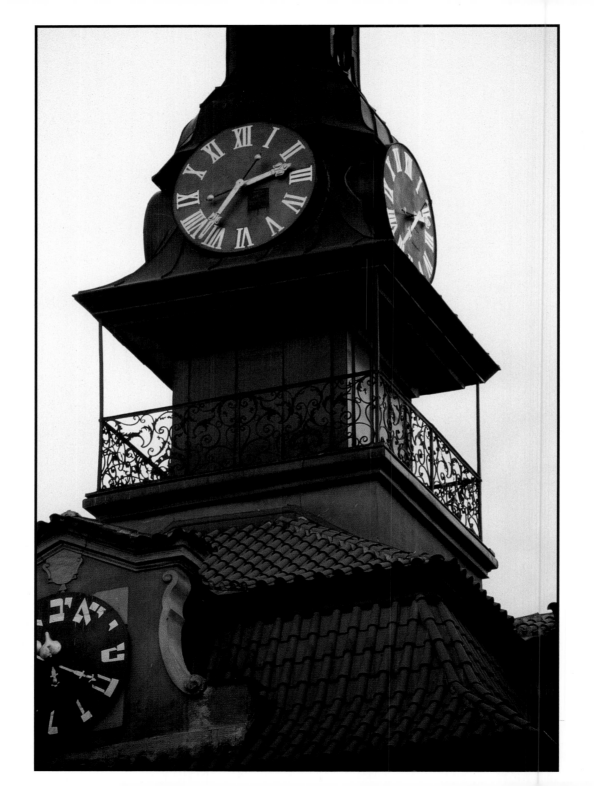

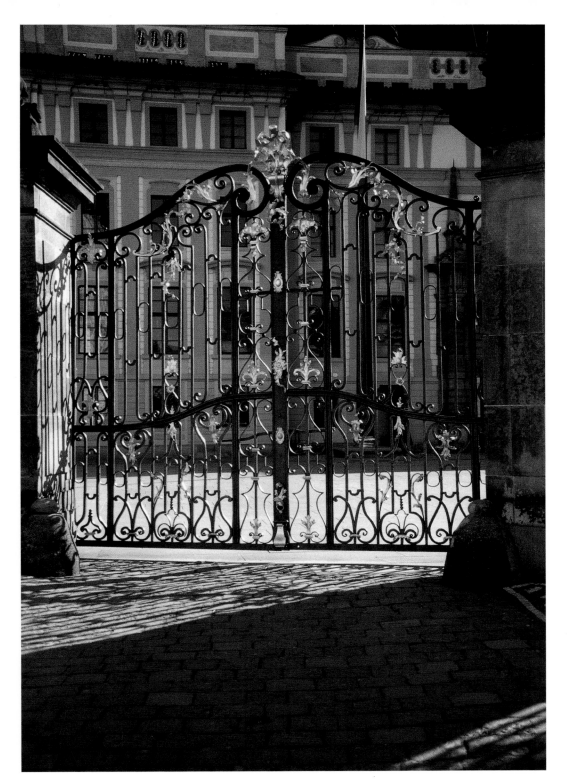

Chapter 5
Gates and Fences

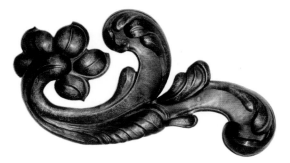

Few artists become nationally or internationally known for the gates and fences they create. Yet the amount of design knowledge, artistry, and work involved are equally, if not more, impressive than that of a painter or sculptor. Add to that an inordinate amount of physical labor. You can't toss the materials in the back of your car, take the project out in the country on a Sunday afternoon, and return with a finished product. Neither can you hammer a nail in the wall and hang up your art for all to admire.

Gates and fences are among the most apparent uses for ironwork. They are so very obvious when one takes the time to look for them and at them. We take fences for granted because most are mundane, sacrificing design to economics and pure function. The examples shown are anything but trite and mundane.

A fence may be the first decorative element we see when approaching a building but we often see through it, or it stops our eye, yet subliminally we know it is there. A gate or fence, well integrated with a building's style, can be a beautiful complement to the architecture. When it is well integrated we see it as a part of the building and not a separate structure.

Arch over the courtyard entry to the Prague Castle, Czech Republic. The Prague Castle courtyard dates from 1753-55. The entire palace area was rebuilt using the then popular late Baroque and Neo-Classical styles. *Photo, author*

Renaissance, Baroque, Rococo, and Elizabethan gates and fences usually had flourishing curves, elegant scroll work, and gold and brass embellishments. Antoni Gaudì leaped across art history and created a new kind of gate for his Park Güell in Barcelona, Spain. In one, a huge bird becomes the gate top and the ironwork's components are not so flourishing as in French style ironwork. Still they have movement and swirls to the point that the word "gaudy" is derived from Gaudì's name. Over time, the word has come to mean showy, overly ornate. Fortunately the artist's name has escaped fitting that definition.

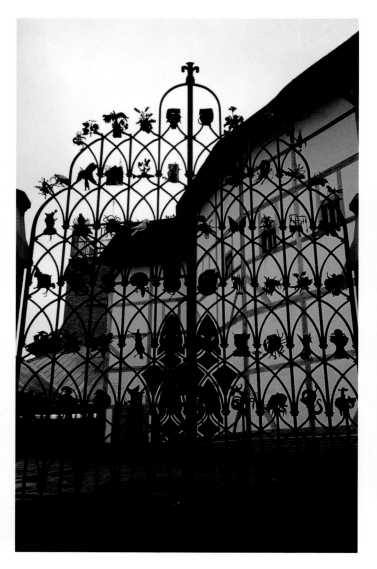

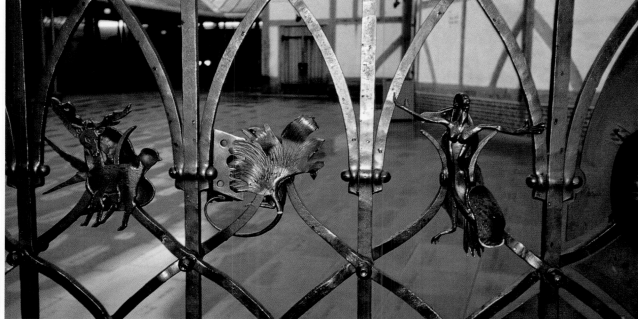

The Bankside Gates at Shakespeare's Globe Theatre, London, England, 1997. A symbol from one of Shakespeare's plays, created by craftsman from around the world, is placed at each intersection. The gate's shape replicates the Gothic arch. *Photo, Don Diehl*

Details from the Bankside Gates at Shakespeare's Globe Theatre, London, England From Left to right: **The Deer** from *As You Like It,* by Steve Davis, Northport, Alabama. The **Conger Eel** from *Pericles,* by Harry Pomfret, United Kingdom. **The Siren** from *The Comedy of Errors,* by Bill Poirrier, United Kingdom. *Photo, Don Diehl*

166

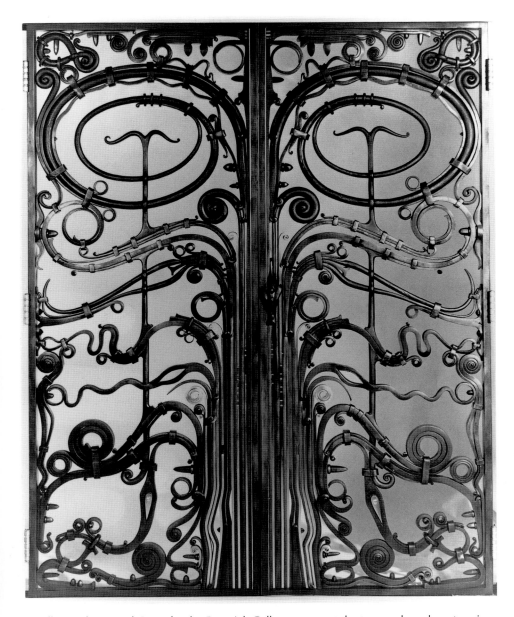

Today's artist may emulate, and often replicate, historical designs with great skill. Or he may build on a design and develop a new direction. He may design something so fantastically different that people will flock to his workshop.

Regardless of design, the function of the gate or fence must be addressed. It can be a pedestrian gate, a garden gate, a driveway gate. If it's a driveway gate, engineering may be required. Depending on space and needs, it can be a one part rolling gate, a two part rolling gate, it can swing open, or it can move up and down, guillotine style. Very often it is electronically controlled so there is much more planning than meets the eye.

Gates are designed to protect, to keep people or animals in or out, to delineate a property line, and/or to establish an entry and exit point. If gates and fences must discourage people from entering, the tops may include some kind of spike or spear that is formidable though decorative. Along with the ironwork's basic design the blacksmith must often design mounting hardware, handles, and locks.

In the following examples, the gates are organized by the design elements. Before drawing a line the artist must decide what elements to use that can be created in iron or another chosen material. The project begins with a sketch, then a blue print with all parts drawn to scale. These may be hand drafted or created on a computer.

A computer enables the blacksmith to work long distance with a client more swiftly than ever before. He can E-mail plans and ideas back and forth and get instant feedback. Even contracts can be signed via the computer. If there are questions, or changes along the way, they can be quickly addressed via E-mail or teleconferencing. Problems can be solved without lengthy and costly time delays.

Artist blacksmiths who vie for commissioned work often must present a proposal to win the contract. This is especially so where public art is concerned. The conditions may require that several proposals from different crafts people be considered before a decision can be made. A committee is often responsible for these decisions rather than the client and the architect.

Albert Paley. Portal Gates for the Renwick Gallery represent the tremendous departure in concept and design made by Albert Paley in 1975. The gates have a classical balanced composition, but vary in their symmetry. A mustache shape is centered in each of the top circles. Circles and coils are repeated throughout using copper and brass with different weights of iron. *National Museum of American Art, Smithsonian Institution, Commissioned for the Renwick Gallery, Washington, D.C.*

Corrina Rising Moon Mensoff and Enrique Vega frequently propose such commissions and two of the drawings from their proposals are shown here. Mensoff created a drawing and a scaled down portion of a gate as a maquette to show the committee how the final piece might look with the materials, coloration, and workmanship involved. A maquette also gives the artist an idea of how much materials will be involved so he or she can determine material costs.

Vega's gate illustrates its design, the elevation and engineering like drawings he needed to show how the different parts would appear and how they would work.

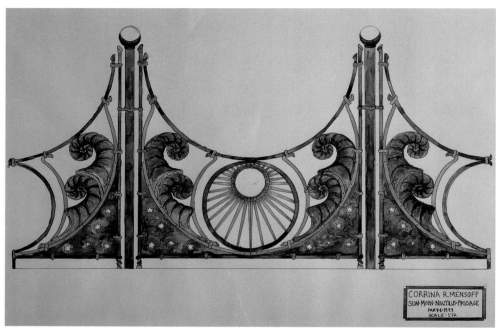

CORRINA R.MENSOFF
SUN·MOON·NAUTILUS·PASSAGE
MAY·1·1999
SCALE·1½

Corrina Rising Moon Mensoff. An artist frequently creates a drawing and a model, or maquette, of a proposed project. This drawing was for a gate proposal to be titled, Sun-Moon-Nautilus-Passage. *Photo, Jill Buckner*

Corrina Rising Moon Mensoff. It was necessary to make a panel that would give the client an idea of how the finished gate will look. Making a panel or a maquette, actual size, or to a smaller scale, also gives the artist an idea of time and materials that will be involved. *Photo, Jill Buckner*

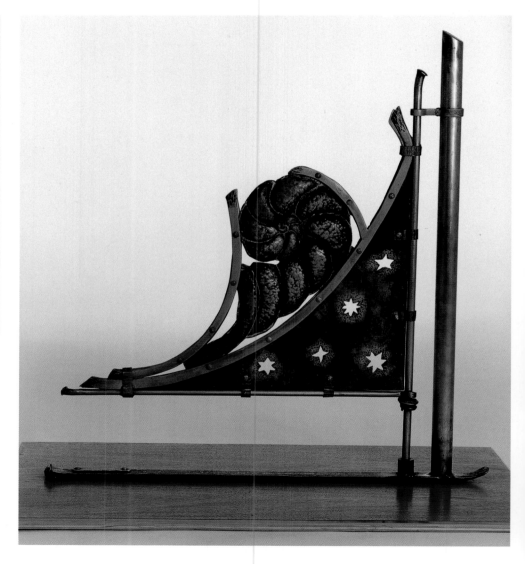

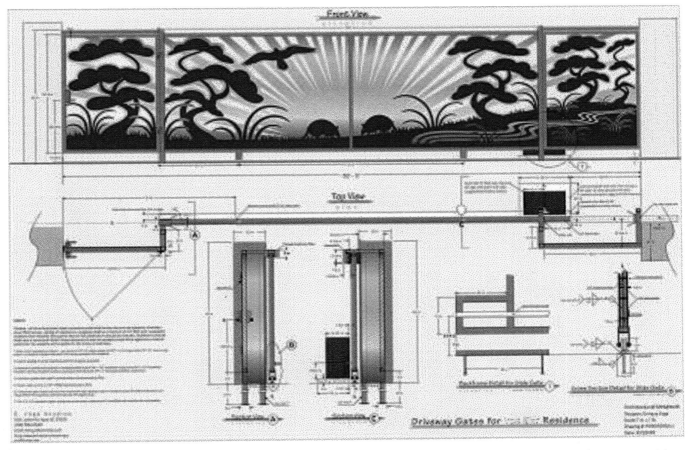

Enrique Vega. Often detailed engineering blueprint drawings are required as in "The Sun Gates" for a driveway in the Dallas, Texas area. *Courtesy, artist*

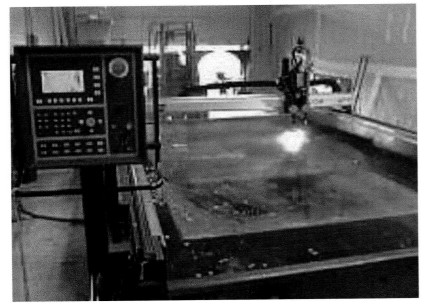

Today's metal workers use a computer controlled plasma cutter to facilitate their work. It saves time and results in a cleaner cut. Enrique Vega used the cutter for "The Sun Gates." *Photo, artist*

Scrolls

Gates and fences often utilize the same scroll elements found in stair railings and doors. These usually are associated with traditional styles used with French, Mediterranean, or Italian architecture. But Christopher Thomson of New Mexico uses scrolls effectively in his modern Corn Plant Gate in a non-traditional arrangement that is fresh and innovative.

The gates from the Castle at Prague, dating from the 1700s, illustrate a traditional style. Other gates from the same Castle, and probably done at a later date, have none of these traditional elements. They are strictly geometric and one of them uses cast elements to establish a theme. If these were uncovered archeologically, the conclusion would be that they were built at different times. That's certainly a logical conclusion with these gates.

Prague Castle gates, Czech Republic. Designers throughout Europe picked up the French gold fleur-de-lis and acanthus leaves, often used in French ironwork. The popularity of these motifs is still evident in work that emulates these historical styles. *Photo, author*

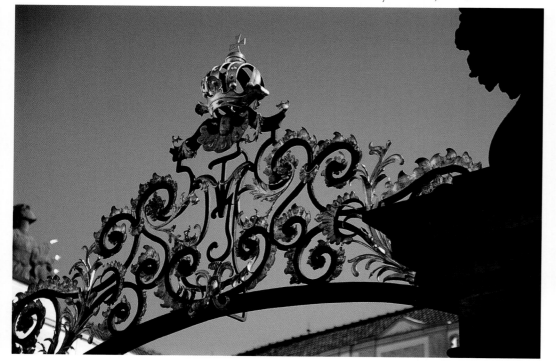

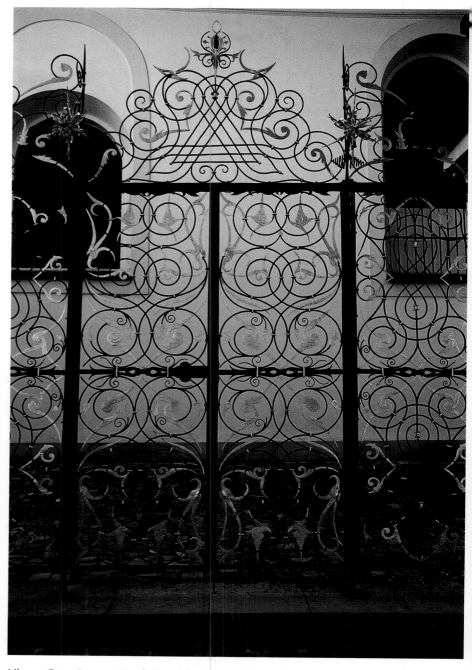

Library Gate, Prague, Czech Republic. A Neo-Classical design with circles and gold accents is used in these gates. Stylistic differences are apparent between this Neo-Classical gate and the Baroque Castle gates by comparing the weight of the iron elements, the ornateness, and the amount of gold embellishment. *Photo, author*

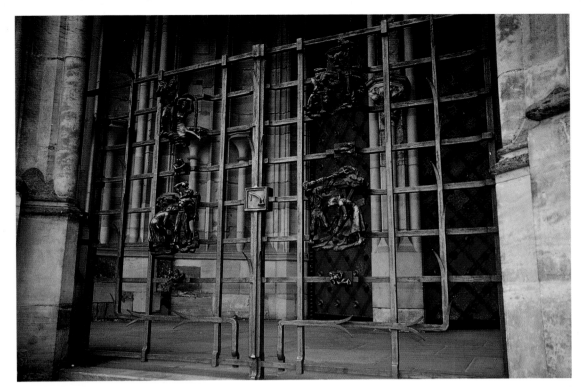

Iron gates with bronze figures, Prague Castle. This gate, composed of squares, is also on the grounds of the Prague Castle. Twelve cast bronze figurative squares adorn three sets of gates. The design in each square represents an activity for each month of the year. The upright bars have protrusions that suggest plants. Although the gate design is based on squares, close study reveals there are many design elements and complex construction details. *Photo, author*

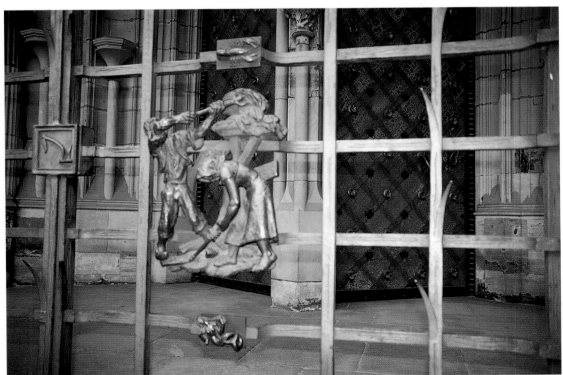

Detail of one bronze square represents farming. Prague Castle, Czech Republic. *Photo, author*

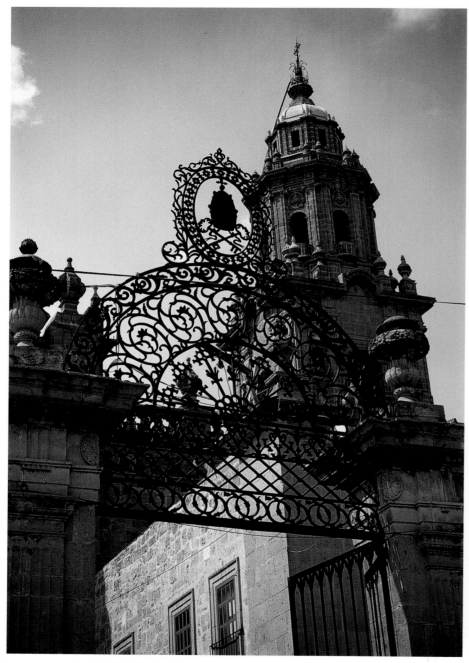

In a modern use of scrolls, Craig Kaviar fashions a gate where the scrolls are light and fanciful as they combine with other curving shapes within the verticals. The hand forged gate lever is textured and as beautifully forged as is each element of his design.

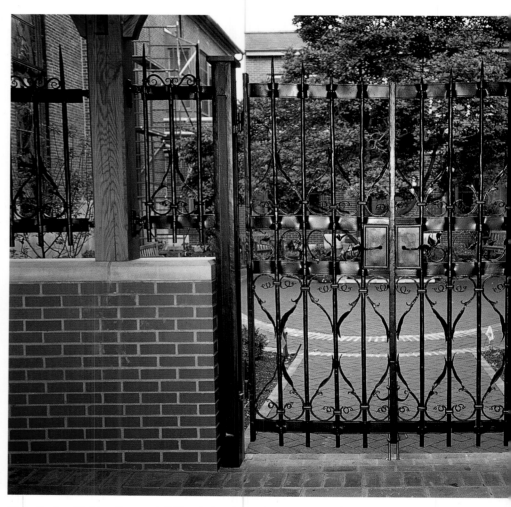

Iron gateway arch to the Plaza de Armas, Morelia, Mexico. Materials and techniques used for ironwork are the same everywhere, but Mexican ironworkers used completely different designs than their European counterparts during the same time period. The motifs may be highly symbolic religious references. *Photo, Bushnell-Soifer*

Craig Kaviar. Cloister Gate and Grilles define the main entrance to the newly renovated Christ Church Cathedral in Louisville, Kentucky. Steel hot-dip galvanized and painted black. Horizontal bars were grooved and hot punched for the vertical bars to pierce. The leafy scrolls banded to the horizontals soften the look and tie in with the courtyard garden. Architect, Peter Richardson, John Milner Associates. 7' high, 6.5' wide. *Courtesy, artist*

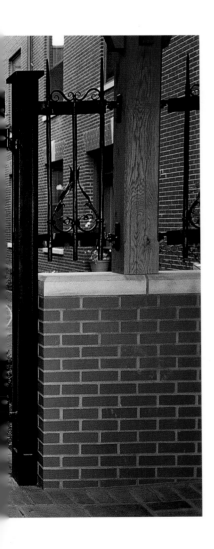

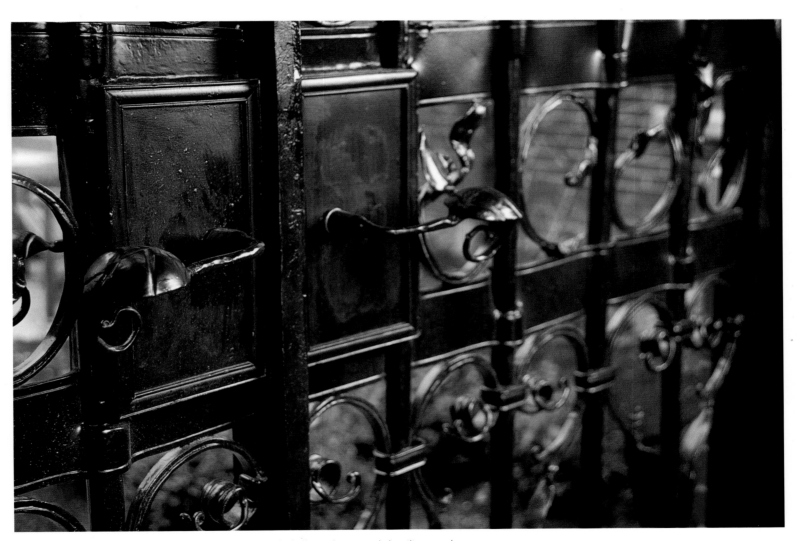

Craig Kaviar. Detail of the Cloister Gate showing the handle and textured detailing on the bars. *Photo, Steven A. Drake*

Geometric: Lines, Circles, Squares

The majority of production type gates and fences consist of straight vertical iron bars welded to a top and bottom horizontal bar. These are the least costly to produce and, often, when they surround a large public area, they are the most functional and economical solution. For every fence project, several codes exist that must be met in their construction. Bars must be a determined distance apart so that children can't get wedged between them. There are codes as to how far the heavier supports must be and how far into the ground these supports must go so the fence can't be knocked or blown over easily.

These same codes and regulations apply to custom gates, especially those used out of doors, and they vary by state and by country.

The labor and equipment involved in making a gate or fence can be daunting. Enrique Vega's Sun gate required 1-1/2 years to complete. It's not unusual to have a project require 3 to 6 months, and hundreds of hours. Robert C. Bentley's workshop shown in the illustration represents only the fabrication area where the piece is finished and assembled. There are also forges where the iron is heated, and hand and power equipment for shaping the metal. Several workers are involved in creating and handling large fence and gate projects such as this.

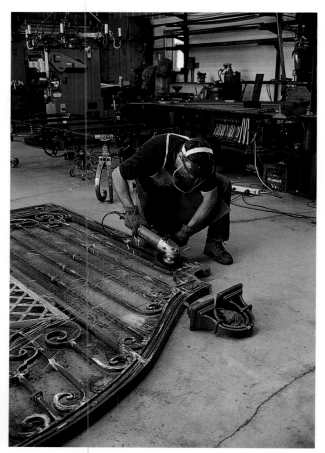

Enrique Vega. "The Sun Gates" installed. This 1–1/2-year project includes the driveway gates, a pedestrian gate on each side, and a matching mailbox. Stainless steel and bronze. A flat bed trailer was required to deliver it from artist's shop in North Carolina to its final site in the Dallas, Texas, area. The entire process of making the gate, including his shop notes, can be found on Vega's Internet site at http://www.artmetal.com/enrique *Photo, Seymour Zweigoron*

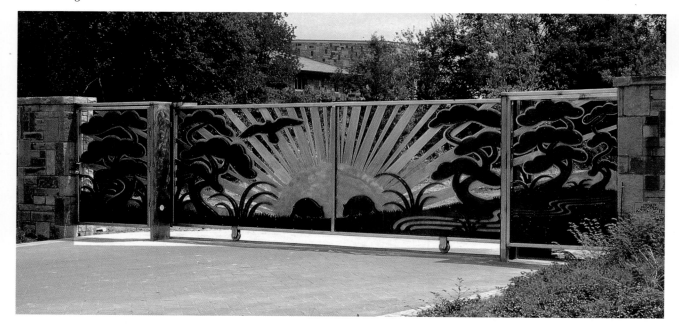

Robert C. Bentley. Gate, in progress, that will become part of the entry to the Weyrich Family Ranch, Paso Robles, California. Russ Windbiel grinds and smoothes the welds. Behind him is an "in progress" table base that will be used in the winery tasting room. *Photo, Bruce Woodworth*

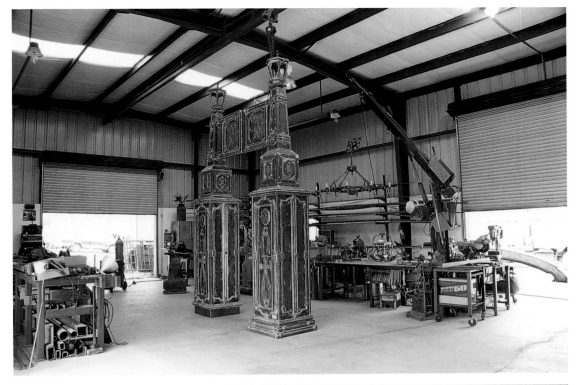

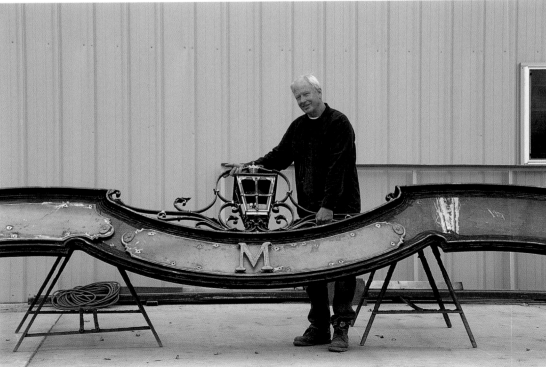

Left: Robert C. Bentley. Supporting pillars for the winery gates must also be forged and fabricated. Large shops and heavy equipment are necessary. *Photo, Bruce Woodworth*

Below left: Every detail of the gate and its surround is hand crafted. Bentley raises the overhead arch with the lantern and the M from the final signage. Before beginning, each element must be drawn to scale and meticulously planned with blueprints. *Photo, Bruce Woodworth*

Below: Robert C. Bentley. The Weyrich Family Entry Gates. *Photo, Bruce Woodworth*

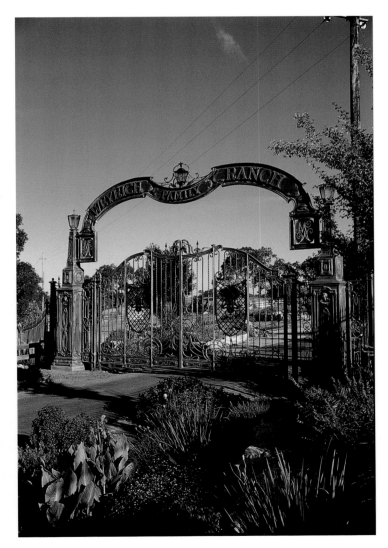

175

Horizontals and verticals dominate the construction of most fences, yet other geometric designs can also be worked in to relieve the monotony of lengthy fences. Some changes are so subtle you have to study the construction to appreciate it. Others are outright visual shifts.

Paul Margett's Gate in the medieval archway entrance to Worcester Cathedral, London, England, relieves the horizontal shapes by adding a curve between each vertical bar, resulting in a curved arch. The pattern of balls and their dimensional holders, representing the Bishop's Coat of Arms, adds a triangular shape to each door. The rivets, too, bring in another shape. By spacing the horizontals at different intervals, additional visual variety is added.

In his fence leading to the Bescot train station, Margetts "peoples" the upright bars with stylized shapes representing passengers walking down the path. Along the length of the fence, individuals and groups of people are suggested: family groups, chattering women, amorous couples, and arguing couples. The red people against the fence's green color is less stark than if the fence were black.

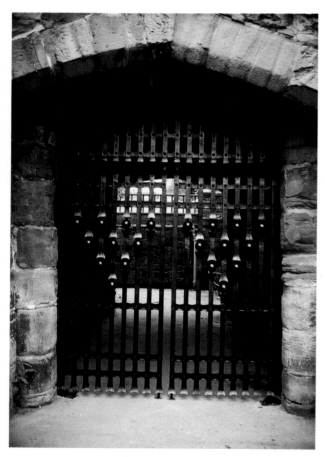

Paul Margetts. Worcester Cathedral Gate. Forged steel gates and overthrow are set within a medieval archway in the original city walls. The roundels (balls) are arranged in a triangular pattern taken from the Bishop's Coat of Arms. *Photo, artist*

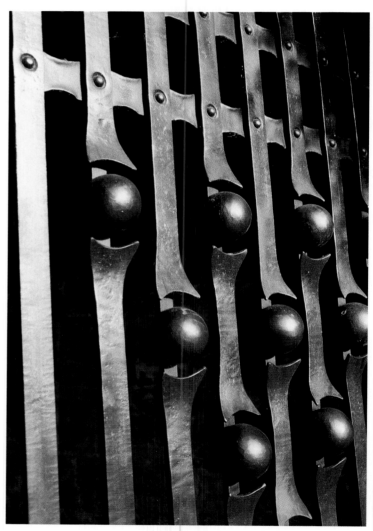

Paul Margetts. Detail shows the forging for the Worcester Cathedral Gate, Worcester, England. The horizontal bars are scalloped to relieve the rigidity and to repeat the circular shape. The emphasized structural riveting becomes a design element as well as joinery. *Photo, artist*

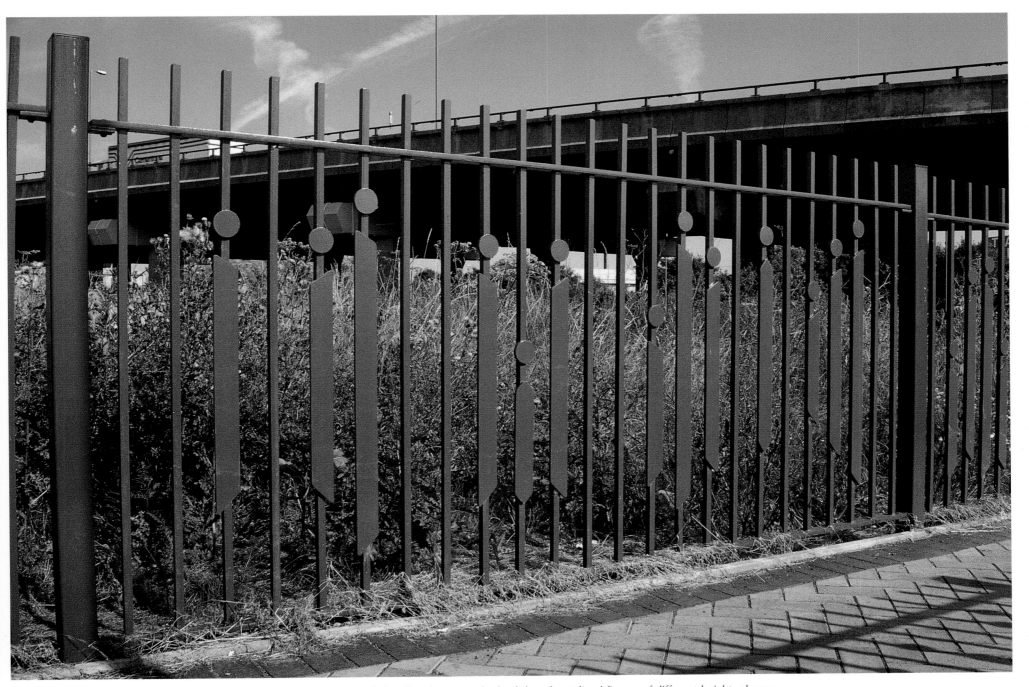

Paul Margetts. The verticality of plain bars becomes the backdrop for stylized figures of different heights along a footpath to the Bescot Train Station, Walsall, West Midlands, England. Because the train station is in an isolated area, the idea was to make the station appear more "peopled." *Photo, artist*

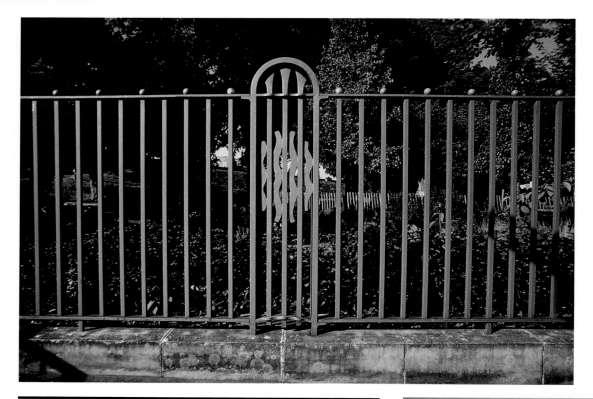

In the Dave John Park fence, Julian Coode breaks up a straight fence by adding a sculptural detail at regular intervals. This area curves inward resulting in a third dimension on an otherwise two dimensional fence. The fence is painted and brass balls are on every other upright.

Julian Coode. Dave John Park fence, Canterbury, England. The simplicity of the straight line with restrained detailing can be seen in this fence. The protruding arched element with the wavy line in the center is curved inward to yield variety and dimension to an otherwise two-dimensional composition. Brass round balls cap every alternating upright. *Photo, artist*

In his additional examples, Coode plays with geometric principles to yield a fool-the-eye arrangement of line in the fence and gates for the Redlees Arts & Crafts Centre in London. By using principles of geometry, he curves the iron so that a two-dimensional plane has the appearance of three-dimensions. In the Tempus Court fence, the linear arrangement of the bars on angles, combined with the curved top edge, is elegant in its simplicity. It is minimally embellished with six unusual flat stainless steel scrolls that represent the ammonite, a seashell form, in each of the wave sections, for a statement in restraint.

Julian Coode. Redlees Arts & Crafts Centre, London, England. This fence, and gates, though physically flat and two dimensional, give the visual impression of being curved and three-dimensional. It's accomplished by slightly curving each vertical bar on a different arc and in a geometrical progression. *Photo, artist*

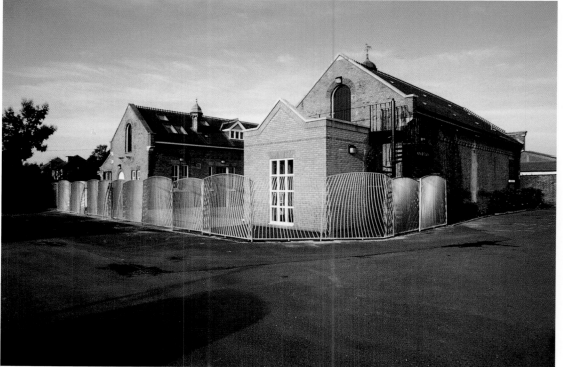

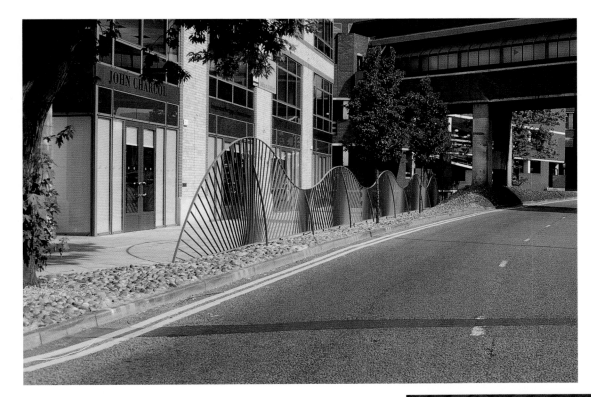

Julian Coode. Coode uses the vertical iron bars in a fan-like arrangement for this screen/fence for Tempus Court, Guildford, England. The top edge is a wave like curve. The vertical supports are also curved. *Photo, artist*

Julian Coode. Detail for the Tempus Court, Guildford, England. Six flattened tightly coiled scrolls, representing a seashell, are placed in opposing directions in each wave section. Coode is a master at rhythm and restraint in his ironwork compositions. *Photo, artist*

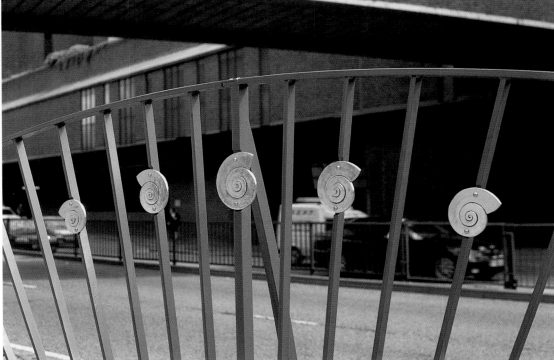

George Schroeder's entry gates to an exclusive Texas housing development alter the character of straight, 1-1/4" round bar by using an industrial 1500 lb. steam hammer to make them into unique curving shapes with a rough texture. The overall wave-like shape of the upright ends replicates the rolling hills of the landscape. The forged steel is finished in a gunmetal blue patina.

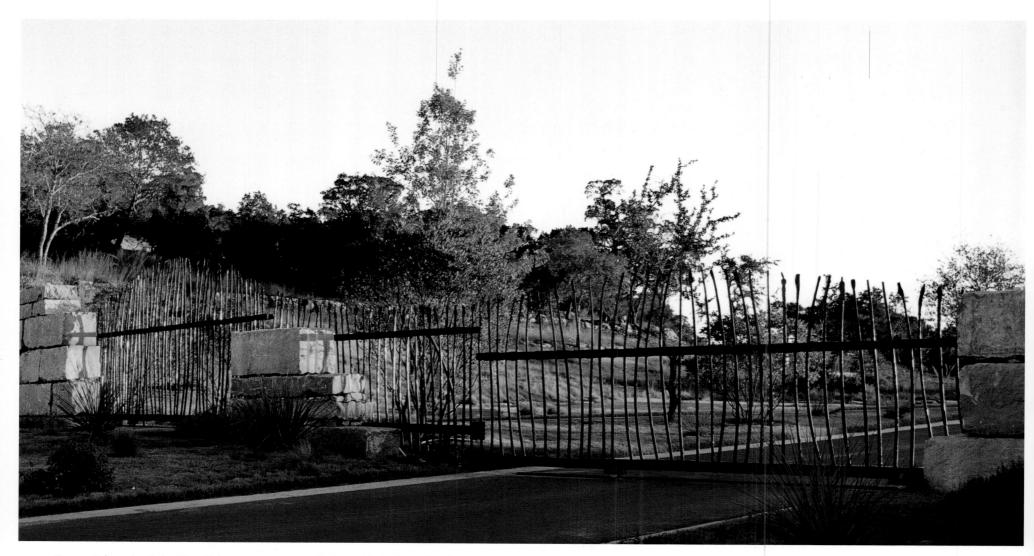

George Schroeder. Lake Flato Driveway entry gates. Each upright is shaped and curved; the top edges form a design that resembles the rolling hills. Architects: Lake/Flato. 58' long, height varies from 5' to 9'. *Photo, Seale Photography*

A round shape, cleverly achieved in different ways, is worked into several examples. Terrence Clark's driveway gates (one of a set of five) are completely hand forged and textured. The rods of the central panel are shaped to form a circle. Bar tops are splayed and pointed for security but they're also attractive. The whole central panel is bent outward to achieve a third dimension. Fittings and light fixtures are also hand forged.

Instead of flattening the bar as Terrence Clark did, John Rausch created a bend in the bar and flattened it on each side of the bend thereby carrying out the circle shapes at the top of the gate. Adam Piper Booth welded a solid circle in the center of his Chelsea gate. The circle passes through each vertical, with detailing around it. The circular form is repeated at the top in a double arc.

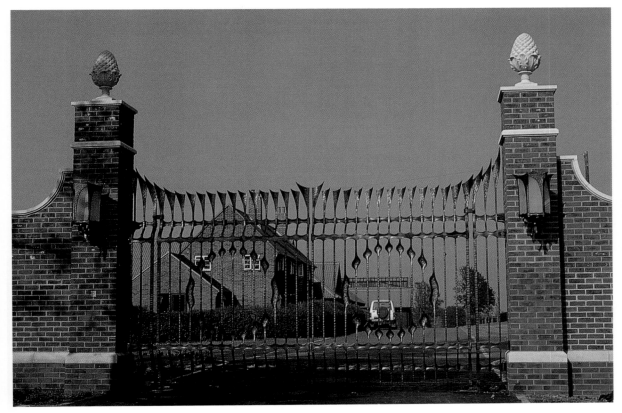

Terrence Clark. Driveway gates. One of a set of five identical house gates for a private stud farm all forged in mild steel. An example of straight lines offset with geometric shapes. The horizontals are shaped, the top ends are splayed to form a pattern, and the central shape is achieved by flattening the rods to create the circular form. Rod areas within the circle are twisted. The central portion is bent forward so it protrudes into another plane from the top and bottom. The artist worked closely with the builder and architect. *Courtesy, artist*

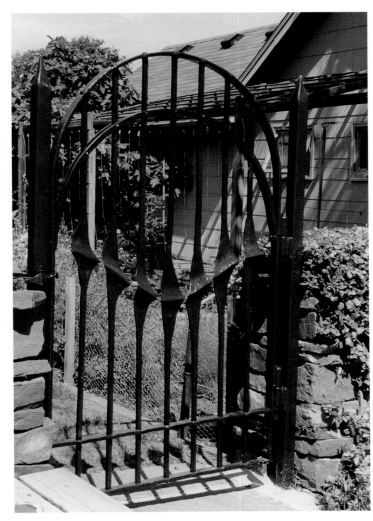

John R. Rausch. Garden gate. An example of a circle within uprights. The circle shape is echoed in the gate top arch. 5.2' high 3' wide. *Photo, Patricia Woelie.*

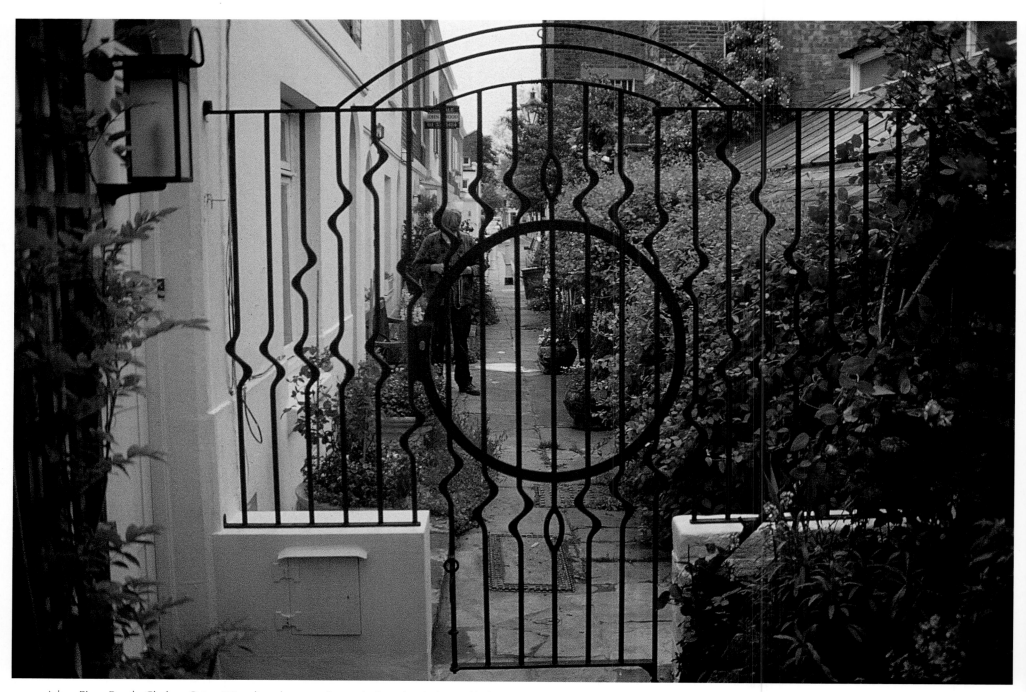

Adam Piper Booth. Chelsea Gates. Wavy lines become the verticals and a circle is added into the two dimensional plane. 6.4' high, 8' wide. *Photo, artist*

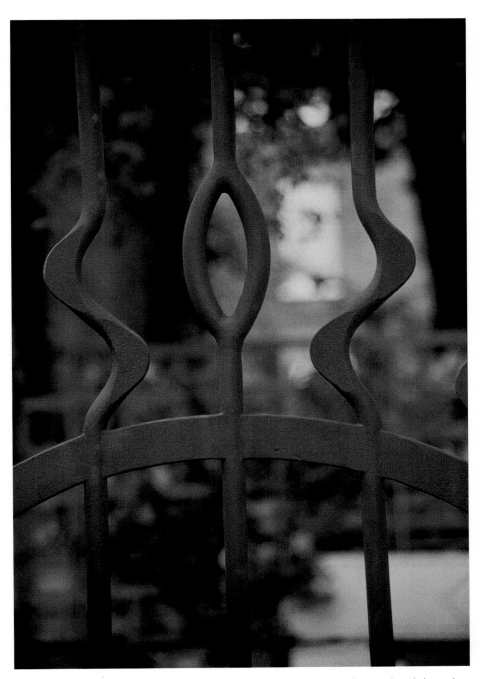

Adam Piper Booth. Chelsea Gates, detail, showing how the iron is flattened and shaped to achieve the wavy line, and how the circle becomes one with the lines. *Photo, artist*

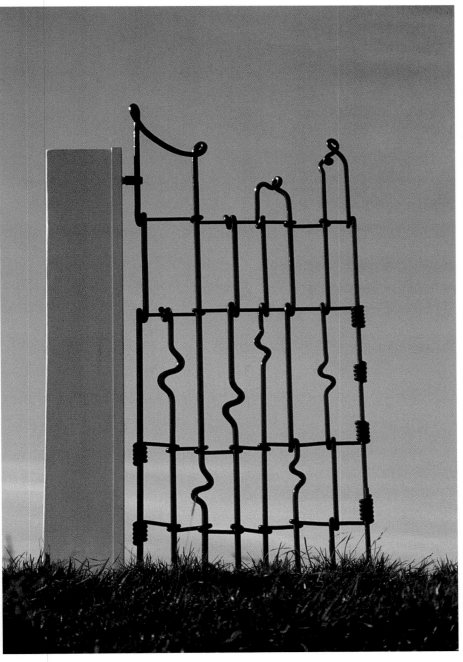

Adam Piper Booth. Knotted gate. Booth knots the wavy lines together to result in a unique design. *Photo, artist*

Squares and rectangles dominate the design in Tom Joyce's Courtyard Gate. It is basically rectangular, but he works in an oval shape. Adam Piper Booth's "Well Door" has folded bars that give it a Mayan appearance. Bending metal like this takes the experience of a master smith who has a mathematical background.

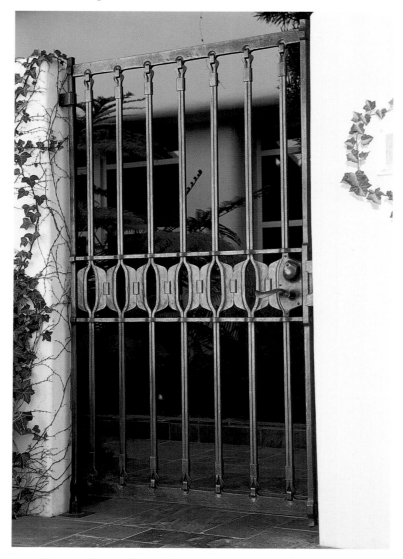

Tom Joyce. Courtyard gates offer a brilliant solution for joining the horizontal bars to the vertical bars at top and bottom. The central detailing captures the negative space in a flowing design. 8' high, 3' wide. *Photo, Tom Brewster*

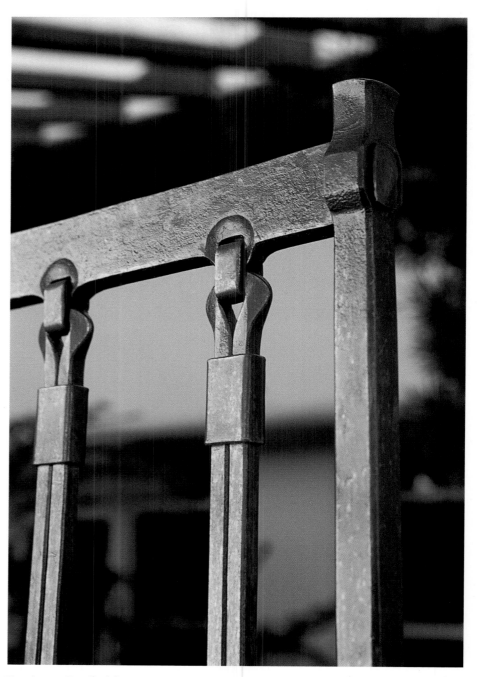

Tom Joyce. Detail of the construction of the courtyard gate. *Photo, Tom Brewster*

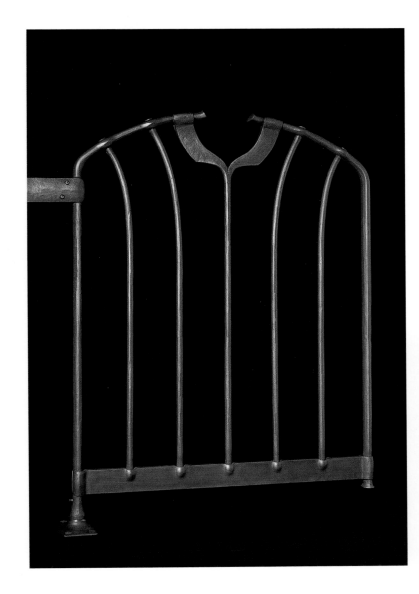

Tom Joyce. Patio Gate. Joyce uses a simple geometry for design but, like much of his work, he also uses unique joinery and impeccable finishes to yield their beauty. 3.5' high, 2.5' wide. *Photo, O. Diaz*

Tom Joyce. Patio Gate crest detail. You can also see, and appreciate, the subtle hammer texturing in the forged mild steel. *Photo, O. Diaz*

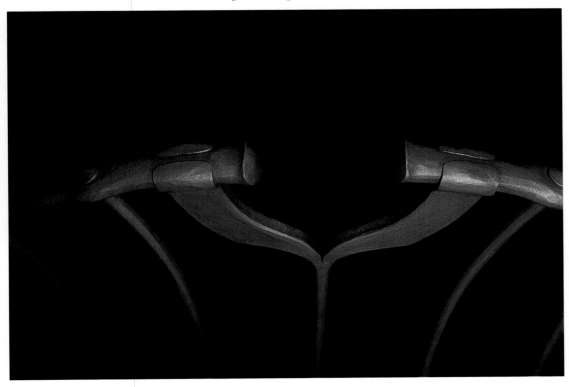

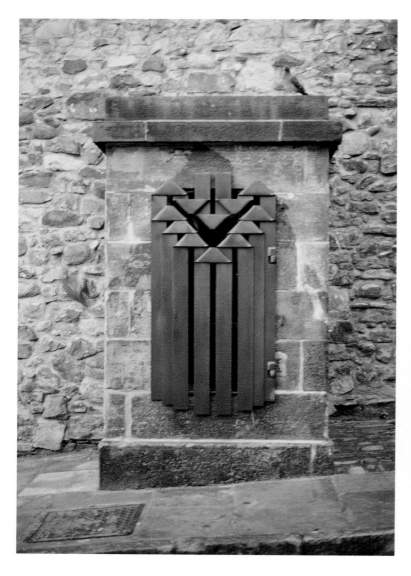

Adam Piper Booth. A door for a well opening is designed with a folded metal technique to result in the chevron-like pattern at the top. 4.6' high. *Courtesy, artist*

Adam Piper Booth. Detail of the folding technique in the well door. *Courtesy, artist*

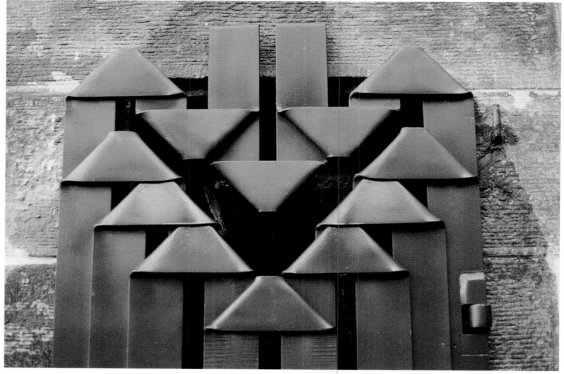

Joel Schwartz's driveway gates have spikes at the top; both the gates' height and the prospect of being impaled on one of the spears would certainly deter any vandal from trying to climb over.

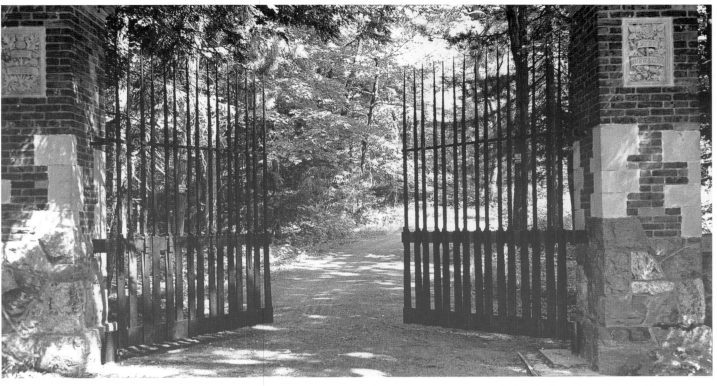

Joel A. Schwartz. Driveway gates. The verticals graduate from wide at the bottom and taper into spears at the top. *Courtesy, artist*

Joel A. Schwartz. Detail of the driveway gate latch construction. *Courtesy, artist*

187

The circle is the gate with additional circles repeated within the gate by Jorgen Harle. To achieve the inner circles, each horizontal is actually two horizontals. Each one has a half circle and pegging, or riveting, with matching forged rivets inserted through holes "punched" in the rods.

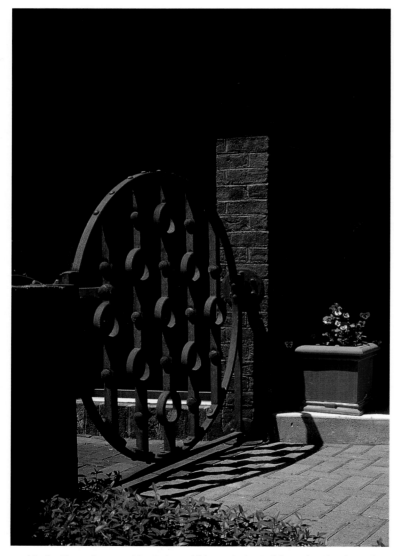

Jorgen Harle. Round gate with circles within a circle. Mild steel with silicon bronze. Forged and fabricated with bronze rivets. 4' diameter *Photo, Dan Eisenhart*

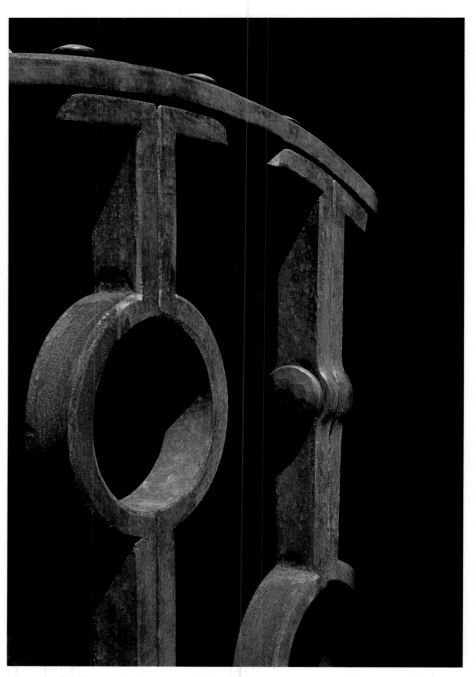

Jorgen Harle. The emphasis on "round" is repeated in rivets used in the joinery. *Photo, Dan Eisenhart*

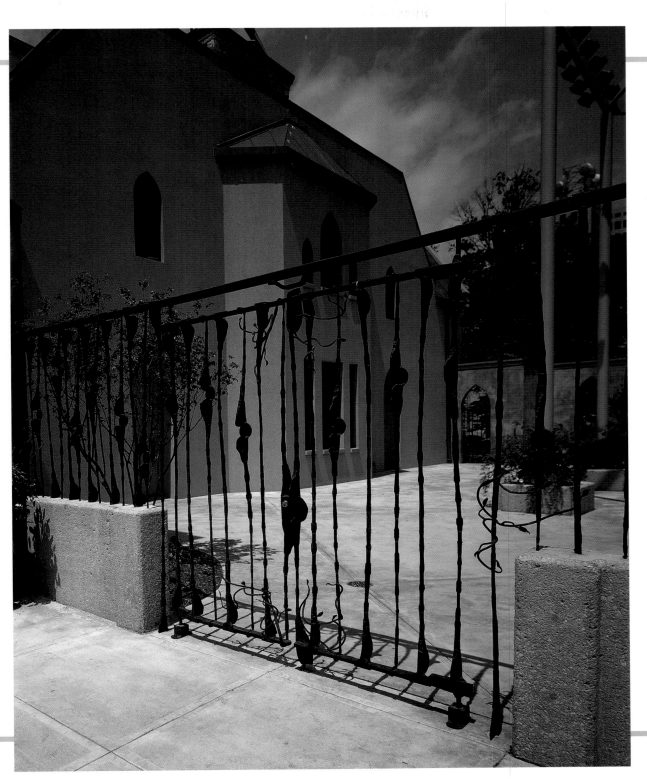

Craig Kaviar. Courtyard gate and fence for the First Unitarian Church, Louisville, Kentucky. When the original church burned to the ground, only a portion of the stone façade stood. Kaviar was commissioned to design and create gates, grilles, and fencing to delineate a new court-yard for a portion of the existing building. The ironwork has a subtle dimensionality created by using flattened and shaped parts of the bars in a more random pattern than a circle. Vines are also added at top and bottom. *Photo, Geoffrey Carr*

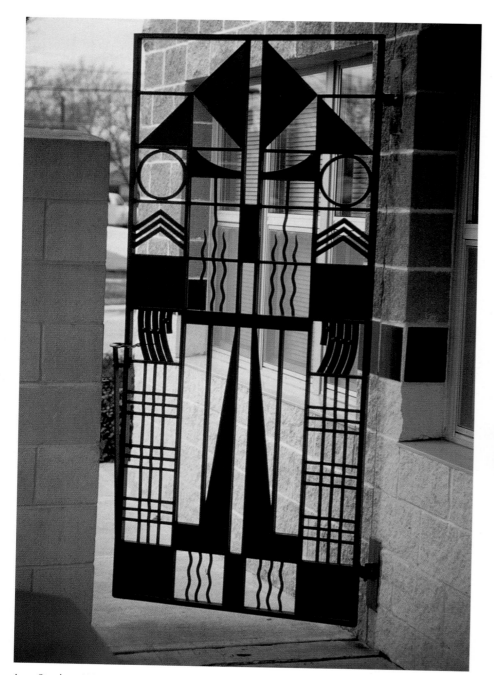

Lars Stanley, AIA. Fireman Gate. Geometric shapes combine in this expression of Art Deco in ironwork. *Courtesy, artist*

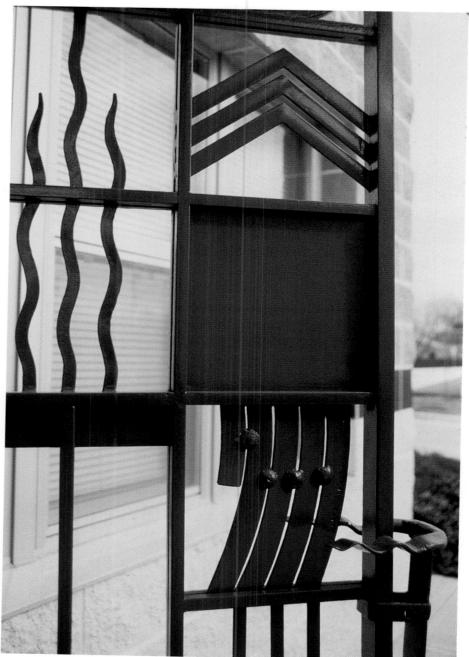

Lars Stanley, AIA. Detail of Fireman Gate. *Courtesy, artist*

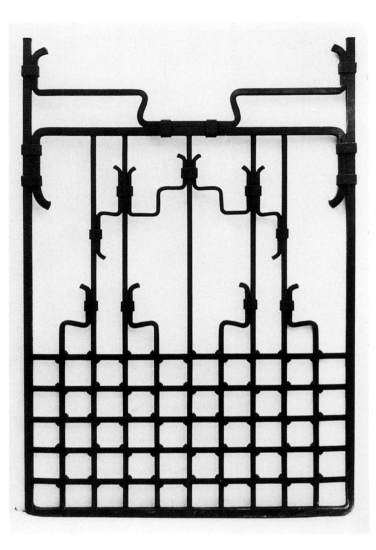

Lars Stanley, AIA. Green Gate. Squares and rectangles are the design elements. Some squares have rounded corners so that the whole appearance is not of perfect squares; rather, each section is a shape within a shape. The ends are purposely left away from the adjacent rod and clipped off to intrude on the negative shapes for design interest. *Photo, artist*

Subtle geometry marks Robert Rotondo's Wood-Prince Gate. He uses the C scroll along the bottom to soften the stark rectangular shapes.

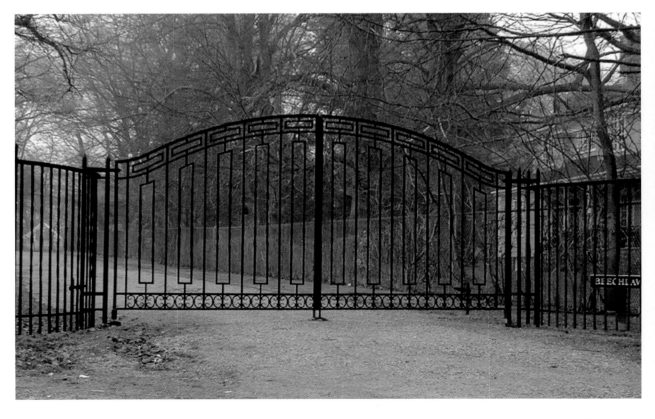

Robert Rotondo. Wood-Prince driveway gates. The design elements are graduated rectangles along the top, repeat rectangles in the center, with C scrolls along the bottom. *Photo, Roger I. Birn*

191

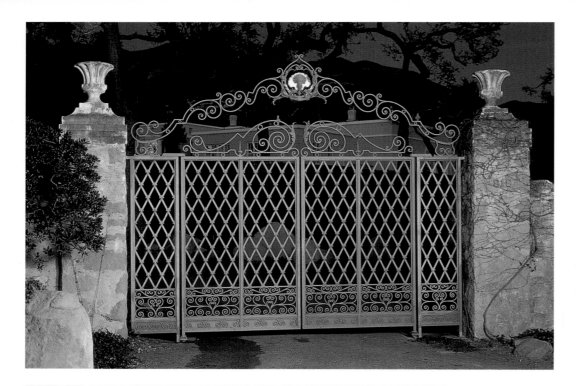

Jean-Pierre Masbanji. The diamond is the dominant design element in these entry gates fitted for an old French estate. A course of scrolls is at the top and bottom. A clamshell with a light in it as at the top and it is surrounded with acanthus leaves. Hot dip galvanized and weather resistant epoxy finish. *Photo, James Chen*

Two gates by The Transfer Company of Tokyo, Japan, use geometry in different ways. The gate by Russell Jaqua is also a symphony in geometric design, relying on the square as the basic building block. Darryl Nelson's bi-folding doors for the Skamania Lodge have squares and rectangles with triangles atop one another representing trees. It is a fitting motif for a lodge at a national forest.

Transfer Co., Kotaro Kurata and Goro Hatanaka. Driveway gate. A repeat of diamonds and triangles with heart shapes along the bottom. Abstract plant shapes are at the top and bottom of the verticals. A coordinated hand forged canopy and signage are in the background. *Photo, Shinichi Sato*

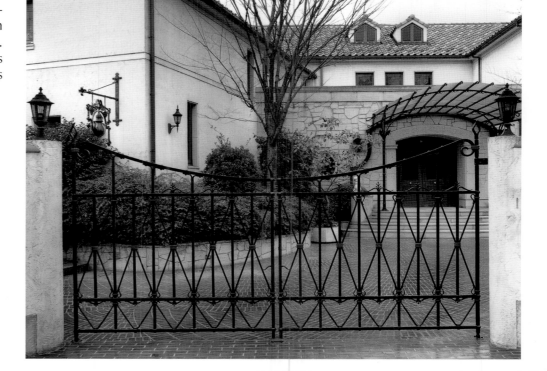

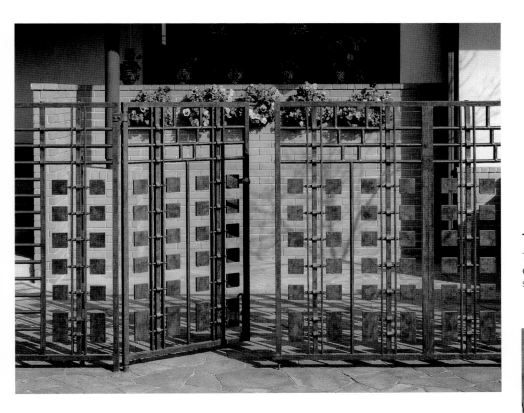

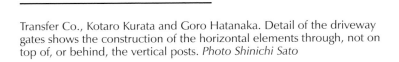

Transfer Co., Kotaro Kurata and Goro Hatanaka. Detail of the driveway gates shows the construction of the horizontal elements through, not on top of, or behind, the vertical posts. *Photo Shinichi Sato*

Transfer Co., Kotaro Kurata and Goro Hatanaka. The squares within rectangles for this driveway gate cast interesting shadows. The artist must be sensitive to the lighting and shadow potential when designing outdoor projects. *Photo, Shinichi Sato*

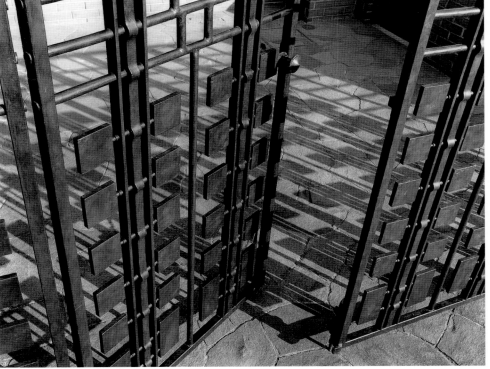

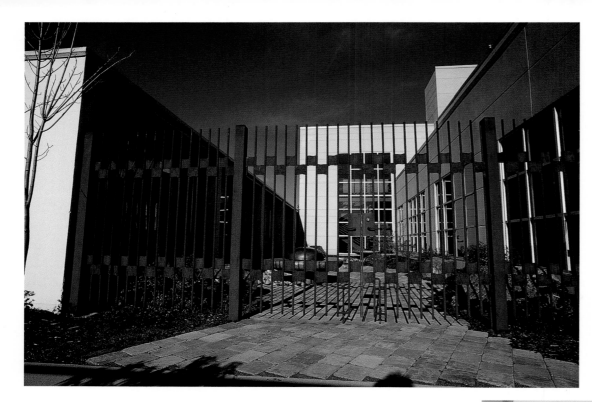

Russell Jaqua. Verticals and squares are the main design elements in this entry to the Malcolm Bruce Courtyard, Jefferson General Hospital, Port Townsend, Washington. *Photo, Robert Gibeau*

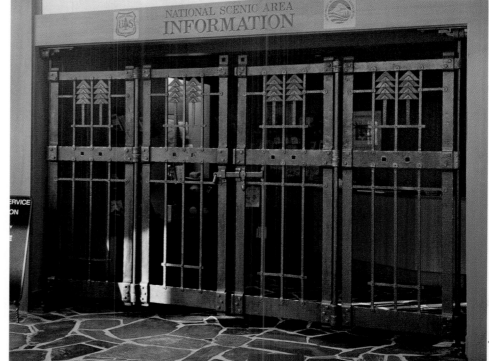

Darryl Nelson. Verticals, squares, and triangles are the dominant design structure in these bi-folding gates for the National Forest Service Information Booth, Skamania Lodge, Stevenson, Washington. 2' high, 12' long. *Photo, artist*

Flat panels of steel are incorporated into Michael Bondi's pierced solid bronze plate gates.

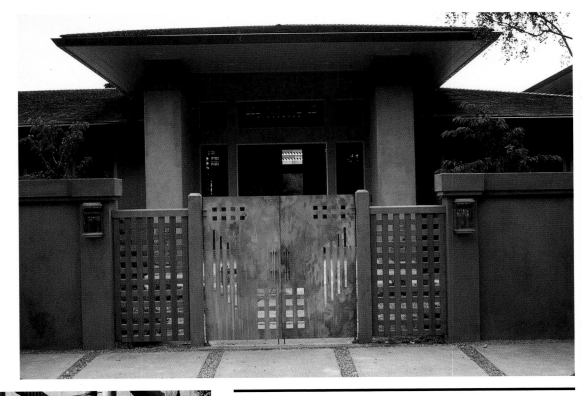

Michael Bondi. Solid areas of iron plate with pierced sections of squares and rectangles, the squares are coordinated with the wood fence and the result is an oriental theme. An antiqued green patina is added. *Photo, artist*

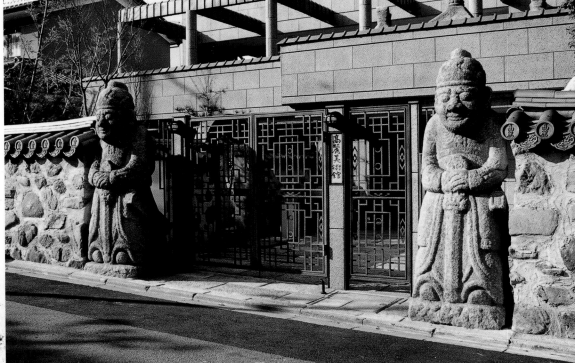

Hiroshi Minamizawa's gates for the Korean Art Museum in Kyoto, Japan, are an expression in metal of the type of design that has been associated with Japanese wood work. (See the Japanese doors and railings in Chapter 4.) It represents an acceptance and increasing use of metal for Japanese architecture and especially where security is also a factor.

Hiroshi Minamizawa. An oriental motif is accomplished with a linear design composed of squares, rectangles, V's, and a few circles. *Courtesy, artist*

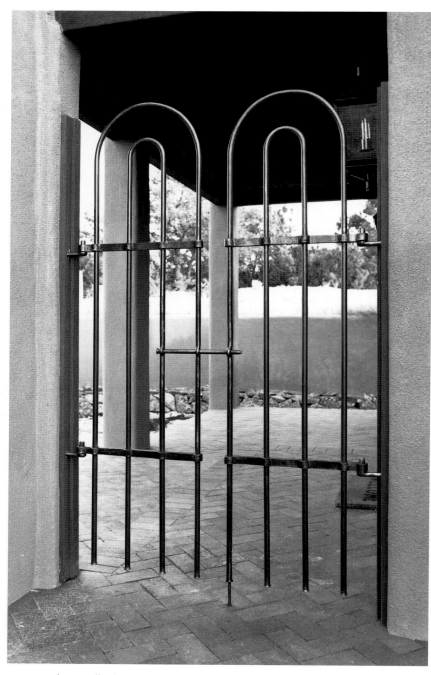

Helmut Hillenkamp. Passageway gates rely on a straight line and a curve for a minimalist design but a maximum effect. Steel is wire brushed and coated with polyurethane. 6' high, 4' wide. *Courtesy, artist*

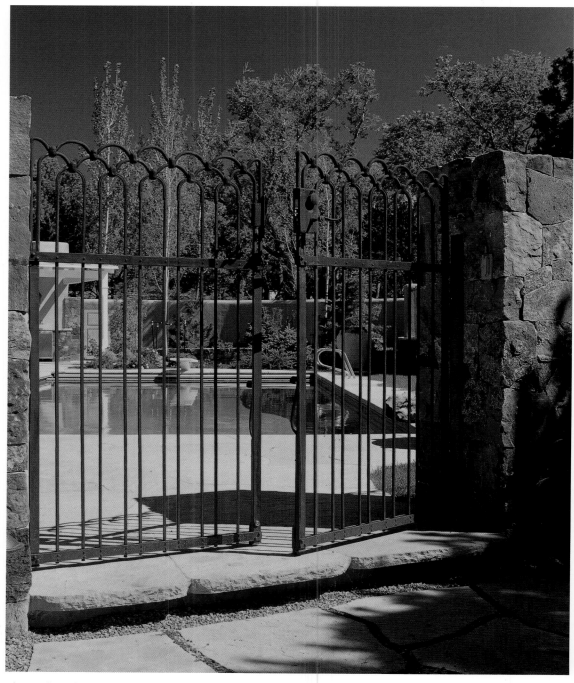

Christopher Thomson. Ripple Gate. The straight line and the arch are combined. By repeating the arch, a fish scale design evolves. *Photo, Peter Vitale*

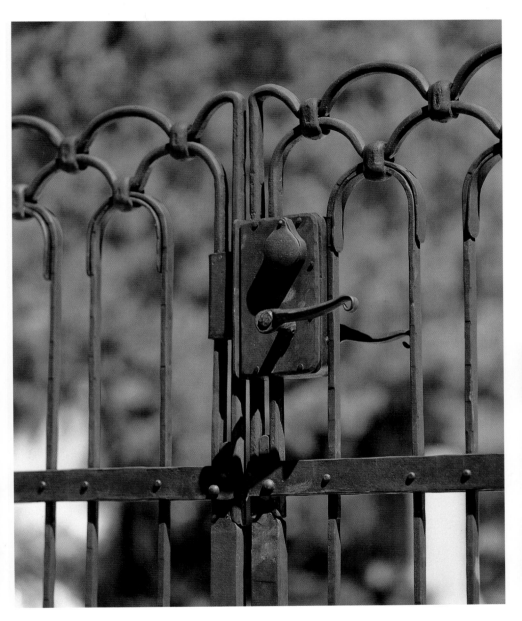

Christopher Thomson. Detail of the Ripple Gate shows the extra support on the arch, the handle, and the use of riveting for design repetition. *Photo, Peter Vitale*

Below: Christopher Thomson. Driveway Scroll gate. A line and an arch with scrolls added. Instead of riveting for details, the horizontal rail is passed through each vertical bar. Every other vertical bar has a twist. The shadows and how they fall are important design considerations. *Photo, Peter Vitale*

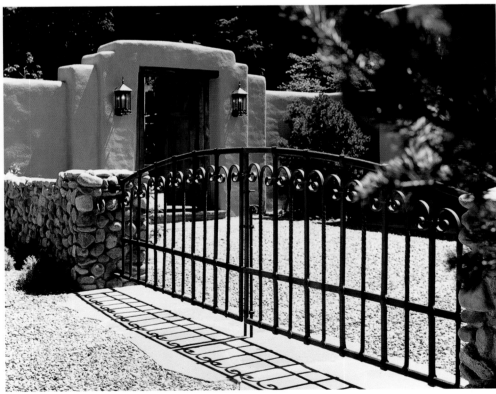

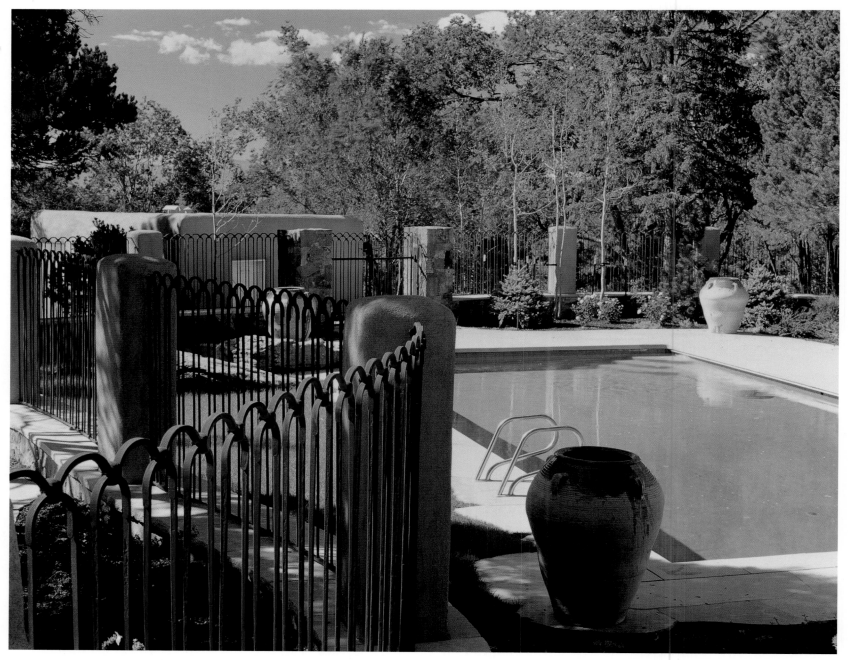

Christopher Thomson. Ripple Fence. The surrounding fence repeats the design in the gate, but with only two arches. The basic shape, though a simple combination of two geometric elements, makes a strong repeat pattern over a large expanse. The New Mexico sun, and its strong shadows, combine for an effective use of fencing. *Photo, Peter Vitale*

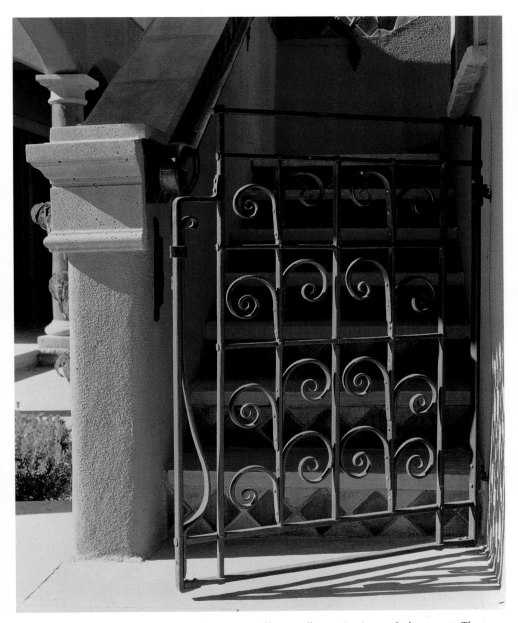

Christopher Thomson. Corn Plant Gate. Offset scrolls vary in size and placement. The top left corner of the gate is inset to accommodate the banister. *Photo, Peter Vitale*

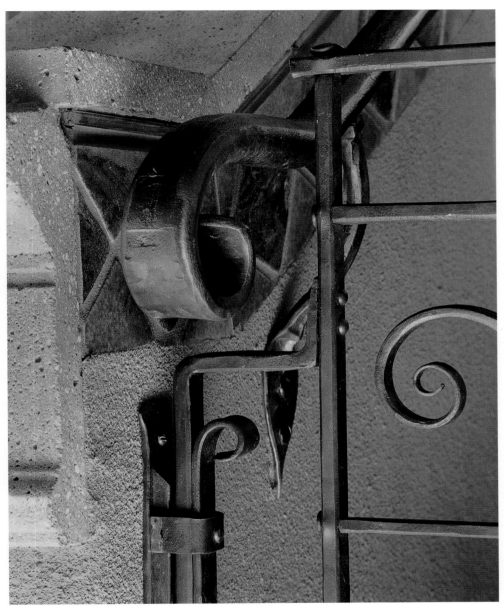

Christopher Thomson. Inset detail of Corn Plant Gate with banister illustrating hand wrought texturing. *Photo, Peter Vitale*

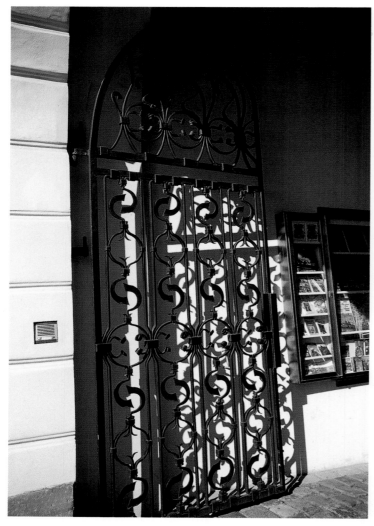

Prague Gate, Czech Republic. Partial circles, or half moon shapes with circles, combine to make an intricate, unusual pattern. *Photo, author*

Close up reveals the banding and the fishtail endings on the scrolls. All construction details must be meticulously worked out. *Photo, author*

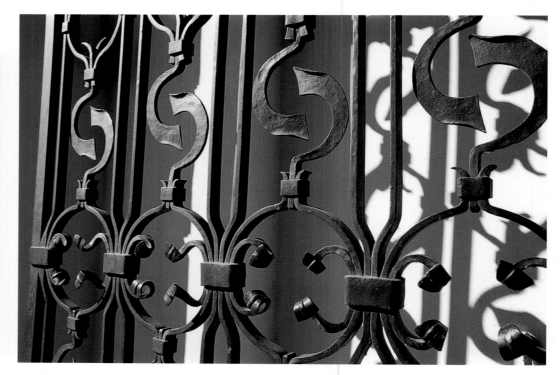

Detail showing how the pattern evolves and progresses, and the arresting shadow that results. *Photo, author*

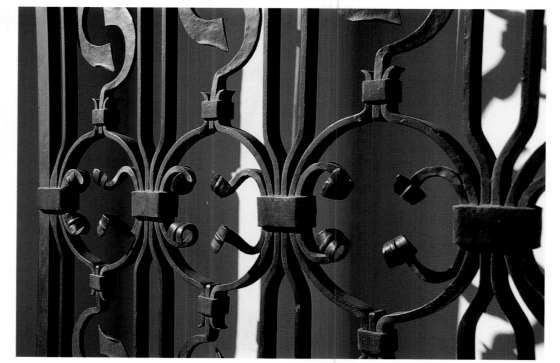

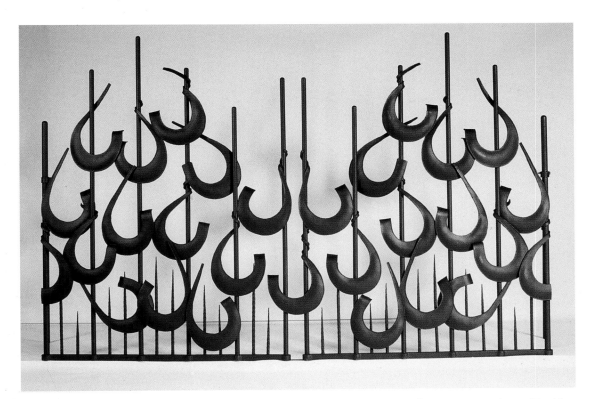

Adam Piper Booth. Antigua Gate. A similar moon, or horseshoe shape, as in the Prague gate, is used in this modern gate in a carefully worked out pattern, but one that gives an almost random effect. Without exterior framing the elements seem to float in space. *Photo, artist*

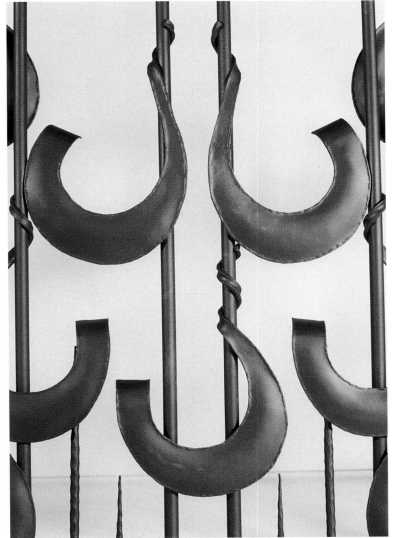

Adam Piper Booth. Antigua Gate detail. Each moon shape is wrapped around the upright bar and welded to another for support. *Photo, artist*

Arcs and Curves

The curved shape worked into arcs seems a natural type of bend to make in iron. And so it is, but combining the curved rods into gates and fences and conjuring up new ways to use curved metal shapes is a perpetual challenge for the smith. The examples illustrate several solutions. The innovations rely on the commission, the problems to be solved, and the ingenuity of the craftsman.

Helmut Hillenkamp uses the smooth curve in exciting relationships for gates and fences. Several gates photographed in Prague also show different uses for the curved shapes, while Adam Piper Booth's gate with horseshoe like shapes could be the perfect gate for entry into a ranch or riding academy.

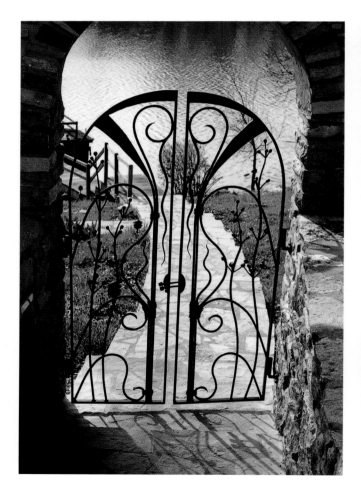

Erika Strecker. The gate relies on curves, scrolls, and ends drawn out to points. Walter Gross III Gate; Burgin, Kentucky. Mild steel. 6' high, 4' wide. *Photo, artist*

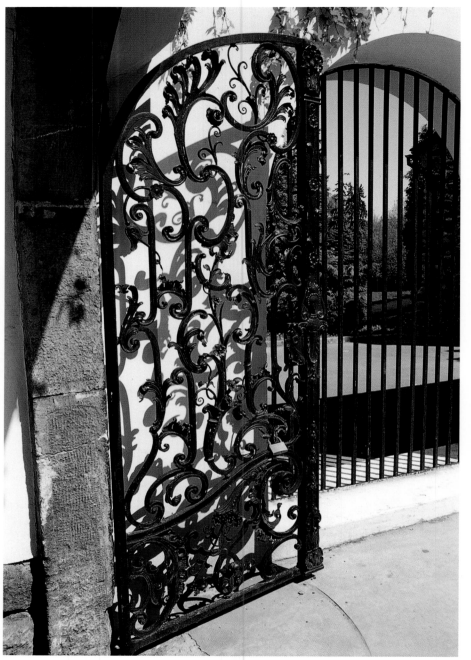

Garden Entry Gate, Prague, Czech Republic. Nary a straight line can be found within the interior frame of this gate that relies on arcs and curves in different weight iron for variety. A few flower forms can be seen and there's a cornucopia at the bottom. A figure with a face appears on the handle. *Photo, author*

Jim Gallucci's Whisper Gates are the entry to "Exploris" a science museum in North Carolina. They had to function as gates for an open courtyard while conveying a sense of welcome to visitors, and a suggestion of the museum's content.

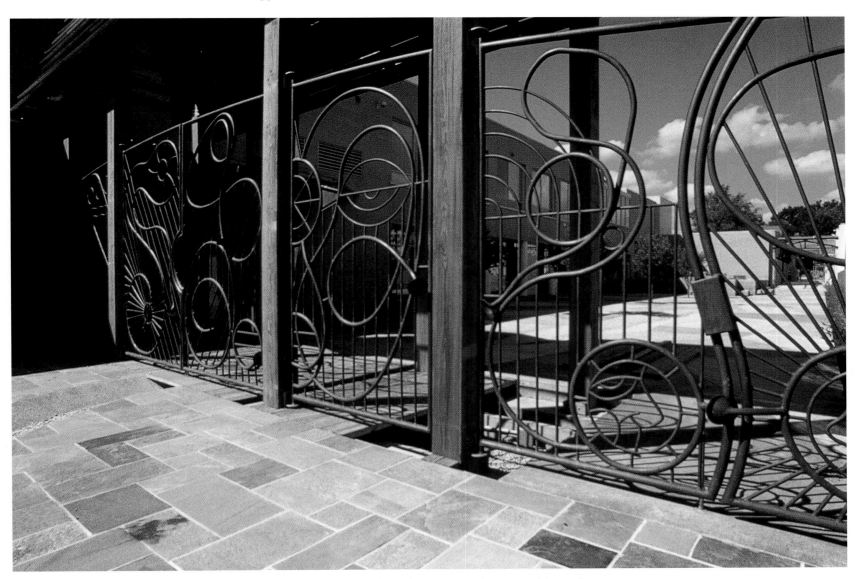

Jim Gallucci. Whisper Gate. Red Brass. An interactive gate that lets sound travel across its 40-foot span without wires. 12' high, 62' wide. *Photo, artist*

Says Gallucci, "The museum uses interactive exhibits so I designed red brass sound tubes winding through the gates creating abstract designs but also carrying visitors voices to either end of the 80' long tubes.

"The physics involved are quite simple," explained Gallucci. "It is the same principle found in musical instruments or the message tubes used on old steamships to talk from the bridge to the engine room. Sound can travel down a tube or pipe a long way if there are no obstructions and the walls of the tube do not absorb the sound. The sound waves bounce off the walls carrying the sound." While testing the system with his ten year old daughter, she whispered to him and her voice came through sharp and clear. She named them "The Whisper Gates."

Gallucci finished the brass with a brown patina to give it an aged look. With millions of people passing by the gates, it was estimated that the finish would have to be redone in about ten to fifteen years and this maintenance cost was added to the budget.

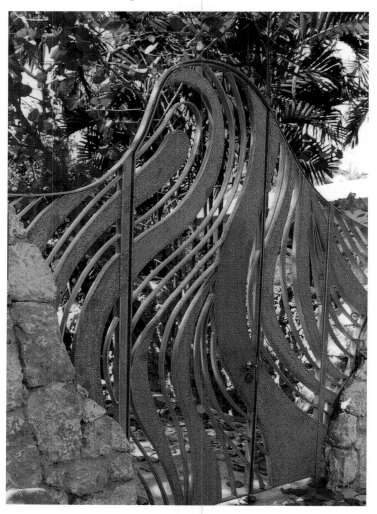

ArtsWork Unlimited. Ghost Gate. Curving elements in different widths and weights in a flowing design. Fabricated from mild steel, using flat bar and 1/8" plate. The plate was textured using the MIG welder with the gas turned off to create a very rough surface. The finish is hot dipped galvanized and left natural. *Photo, artist*

Joseph Miller. Curves and scrolls are used exclusively for this gate at the Hyatt Regency Hotel, Wichita, Kansas. *Photo, Jennifer Malling*

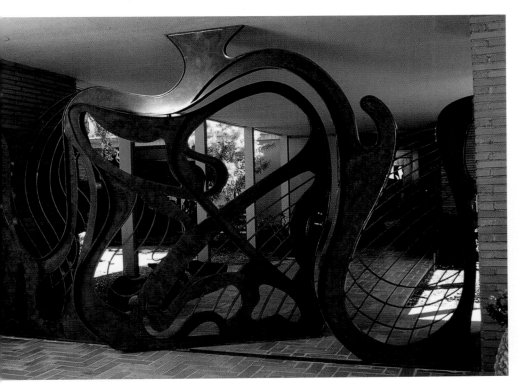

ArtsWork Unlimited. Pivot gate with curves and flat areas. Aluminum. Designed by the architect, James Loyd, with intersecting lines, amoeboid positive and negative spaces. *Photo, artist*

Joseph A. Bonifas. Transportation Portico. A design based on elements from an old "Shay Engine" steam engine built in Lima, Ohio. Two horizontal bars separate the curves at the top from the rounded arches at the bottom that represent the train's cowcatchers. Building railroad engines was one of two industries responsible for the city's development. 8' high, 6' wide. *Entry gates to ArtSpace, Lima, Art Association, Lima, Ohio. Photo, Michael Lawson*

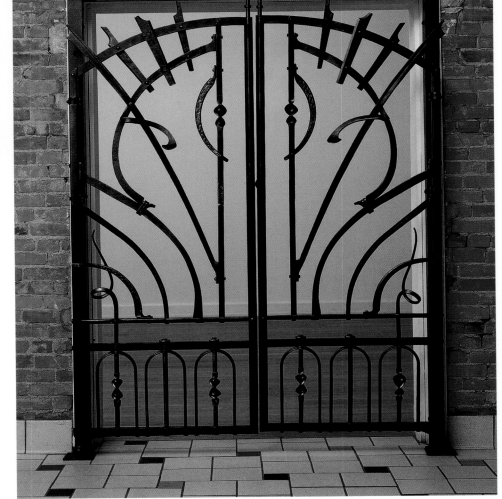

Flowers, Leaves, Trees, Landscapes

Hail the ironwork garden gate. It's like an artist's canvas for the iron-worker and can be a source of delight and pleasure for those who use it. Here, the artist's imagination can run wild. Plants, bugs, small animals, anything one finds in a garden can blossom on a gate. And they do.

Animals and fish are all fair game for the blacksmith's talents. Plant and animal forms free the artists' creative reins by following the lead of nature itself. Gates very often are not symmetrical with one side mirroring another, although they can be. They can enjoy informality. They can be whimsical.

At the same time, they are a way of obstruction or passage, a means of confinement or release.

Just as landscapes intrigue the painter, the artist in iron can also create landscapes. Driveway gates provide a large canvas for their art. The design for Jeffrey Funk's driveway gates for a Boca Raton, Florida, estate is a liberally stylized buttonwood mangrove tree, with the vertical elements representing falling water. The design draws from the Florida landscape and the client's interest in Asian artwork. It has the feeling of a Japanese bonsai plant in the way it is shaped to fit the space.

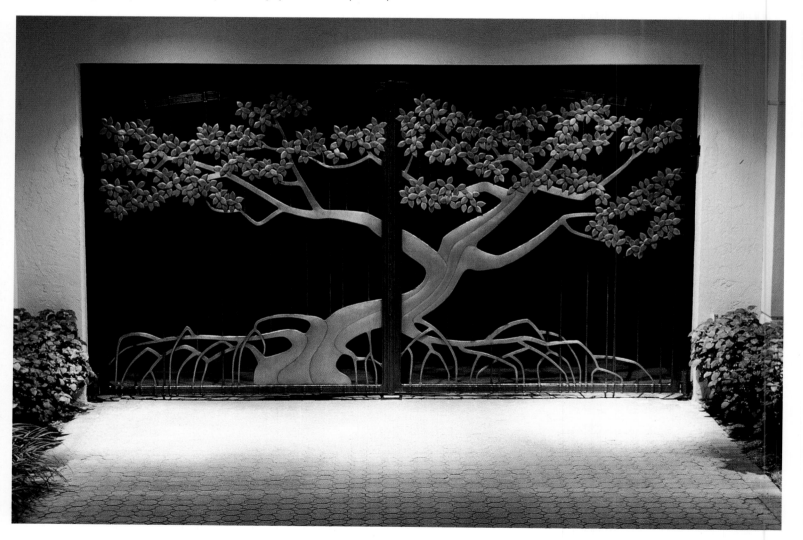

Jeffrey Funk. "Tree" gates for an estate, Boca Raton, Florida. Forged and fabricated from stainless steel and silicon bronze, patinated, and lacquered. The gates are automatically operated by an in ground electro-hydraulic opener which drives through a small floating axle in the lower hinge. 9' high, 18' wide. *Photo, artist*

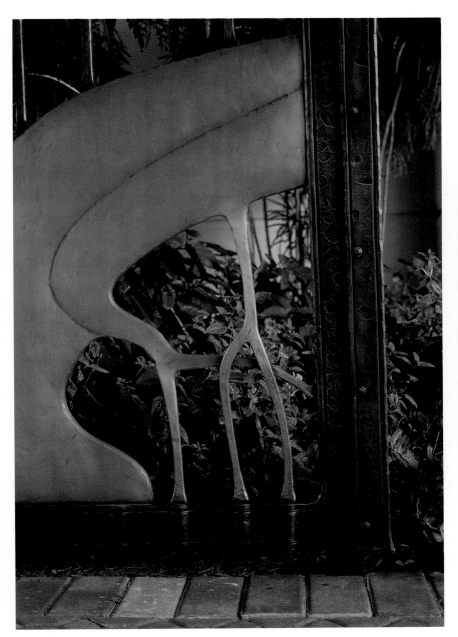

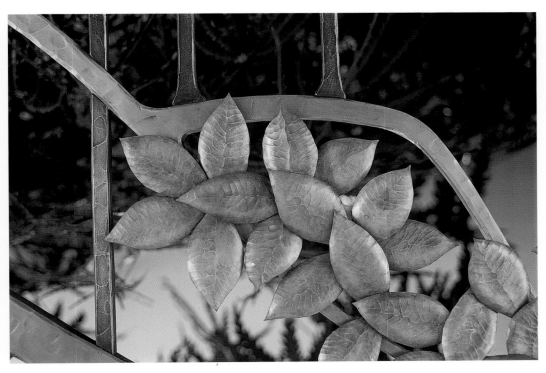

Jeffrey Funk. Details of "Tree" gate. *Photo, artist*

Jeffrey Funk. Details of "Tree" gate show the fine hand forged texturing of every piece, including the horizontal and vertical bars. *Photo, artist*

By contrast, Lars Stanley's "Zilker Gates" are as loaded with floral images as a garden itself. The images appear to grow wildly but the design is carefully organized and the gates are balanced and symmetrical. That's not an easy feat with a project this size.

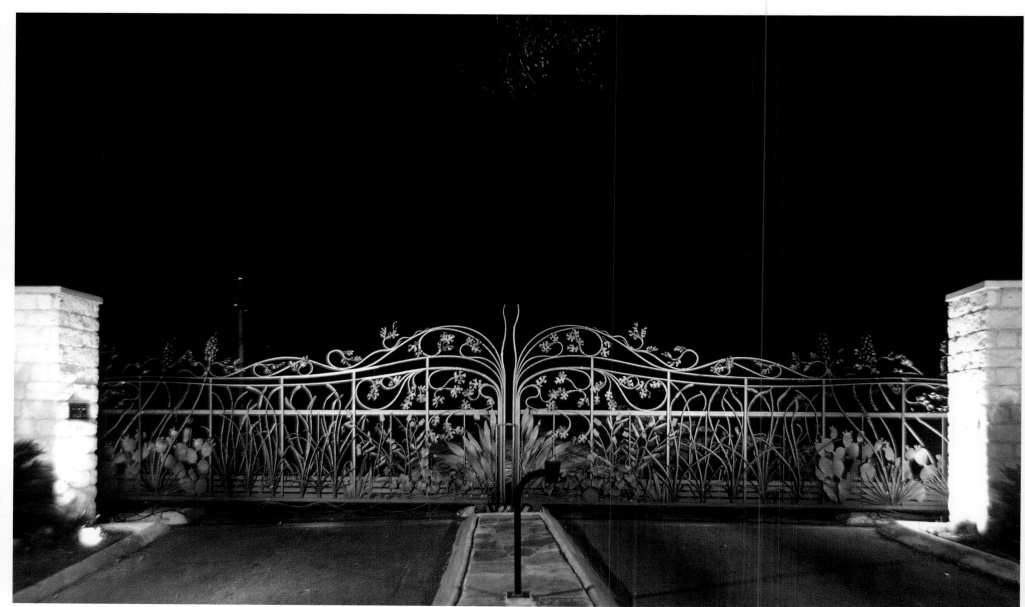

Lars Stanley, AIA and Louis G. Herrera, Jr. Zilker Botanical Gardens main entry gate. *Photo, AtelierWong*

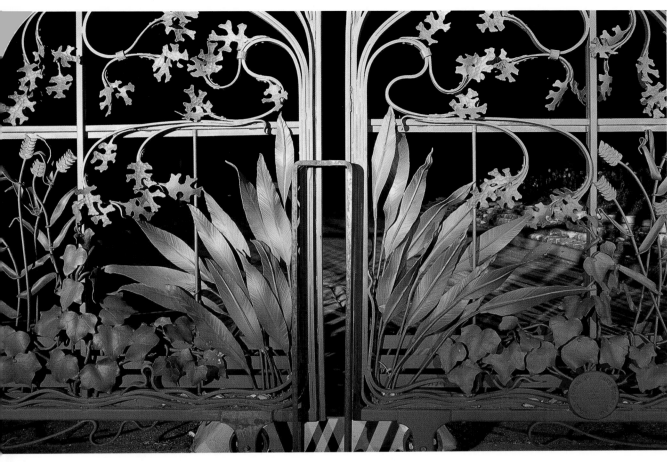

Lars Stanley, AIA and Louis G. Herrera, Jr. Zilker Botanical Gardens gate, central detail. *Photo, AtelierWong*

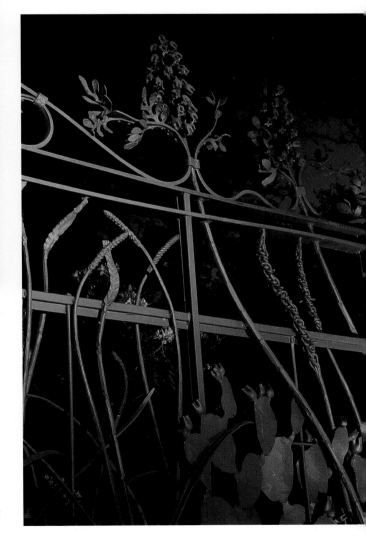

Lars Stanley, AIA and Louis G. Herrera, Jr Zilker Botanical Gardens gate, central detail. *Photo, AtelierWong*

209

Did we say the artist draws from paintings as well as nature? Dimitri Gerakaris' "Iris Gate" looks like it jumped off the Vincent Van Gogh "Iris" canvas painted in May, 1889. It also could have been taken from a Japanese woodcut by Katsushika Hokusai, titled "Iris and Field Cicada" from 1832.

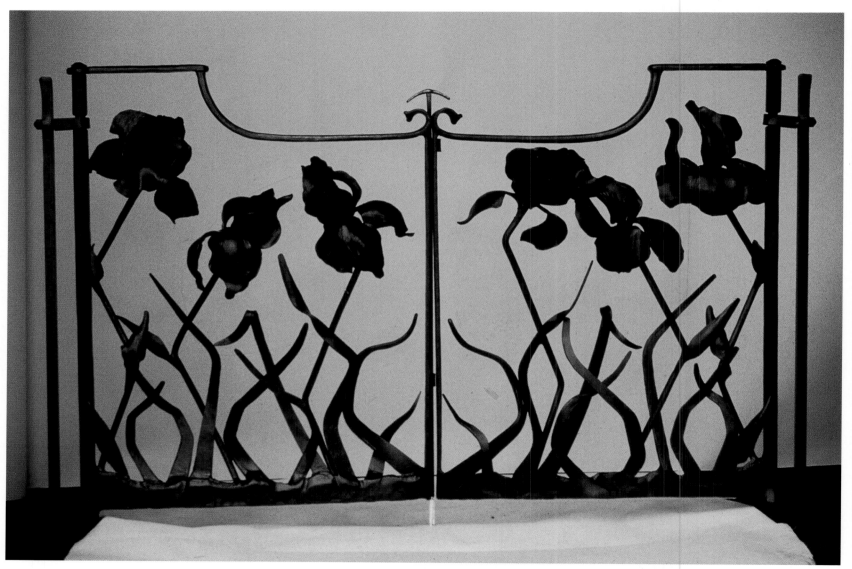

Dimitri Gerakaris. Iris gate. Initially, the gates appear symmetrical but closer observation shows that the flowers are blooming in different shapes as they do in nature. A hexagonal pattern was designed into the leaf sections to provide a sense of geometry and order, and as a counterpoint to the flowing floral portion. *Photo, artist*

Enrique Vega's driveway gates are like a landscape painting with the sun radiating out from the center. Armadillos forage in the earth beneath. This project involves four gates; the two main automobile access doors and two pedestrian gates, one on each side.

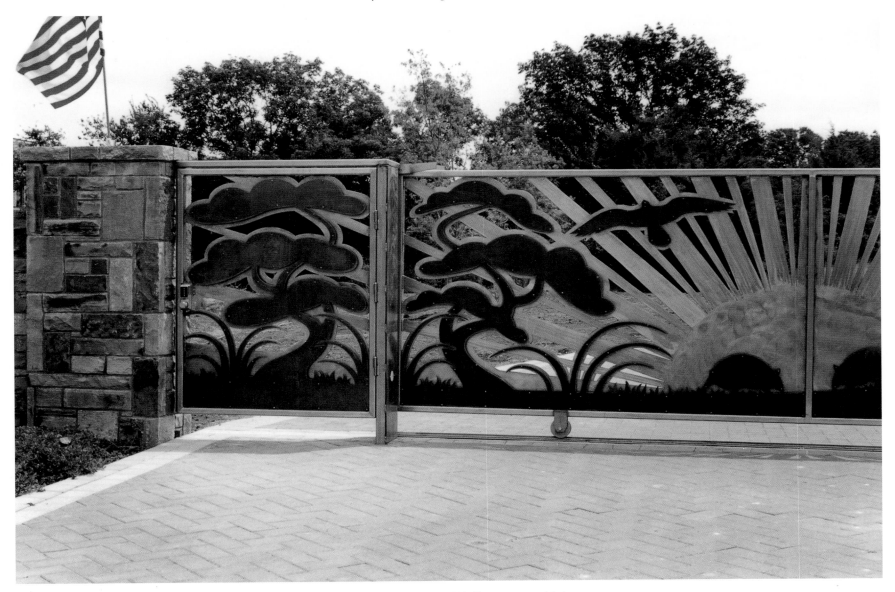

Enrique Vega. "Sun Gates" detail of the left drive gate and one pedestrian gate (page 169). Trees, grass, a bird and an armadillo in the left panel of the driveway gate. Each pedestrian gate is like a separate landscape. *Photo, Seymour Zweigoron*

Enrique Vega also fills his "Tree of Knowledge" gate with symbolism. The apple and seed pod were hand raised from soft brass, a technique used to cold form objects with repeated blows using specialized hammers and stakes. The serpent was hot forged from solid copper and brass, and finished with a patina.

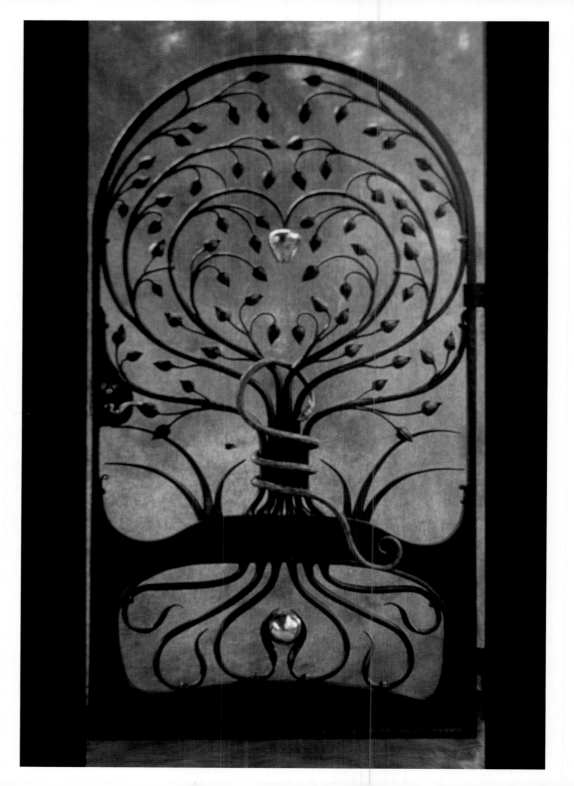

Enrique Vega. "Tree of Knowledge Gate." Forged steel, copper, and brass. 8' high, 4' wide. *Photo, artist*

Alber De Matteis tackles the landscape as a three-dimensional painting though it is two-dimensional. The gate is the entrance to the Carley's Magical Gardens at Children's Hospital and Health Center in San Diego, California. He uses iron to simulate a stone walkway over a bridge with handrails and trees, and a pony-tailed girl running. The fence continues the landscape of the gate.

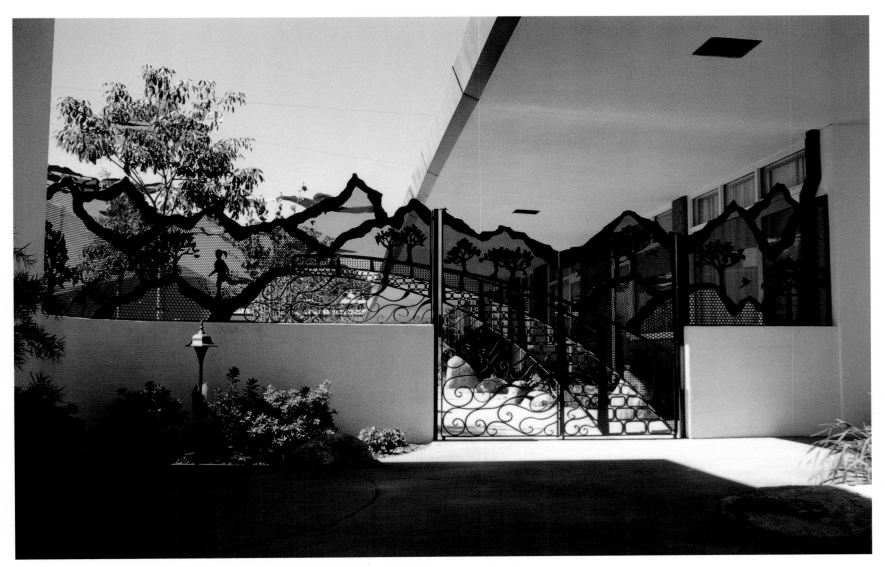

Alber De Matteis. Landscape gate and fencing. Entry to a children's garden in a San Diego, California, children's hospital. *Photo, artist*

"The Pilgrim's Way" by Terrence Clark is layered to achieve a three dimensional composition. The pictorial image illustrates the pilgrim on his journey as the sun rises behind the gate. The tree and the pilgrim are attached to the front of the gate. Grass, flowers, and birds are "drawn" into the iron as they might be on a canvas.

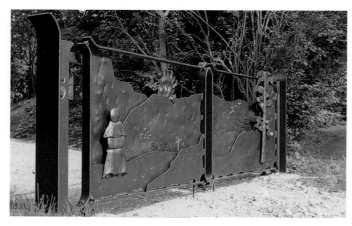

Terrence Clark. "The Pilgrim's Way". A solid area is appropriate for this "story" gate that illustrates the pilgrim on his journey as the sun rises. Made from sheet steel sprayed to give it a burnished look. *Courtesy, artist*

Chris Axelsson and John Boyd Smith use a palette of leaves and flowers in their gates but have handled them very differently. Axelsson's gate is symmetrical with all the vines and leaves held together by scrolls. The latch is a carved animal head.

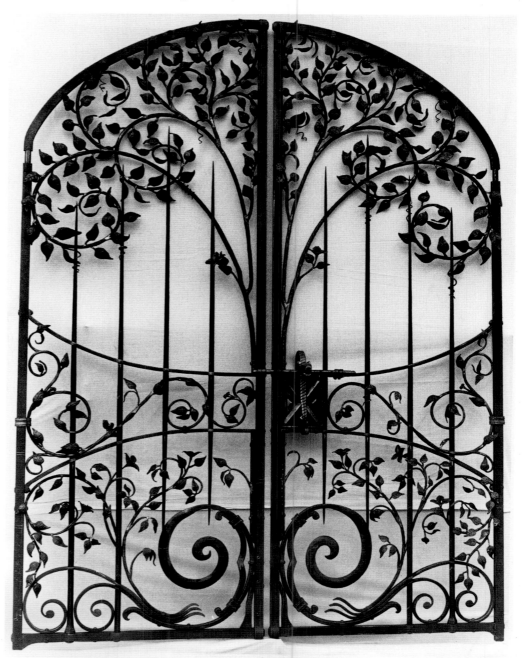

Chris Axelsson. "Enchantment" courtyard gates. Forged mild steel with oxides. Leaves and scrolls are used in a symmetrical arrangement. Mortise and tenon framework with rivet construction. The wolf head latch closure will supposedly deter deer from entering into this Pebble Beach, California, location. *Photo, artist*

214

Smith's "Camellia Tree" driveway gates are asymmetrical. The flowers and leaves are incredibly complex. No two flowers are exactly alike, thanks to the art of hand forging. The radio-controlled gates on rollers are hydraulically operated from the main house or from an automobile. The gates, weighing over 3,000 pounds, are for the property of a camellia flower breeder. Luckily Smith has a degree in mechanical engineering. He began forging at an early age, a tradition handed down from his great-great grandfather, a renowned Irish gunsmith, Patrick Hoy.

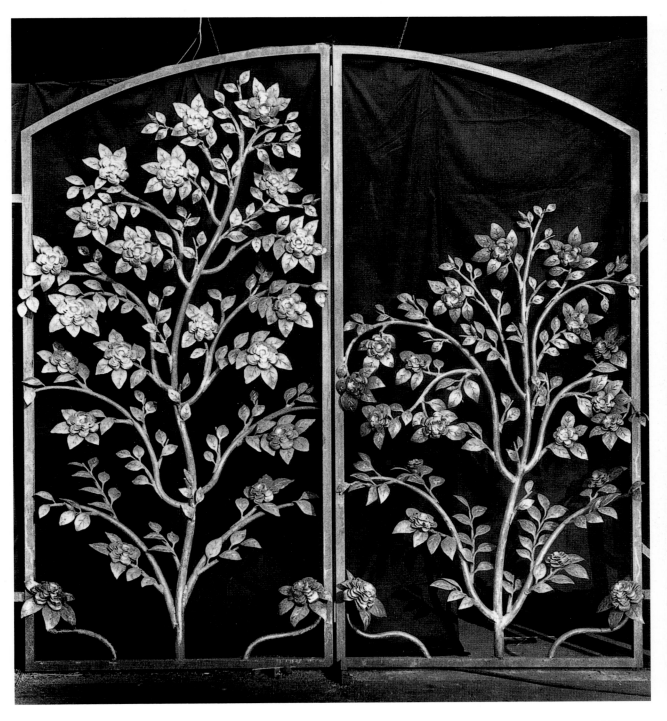

John Boyd Smith. Camellia Tree driveway gate is an effective use of an asymmetrical design. Mild steel. The two flowering camellia tree gates were commissioned by an internationally renowned camellia breeder/grower. 8' high, 8' wide. *Photo, Rhonda Nell Fleming*

Philodendron leaves are the structural elements in ArtsWork Unlimited's aluminum asymmetrical "Leaf Gate" that is the entry through a stone wall for an historical home in Coconut Grove, Florida. The same flowing concepts are in the "Ghost Gate" and the "Pivot Gate." They do not use an obvious object of nature; the artist's use of natural shapes is carried into his abstract work.

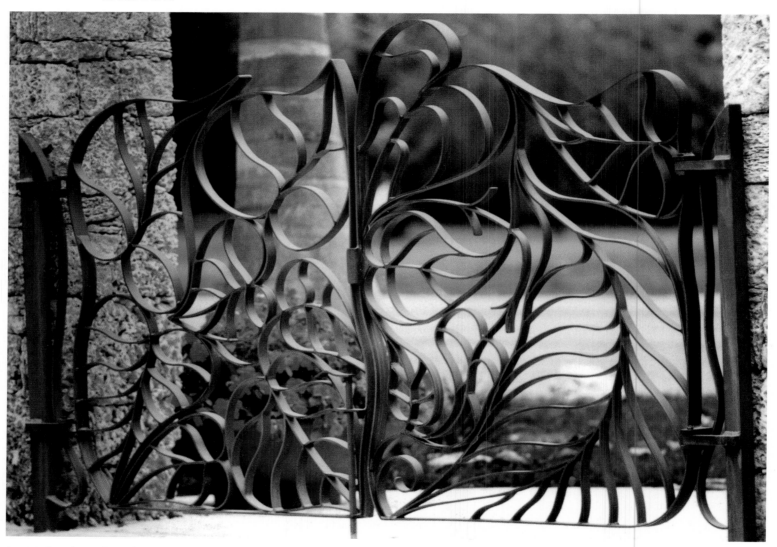

ArtsWork Unlimited. Leaf Gate designed after the "Monstereo Deliciousus" or Philodendron leaf. It was designed by the customer and fabricated from hand bent pieces of 3/8" X 1-1/2" aluminum flat bar, beveled, welded, and blended so the lines flow together. The design relies on asymmetry and undulating curves for its movement and interest. *Photo, Phil Heermance*

It's fitting that Robert C. Bentley has a grape vine with a grape cluster as the central decoration for driveway gates leading into a winery. In another gate, Bentley created a woven metal basket filled with a bouquet of metal flowers.

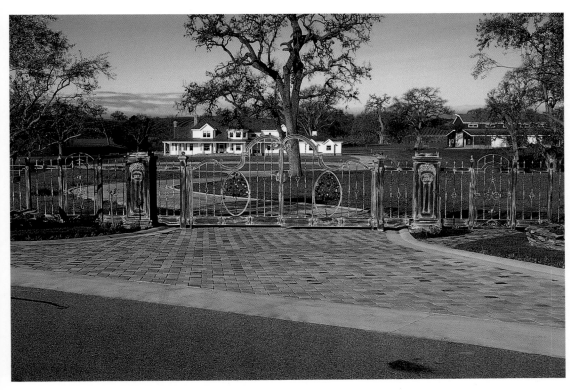

Robert C. Bentley. Driveway and pedestrian gates, and fence for a winery. *Photo, Bruce Woodworth*

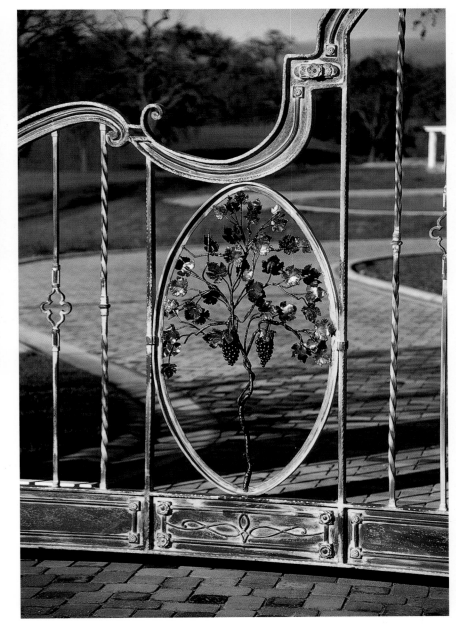

Robert C. Bentley. Floral detail with grape cluster. *Photo, Bruce Woodworth*

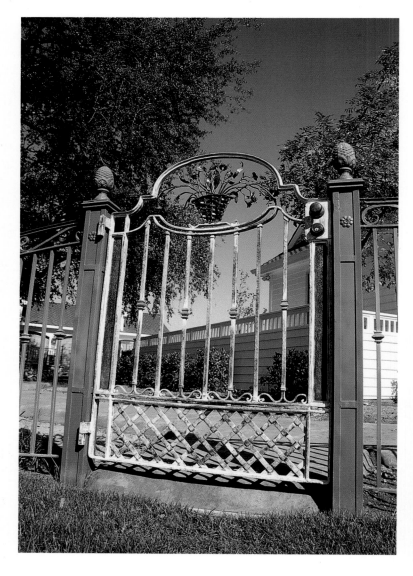

Robert C. Bentley. Floral Basket gate.
Photo, Bruce Woodworth

Robert C. Bentley. Detail of the woven basket; metal is woven to simulate a woven reed basket. *Photo, Bruce Woodworth*

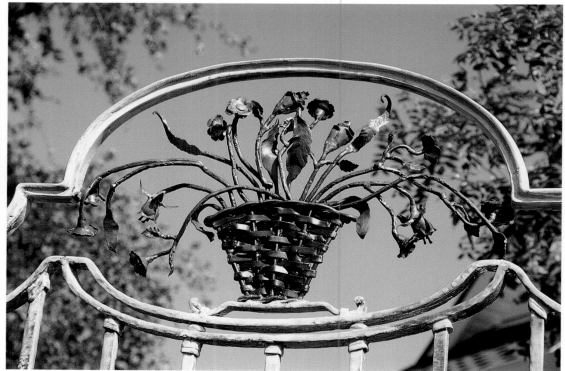

Other examples illustrate the variety that can be achieved in the types of flowers used, and how they're designed into gates and fences.

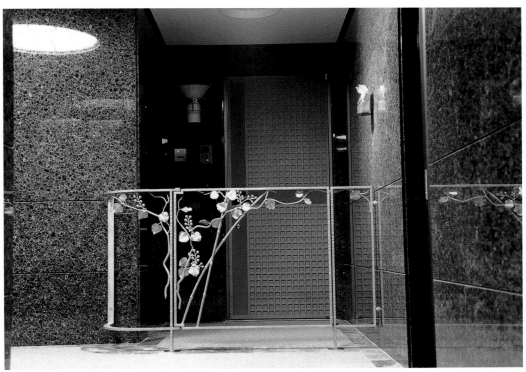

Hiroshi Minamizawa. Ornamental entry gate to an office. The reflective marble wall mirrors the gate that is made with minimal elements for maximum beauty. *Courtesy, artist*

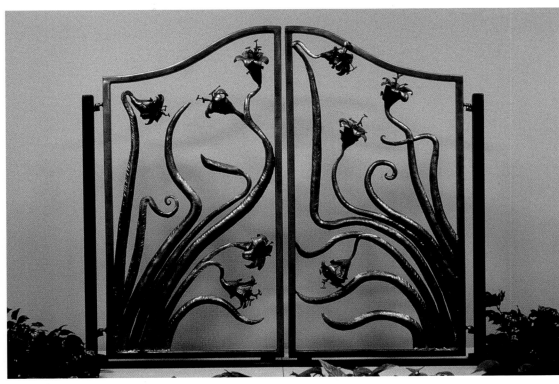

Greg Leavitt. A pair of garden gates; each gate half is slightly different though they repeat the same flowers. *Photo, artist*

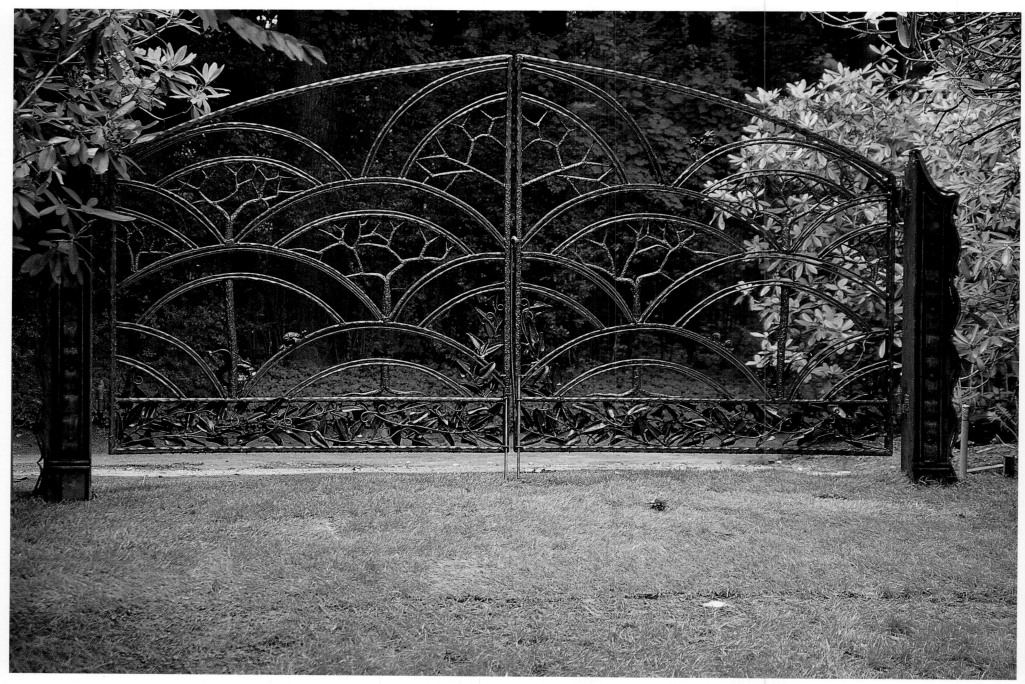

Greg Leavitt. Garden gate with a ladybug. *Photo, artist*

220

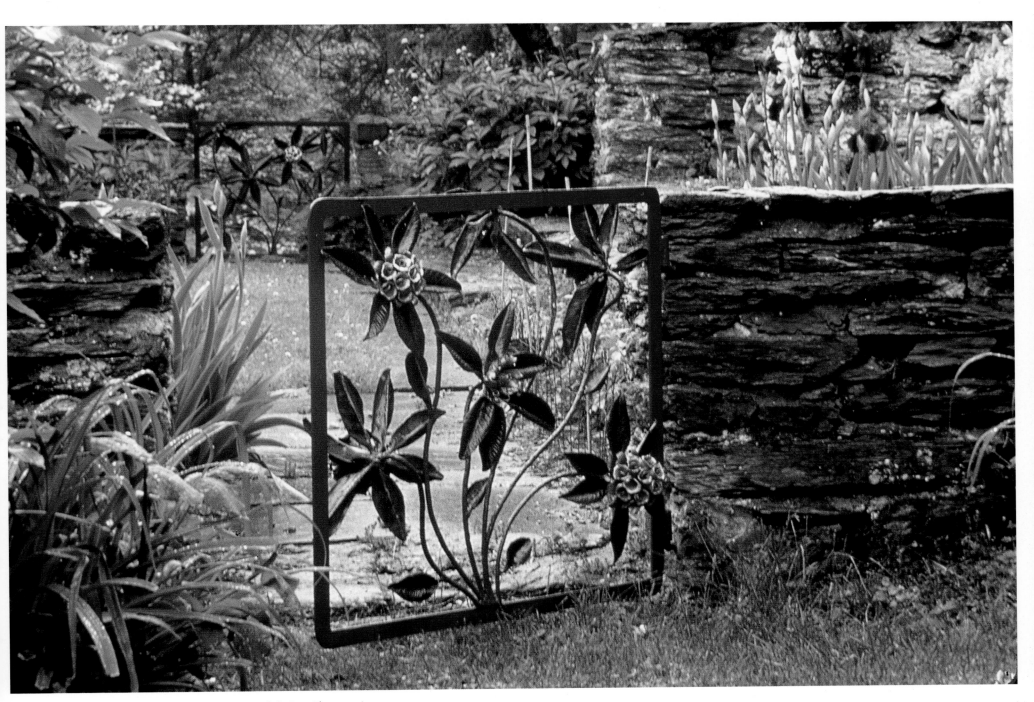

Greg Leavitt. Garden gate with asymmetrical design. *Photo, artist*

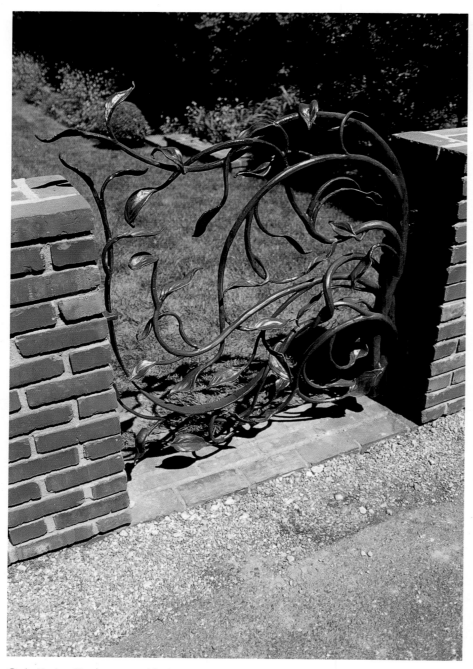

Craig Kaviar. Garden gate with an asymmetrical design within a curved frame. Painted green. *Photo, artist*

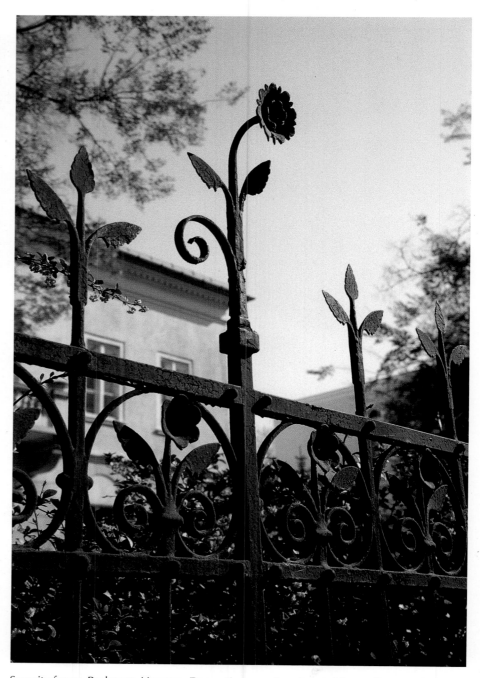

Security fence. Budapest, Hungary. Decorative security gates and fences line a main street with embassies and mansions. Leaves with spears at the top are interspersed with a flower at the support bars. *Photo, author*

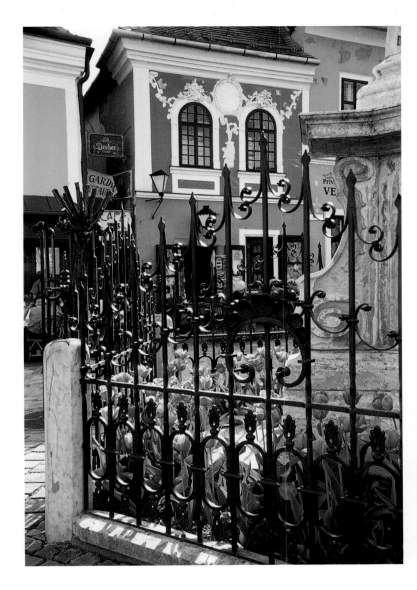

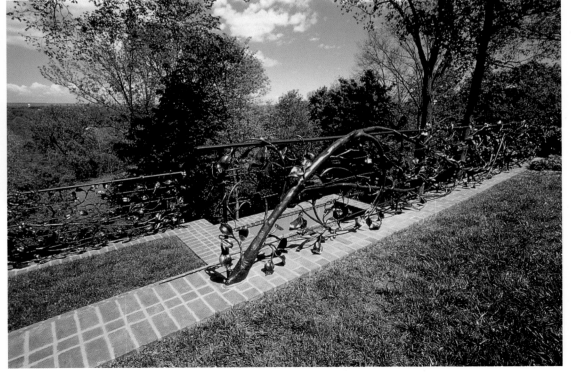

Szentendre, Hungary. Cast and forged iron fence with spikes in a central square. Scrolls and ovals with anthemia. The uprights are at different heights for a scallop effect. An iron fence also surrounds the tree at left. *Photo, author*

Craig Kaviar. Vine rail fence was created for a private terrace garden on a cliff overlooking the Ohio River in Louisville, Kentucky. The design was taken from vines growing wild around the garden. The rail provides a visual and a physical barrier separating the sculpted garden from the wild forest. It also prevents viewers from falling off the cliff. Designed in collaboration with landscape architect J.P. Shadley of Carol R. Johnson & Assoc. 2.6' high, 72.5' long. *Photo, artist*

Animals, Birds, Insects, and Fish

Animals, birds, insects, and fish are all fair game for the blacksmith's art. These objects may be forged from sheet or bar, hammered in a repoussé technique, or cast.

Today, many items can be purchased from companies that specialize in providing such objects to the industry. They may be hand forged, or, when multiple copies of an item are required for a long expanse of fencing, as in the fence from Budapest, more likely they are cast. That's true for the anthemia in the fence from Szentendre. It is more time and cost effective to use cast elements or factory produced forged elements rather than to make each one in a small workshop.

Phil Alan Simpson's painted "Dog Gate" uses assorted, hand forged, delightful objects that might keep a dog jumping with joy: flowers, a worm, a dog bone. A small dog and a turtle inhabit his gate designed to keep a pet penned in or out as the case may be.

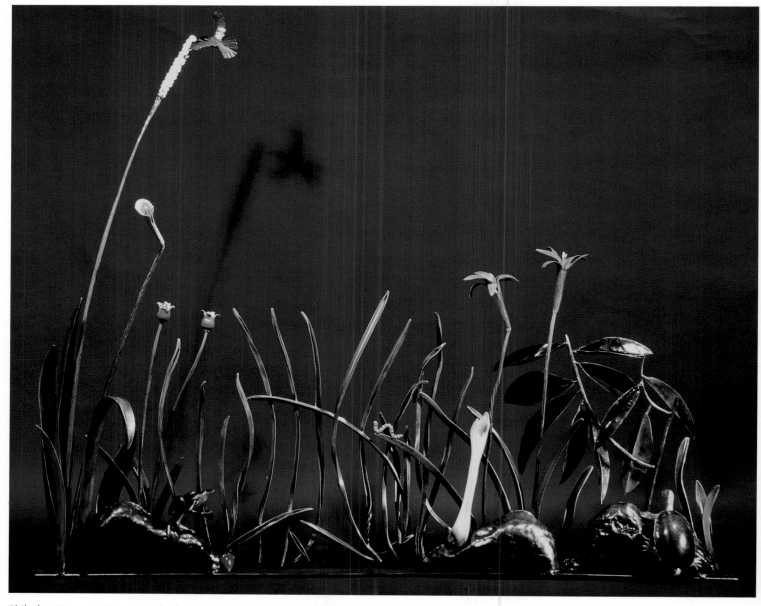

Phil Alan Simpson. Dog gate. The lucky dog that has to deal with this gate will be able to study animals, insects, and plants, but he might be frustrated if he tries to gnaw on the bone. Painted iron. 5′ high, 6.5′ wide. *Photo, Asen Seale*

The large courtyard gate of Hotel Három Gúnár, Kecskemet, Hungary, has birds and fish on the gate. The top of the gate is symmetrical with an intricate design using curves, arches and scrolls. The birds are logically at the top and the fish at the bottom. Frederic Crist's individually carved and different animal heads are decorative and functional. Their spiked ears are meant to keep out intruders and maybe their fierce countenances will help. Joseph Miller has a completely different use for animal heads as decoration on the center of a gate opening into a hotel bar.

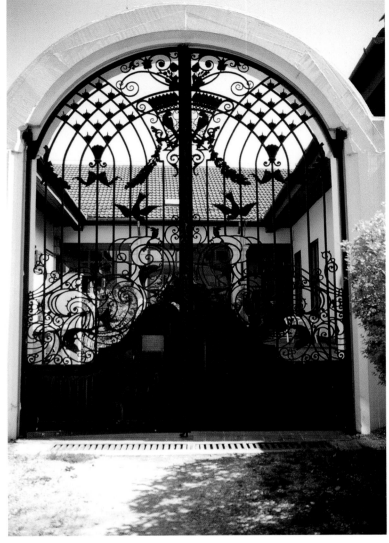

Hotel Három Gúnár. Gate with birds, butterflies, and fish. Kecskemet, Hungary. *Photo, author*

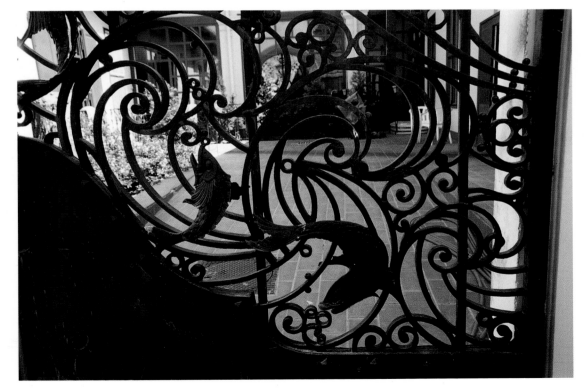

Hotel Három Gúnár. Detail of fish and scrollwork. Kecskemet, Hungary. *Photo, author*

225

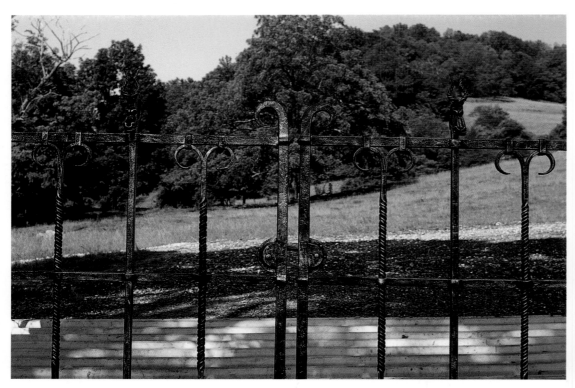

Frederic A. Crist. Entrance Gate with animal heads. The ears serve as spikes. Each twisted upright is split at the top and curved into a gracefully pointed, but potentially damaging, end. *Courtesy, artist*

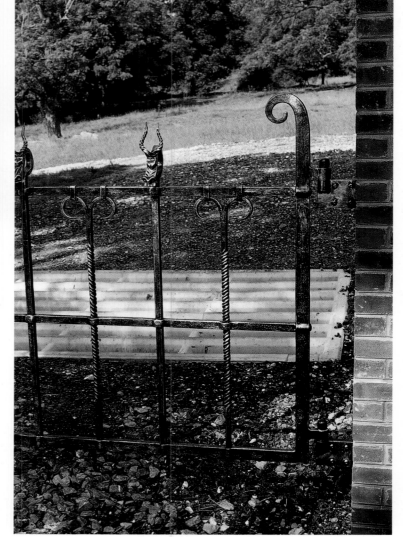

Frederic A. Crist. Detail of Entrance Gate showing the animal heads, the twist of the bars, and the mounting hardware. Note that each upright pierces the horizontal support. *Courtesy, artist*

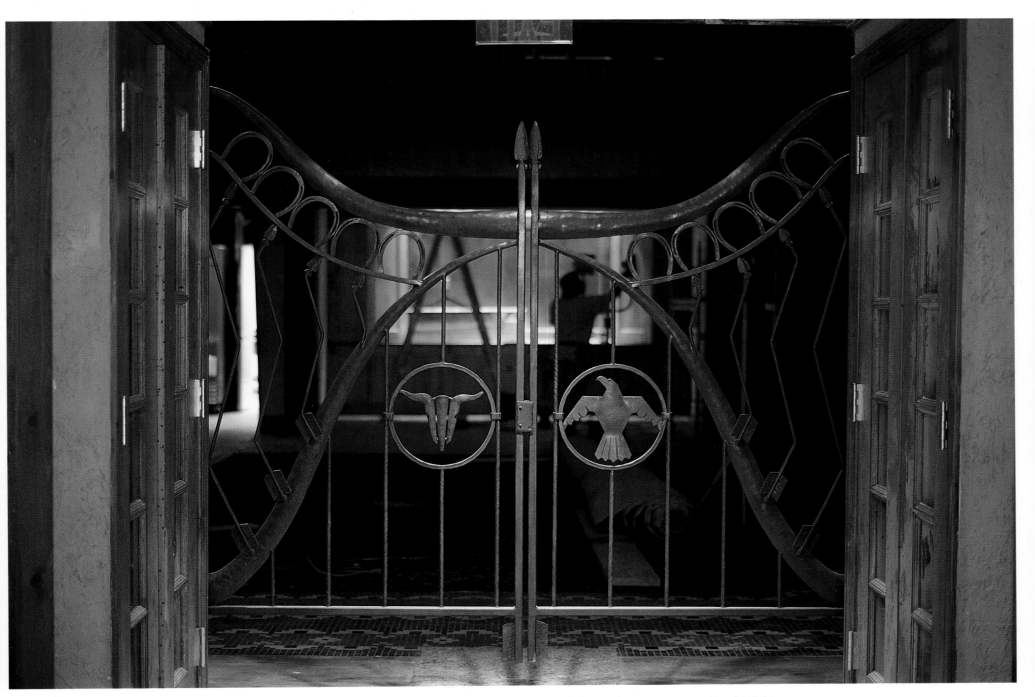

Joseph Miller. The cow and eagle symbols are in a gate to a western style bar in the Hyatt Regency Hotel, Wichita, Kansas. *Courtesy, artist*

Greg Leavitt's Peacock Gate has a couple of birds on each side with their tails spread to fill out the space. The tails are a perfect reason for using brass for the color change, and for the eyes. It takes a masters hands to be able to manipulate the metal in such graceful forms that appear so light yet are made of sturdy steel designed to last a long time in an outdoor environment.

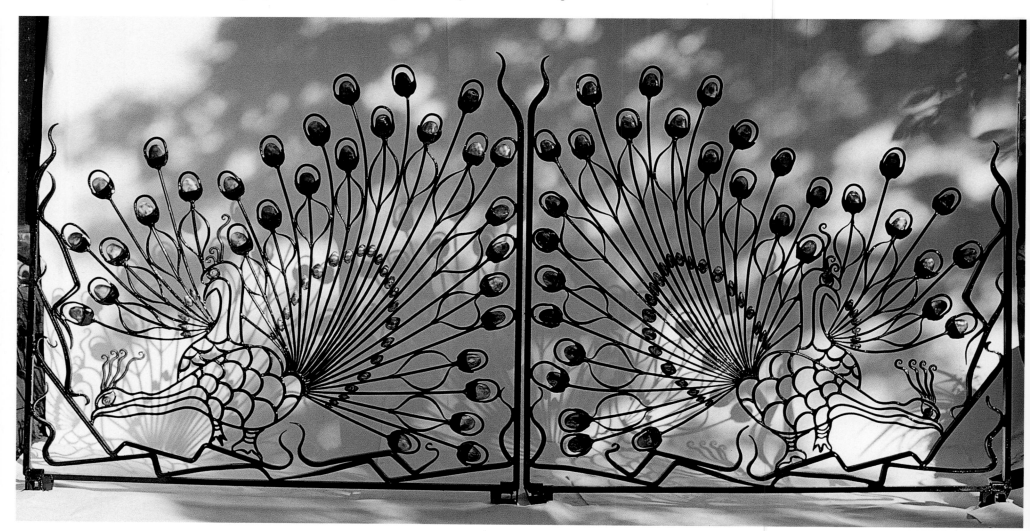

Greg Leavitt. Peacock Gate; the creature IS the gate rather than having a figure overlaid or inserted among scrolls and bars. *Courtesy, artist*

The rounded forms in Jan Pearson's "The Buffalo Hunt Gates" utilize his blown metal technique. Shapes are welded together leaving a small space between them for an air hose. When air is pumped into the pieces, they inflate and shape the metal; then the seams are welded together.

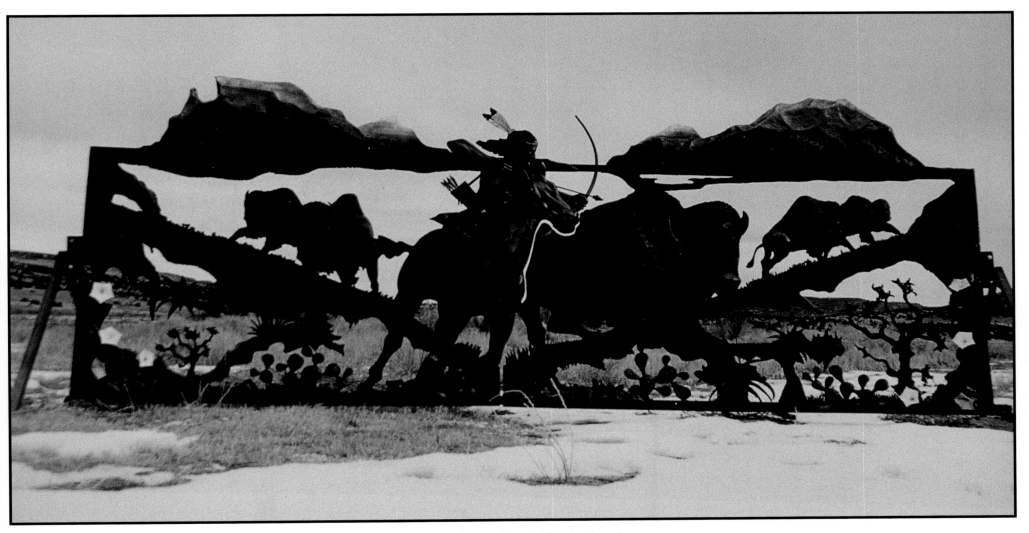

Jan Pearson. "The Buffalo Hunt Gates" are created with a blown steel sculpture technique the artist first developed in 1987 that gives the animal bodies a rounded three-dimensionality. This commissioned piece demonstrates broad ranging possibilities for sculpting metal directly using the unique method. *Photo, artist*

Nature has created so many types of fish that the blacksmith need only observe them in an aquarium or a book to find one that fits the scene. And even if he's not true to its form, almost any variation will do in the scheme of things. Usually gates with fish are used where there is water or where fish inhabit an area such as an aquarium, or just for people who like fish shapes. Clint Wright's gate with fish, a seahorse, starfish, coral, and seashells is for a home overlooking the ocean. Carl Glowienke specializes in sea life gates. He has named his company Sealife Studio, and most of his clients live along the southern California oceanfront. And Stefan and Elisabeth Steinmetz's "Dance of the Fish Gate" is for a client on their northern New Zealand peninsula.

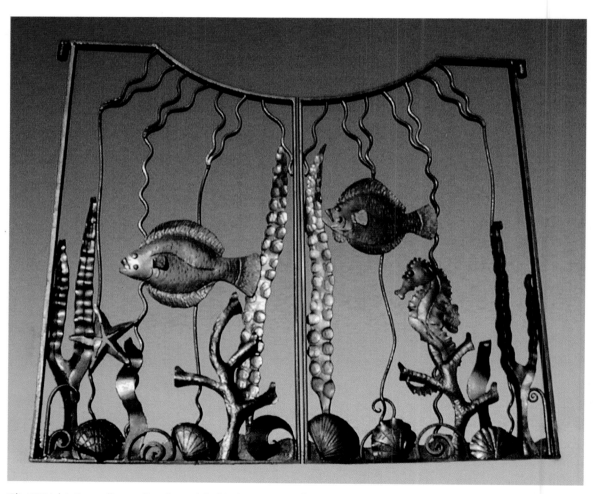

Clint Wright. Seawall gate. Sea forms inhabit this gate installed between two walls that overlook Fisher's Island Sound, Connecticut. The fish and much of the foliage is plasma-cut from 1/8" steel and each piece is hot modeled and tooled with chisels and punches. The gate is primed and painted. 3'4 ' high, 3' wide. *Photo, artist*

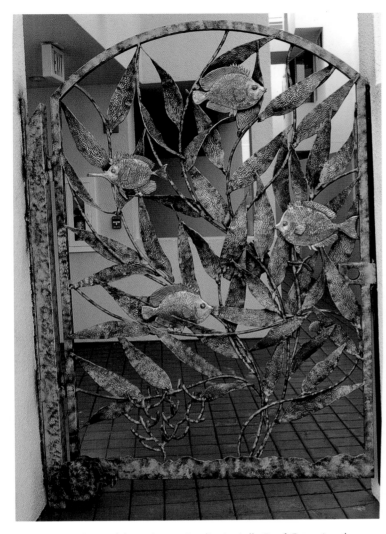

Carl Glowienke-Sealife Sculpture Studio. La Jolla Reef Gate. Another interpretation of fish for a small gate. Bronze and steel polychrome. The fish are steel with crystal eyes. *Photo, artist*

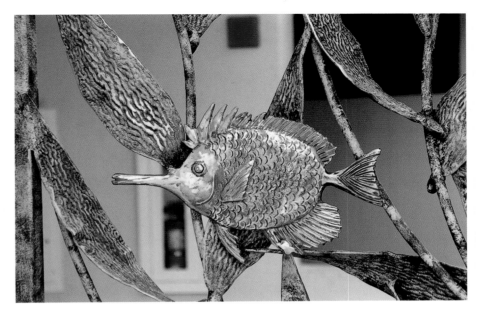

Carl Glowienke-Sealife Sculpture Studio. La Jolla Reef Gate, detail. The fish is bas-relief cast bronze. *Photo, artist*

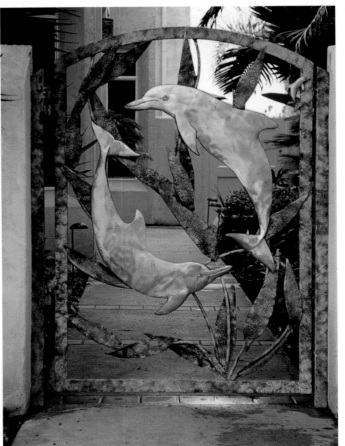

Carl Glowienke-Sealife Sculpture Studio. Rhythm of the Sea. Cast bronze dolphins. Polychromed. 5.2' high, 3.8' wide. *Photo, artist*

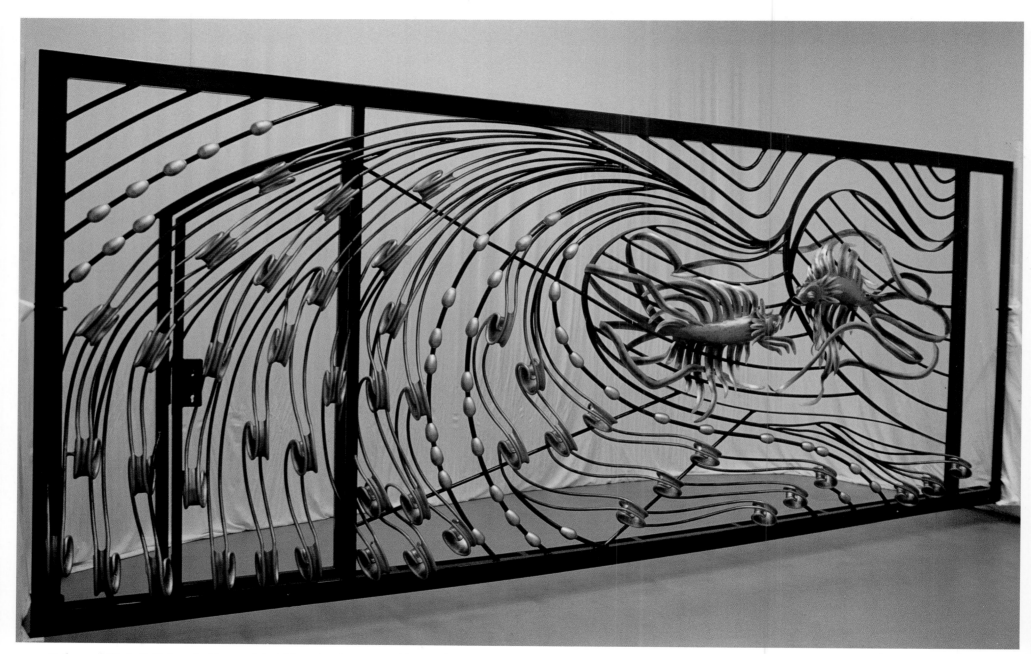

Stefan and Elisabeth Steinmetz. Dance of the Fish pedestrian gate and fence. The gate slides. *Courtesy, artists*

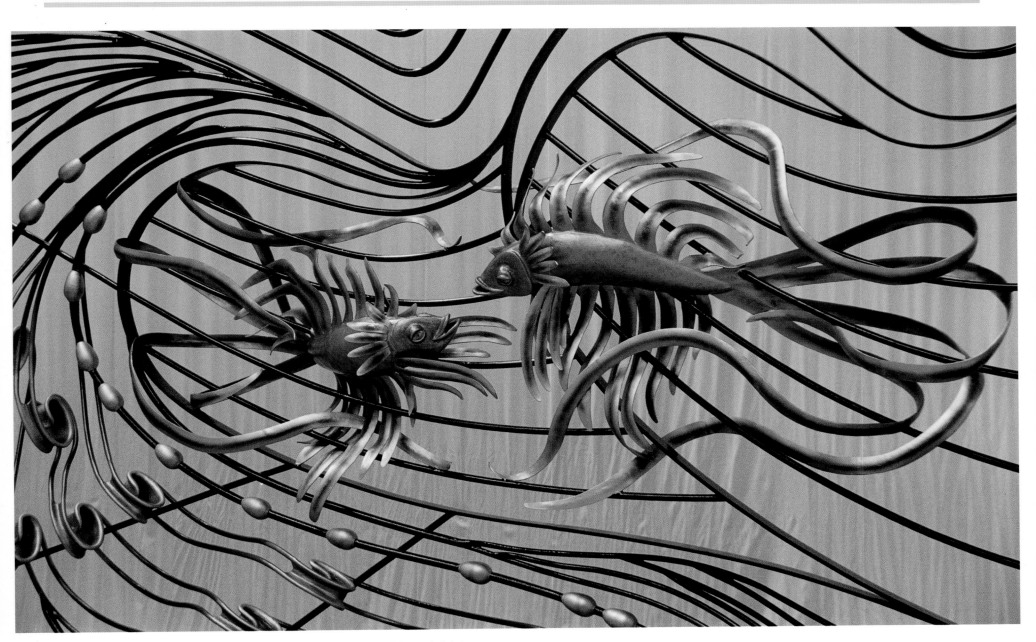

Stefan and Elisabeth Steinmetz. Dance of the fish gate, detail of the fish. Each fish is
constructed from steel and painted. *Courtesy, artists*

Selected Bibliography

Andrews, Jack. *Edge of the Anvil*. Ocean City, Maryland: Skipjack Press, 1991.

Andrews, Jack. *Samuel Yellin, Metalworker*. Ocean City, Maryland: Skipjack Press, 1992.

At the End of the Century, One Hundred Years of Architecture. Los Angeles: MOCA and Harry Abrams, 1998.

Baur-Heinhold, Margarete. *Decorative Ironwork*. Atglen, Pennsylvania: Schiffer Publishing, Ltd., 1996.

Bennett, Malcolm. *The Bankside Gates at Shakespeare's Globe, a Guide*. London: Communication Dept., Shakespeare's Globe, 1999.

Bondi, Stephen. *Monographs on Mazzucotelli*. San Rafael, California: Desktop published on order.

Bondi, Stephen. *Alessandro Mazzucotelli, The Wrought Iron of Casa Ferrario*. San Rafael, California: Desktop published on order.

Budapest- Knopf Guide. New York: Knopf Publishers, 2000.

Campbell, Marion. *Decorative Ironwork*. New York: Harry N. Abrams, Inc., 1997.

Chatwin, Amina. *Into the New Iron Age*. Cheltenham, Great Britain: Coach House Publishing, 1995.

Clouzot, Henri. *Art Déco Decorative Ironwork*. New York: Dover Publishing, 1997.

Condit, Carl. *The Chicago School of Architecture*. Chicago, Illinois: The University of Chicago Press, 1964.

Exhibition Catalog. *Decorative Metalwork in Architecture*. Katherine E. Nash Gallery, University of Minnesota, 1986.

Fahr-Becker, Gabriele. *Art Nouveau*. Germany: Konemann Verlag, 1997.

Höver, Otto. *Style in Decorative Wrought-Iron Work, The Encyclopedia of Ironwork*. New York: Universe Books, 1962.

Geerlings, Gerald K. *Wrought Iron in Architecture*. New York: Dover Publications, 1983.

Joyce, Tom. *Life Force at the Anvil, The Blacksmith's Art from Africa*. Asheville, North Carolina: ABANA & University of North Carolina at Asheville, 1998.

Kahr, Joan. *Edgar Brandt, Master of Art Déco Ironwork*. New York: Harry N. Abrams, 1992.

Meilach, Dona Z. *Decorative & Sculptural Ironwork*. 2nd printing. Atglen, Pennsylvania: Schiffer Publishing Ltd., 1999.

Meilach, Dona Z. *The Contemporary Blacksmith*. Atglen, Pennsylvania: Schiffer Publishing Ltd., 2000.

Meilach, Dona Z. *Direct Metal Sculpture*, Revised Edition. Atglen, Pennsylvania: Schiffer Publishing Ltd., 2000.

Permanyer, Louis. *Barcelona Art Nouveau*. New York: Rizzoli, 1999.

Pevsner, Nicholas. *Pioneers of Modern Design*. New York: Penguin Books, 1960.

Soukup, Vladimir. *Prague Eyewitness Travel Guide*. New York: DK Publishing, 1999.

Southern Highland Craft Guild. *Samuel Yellin Metalworkers; Three Generations*. (Exhibit Catalog.) Asheville, North Carolina: Folk Art Center, 1998.

Southworth, Susan and Michael. *Ornamental Ironwork*. New York: McGraw Hill, 1978, 1992.

Tijou, Jean. *Columbia Encyclopedia*. Sixth Edition. New York: Columbia University Press, 2000.

Whitaker, Francis. *Beautiful Iron*. Carbondale, Colorado: Whitaker Foundation, 1997.

Zerbst, Rainer, Francoise Rene Roland (photographers). *Gaudi*. Taschen America, 1999.

Resources

Organizations

ABANA Artist-Blacksmith's Association of North America
PO Box 206
Washington, MO 63090
Tel: 314-390-2133
http://www/abana.org

American Craft Council (ACC) Information Center
72 Spring St
New York, NY 10012
Tel: 212-274-0630

Australian Blacksmiths Association
RMB 1155 Tongala
Victoria, Australia 3621
Tel: 03-58-590736
Wake@River.net.com.au

BABA - British Artist Blacksmith Association
111 Main Street
Ratho, Newbridge, Midlothian. EH28 8RS.
Scotland
E-mail phil@rathobyres.demon.co.uk
Fax: 01-31-333-3354
http://www.baba.org.uk

Crafts Council of Great Britain
44a Pentonville Road, Islington,
London N1 9BY, England
Tel: 0171-278-7700
http://www.craftscouncil.org.uk

Irish Blacksmith Organization
Anna O'Donoghue
21 Healy Terrace
Bellina Co. Mayo, Ireland
Fax: 353-96-72666 Tel: 353- 96 70998

NOMMA-National Ornamental & Miscellaneous Metals Association
532 Forest Parkway, Suite A
Forest Park, GA 30297
Tel: 404-363-4009   Fax :404-366-1852
http://www.nomma.com

Internet Resources

A Search for architecture, Art Nouveau, Baroque, Art Deco, and other art styles will bring up a wonderful list of resources. Other words to use in a search are "blacksmithing" and "ironwork." Many blacksmiths have personal sites and a search under the artist's name will yield their Internet address, site, and links to other sites.

These sites provide links to a variety of other related sites, host chat and discussion groups, current events, photos of work, artist listings, book lists, and more. Additional resources are in the Bibliography.

Amazon Books
Search using the words: blacksmith, blacksmithing, ornamental ironwork
http://www.amazon.com

Anvil Fire
http://www.anvilfire.com

Architecture.
http://www.greatbuildings.com/architects.html

ArtMetal Village
http://www.artmetal.com

Lamour, Jean.
http://franceguideprestige.com/nancy/htm

Metal Web News
http://www.mindspring.com/~wgray1

University of Georgia Center for Continuing Education. Forge & Anvil: a television series on blacksmithing 1966.
http://www.gactr.uga.edu/forge/

Winikoff's Virtual Junkyard For Blacksmiths
http://www.keenjunk.com

Touchmark Registration
anvilfire! Touchmark Registry
1684 Mitchell Mill Rd. Gladys, VA 24554-2938
http://www.anvilfire.com

Museums and Places to See Ironwork
The only United States museum devoted solely to ironwork as an art form and medium is:
The National Ornamental Metal Museum
374 Metal Museum Drive
Memphis, TN 38106-1539
Tel: 901-774-6380
http://memphisguide.com/NOMN.html

Other museums and historical sites will have some ironwork. You'll find a comprehensive list of the museums, their holdings, and the ability to search by type of objects at:
WWW. Virtual Library: Museums Around the USA
http://vlib.org

Here are a few ideas for ironwork sources. Often a walk around a city's old towns and centers will reveal a wealth of historical ironwork. New buildings may have more modern examples. Look for fences, gates, door hardware and decoration, balcony railings, building enhancements. "Pioneer" museums in the historical area of many cities.

20th Century Museum of History and Technology, San Bernardino, CA
Art Institute of Chicago, Chicago, Illinois (Especially the arms and armor collection.)
Barcelona, Spain
Biltmore House, Asheville, North Carolina
Folk Art Museum, Asheville, North Carolina
New Orleans, Louisiana
Shelburne Museum, Shelburne, Vermont
Victoria and Albert Museum, London, England
San Francisco, California
Also: cathedrals, banks, contemporary buildings, and residences.

Education Opportunities
ABANA Journeyman Program (See ABANA above)
International College of French Wrought Ironwork,
Maison des Compagnons du Devoir,
Chemin de Reims,
51140 Muizon, France
Fax: 01033 26029639
Tel: 01033 26020931

California Blacksmiths Association
P.O. Box 438
Mokelumne Hill, CA 95245
Tel: 530-666-7541
Tel: 650-323-1002

John C. Campbell Folk School
One Folk School Rd.
Brasstown, N.C. 28902-9603
Tel: 800-365-5724
http://www.grove.net/~jccfs

Heritage Blacksmith Association
331 Cotlow Road
Victoria, B.C. V9C 2E9, Canada
Tel: 250-478-1737
blacksmith@pacificcoast.net

Michigan Artist Blacksmith Association—ABANA Chptr
P.O. Box 16

Royal Oak, MI 48068
Tel: 248-547-9607
mbalent@juno.com

NOMMA
804-10 Main St. Ste. E
Forest Park, GA 30050
Tel: 404-363-4009
nonmainfor@aol.com

Northwest Blacksmiths Association (Hot Iron News Quarterly)
616 East Rockwood Boulevard
Spokane, WA 99203
Tel: 509-624-0100

Ozark School of Blacksmithing
HC 87, Box 5780
Potosi, MO 63664
Tel: 573-438-4725

Penland School of Crafts
PO Box 37
Penland, NC 28765-0037
Tel: 828-765-2359

Peters Valley Craft Education Center
19 Kuhn Rd.
Layton, NJ 07851
Tel: 973-948-5200
http://pvcrafts.org

Touchstone Center for Crafts
The Hart Moore Blacksmith Studio
1-49 Wharton Furnace Rd.
Farmington, PA 15437
Tel: 800-721-0177 or 724-329-1370
www.touchstonecrafts.com

Turley Forge
RR 10 Box 88C

Santa Fe, NM 87501
Tel: 505-471-8608

The Venice European Centre for the Skills of Architectural Heritage Conservation.
Al Direttore
Del Centro Europeo di Venezia per Mestieri, della Conservazione, del Patrimonio Architettonico,
Isola di San Servolo,
Casella Postale 676, I-30100
Venezia, Italy

The Wareham Forge
The Hamlet of Wareham,
R.R. #2 Proton Station, Ontario
N0C 1L0, Canada
Tel: 519-923-9219
http://Wareham.Forge@Headwaters.com

Yucaipa Valley Forge
12874 2nd Street
Yucaipa, CA 92399
Tel: 909-797-3279   Fax: 909-797-3279
tito@cybertime.net   www.yucaipaforge.com

Publications

The Anvils Ring
published by ABANA (see organizations, above)

Anvil Magazine
P.O. Box 1810
Georgetown, CA 95634
Tel: 800-94-ANVIL

ARCHI-TECH Magazine
P.O. Box 10915
Portland, ME 04104
Tel: 207-761-2177   Fax 207-761-5921
http://architechmag.com

Blacksmith's Gazette
950 Falcon Road
Camano Island, WA 98292
Tel and fax: 360-387-0349
Fholder@sos.net
http//:www.skagit.com/blacksmith

Blacksmith's Journal
P.O. Box 193
Washington, MO 63090
Tel: 800-944-6134
http://www.blacksmithsjournal.com

Fabricator Magazine
National Ornamental & Miscellaneous Metals Assn.
532 Forest Parkway, Suite A
Forest Park, GA 30297
Tel: 404-363-4010   Fax: 404-366-1852
http://www.nomma.com

Hammer's Blow
published by ABANA (see organizations, above)

Metalsmith
710 East Ogden Ave., Ste. 600
Naperville, IL 60563
Tel: 630-579-3272   Fax: 630-369 -2480

Traditional Building Magazine
69A Seventh Avenue, Brooklyn, New York 11217
Tel: 718-636-0788   Fax: 718-636-0750
http://www.traditional-building.com

Video Tapes

Blacksmith's Journal Techniques. Vol. 1 and Vol. 2.
Blacksmith's Journal. PO Box 193,
Washington MO 63090
Tel: 800-944-6134
http://www.blacksmithsjournal.com

Forged Elegance - Cyril Colnik
Bighorn Forge
4190 Badger Rd.
Kewaskum, WI 53040
Tel:414-626-2208

Marketing

The Guild
931 E. Main Street, #106,
Madison, WI 53703-2955
Tel: 800-969-1556 or 608-256-1990
Fax: 608-256-1938
info@guildsourcebooks.com
http://www.guildsourcebooks.com/contact.htm

Index